Managing Humanitarian Innovation

Praise for this book

'Eric and Abigail have done an excellent job in drawing together leading experts across a broad range of innovations that are already being implemented in the "for profit" world and demonstrating how these could be successfully employed to improve the effectiveness and efficiency of humanitarian preparation and response activities.'
Peter Tatham, Professor of Humanitarian Logistics, Griffith Business School, Griffith University, Australia

'Never before in the history of modern humanitarian action has there been such a compelling case for bringing together the abiding values and objectives of humanitarianism with profoundly transformative innovation and innovative practices. Managing Humanitarian Innovation not only captures that conceptual need, but also provides a clear and practical road map for meeting that need.'
Randolph Kent, PhD, Visiting Professor, African Leadership Centre, King's College London

'The humanitarian profession is going through a dramatic transformation, with new technologies, players, and approaches being introduced on a seemingly daily basis. Managing Humanitarian Innovation boldly takes stock of these changes and offers readers new conceptual frameworks and practical tools that are designed to make the most use of these emerging opportunities in the service of people most in need during disasters. Based on real case studies and forward looking, this is a 'must read' for aid workers, donors, government officials, and innovators drawn to the humanitarian calling.'
Nicholas Haan, VP of Impact and Faculty Chair of Global Grand Challenges, Singularity University

'It is rare that one find a book on humanitarian aid that is relevant to both academic and practitioner audiences. Managing Humanitarian Innovation does an excellent job giving insights and practical solutions to both audiences. Even more important it is inspirational and helps further the important discourse on innovation – one of the most important policy and operational areas facing humanitarian aid today.'
Kirsten Gelsdorf, Director of Global Humanitarian Policy and Professor, University of Virginia. Former Chief of Policy Analysis and Innovation, UNOCHA

'This book sets a new standard for combining theory and practice with a view of what's to come. It weaves together direct experience on-the-ground, unique ways of thinking and pathways to achieving extraordinary results. Eric and the various contributors have achieved this knowledge far from cosy institutes, but by being directly involved in the mud and sweat of humanitarian crises. It will surely be an inspiration for the pioneering approaches so badly needed in our sector.'
Giorgio Trombatore, Country Director, South Sudan, Relief International

Managing Humanitarian Innovation
The cutting edge of aid

Edited by
Eric James and Abigail Taylor

Practical Action Publishing Ltd
Rugby, Warwickshire, UK
www.practicalactionpublishing.org

© Practical Action Publishing, 2018

The moral right of the editors to be identified as editors of the work and the contributors to be identified as contributors of this work have been asserted under sections 77 and 78 of the Copyright Design and Patents Act 1988.

All rights reserved. No part of this publication may be reprinted or reproduced or utilized in any form or by any electronic, mechanical, or other means, now known or hereafter invented, including photocopying and recording, or in any information storage or retrieval system, without the written permission of the publishers.

Product or corporate names may be trademarks or registered trademarks, and are used only for identification and explanation without intent to infringe.

A catalogue record for this book is available from the British Library.

A catalogue record for this book has been requested from the Library of Congress.

ISBN 978-185339-954-1 Paperback
ISBN 978-185339-953-4 Hardback
ISBN 978-178044-954-8 eBook
ISBN 978-178044-953-1 Library Pdf

Citation: James, E. and Taylor, A. (eds) (2018) *Managing Humanitarian Innovation: The cutting edge of aid*, Rugby, UK, Practical Action Publishing, <http://dx.doi.org/10.3362/9781780449531>

Since 1974, Practical Action Publishing has published and disseminated books and information in support of international development work throughout the world. Practical Action Publishing is a trading name of Practical Action Publishing Ltd (Company Reg. No. 1159018), the wholly owned publishing company of Practical Action. Practical Action Publishing trades only in support of its parent charity objectives and any profits are covenanted back to Practical Action (Charity Reg. No. 247257, Group VAT Registration No. 880 9924 76).

The views and opinions in this publication are those of the author and do not represent those of Practical Action Publishing Ltd or its parent charity Practical Action. Reasonable efforts have been made to publish reliable data and information, but the authors and publisher cannot assume responsibility for the validity of all materials or for the consequences of their use.

Cover photo shows local manufacturing in Nepal. Credit: Field Ready
Typeset by vPrompt eServices, India

Contents

List of Tables, Figures, and Photos	viii
Acronyms	ix
Preface	xi
Acknowledgements	xii
About the editors	xiii

Part I: Setting the context

1. Introduction: Key concepts and definitions   3
   Eric James

2. A humanitarian innovation primer   11
   Nezih Altay

3. The potential of innovation: Relief aid of the future   21
   Mickey McManus

Part II: Understanding humanitarian innovation and the challenges it raises

4. How change happens and the process of humanitarian innovation   27
   Eric James and Abigail Taylor

5. Problems and potential   45
   John Bessant

6. Innovation lifecycle and the missing middle   51
   Ian Gray and Dan McClure

7. Complexity theory and humanitarian relief   61
   Jenny MacCann

8. Knowing for the twenty-first century: Reflexivity and rigour   69
   Robert Chambers

Part III: Organizing humanitarian innovation

9. The leadership and management of innovation 77
   Eric James

10. Understanding change: How does change happen? 89
    Duncan Green

11. Ethical and responsible use of ICT 93
    Nathaniel Raymond

12. Building partners for innovation (and resilience) 99
    Justin Henceroth and Ashley Thompson

13. Influencing innovation adoption using the matrix of influence ... 111
    Duncan McNicholl

Part IV: Lessons from the frontline

14. Additive manufacturing and humanitarian aid 117
    Brenna Sniderman, Parker Baum and Vikram Rajan

15. Humanitarian innovation labs: Bridging innovators and
    humanitarian challenges 133
    *Kate Wharton, Adam Arabian, Dave Levin, Jamil Wyne,
    with William Altman and Natalie Chang*

16. Lessons learned from the Nepal innovation lab 143
    Sebastien Maupas, David Kaldor, and Jennifer MacCann

17. Turning a conversation into an opportunity 151
    Abi Bush

18. Collaboration and the importance of process 157
    Robin Borrud and Stephanie Gliege

19. Three-stage design process 163
    Desiree Matel-Anderson

20. Design identification: Planting the seeds of empathy 167
    Rich Lehrer and Annie Johnson

21. Open-source 3D printing 171
    Joshua M. Pearce

22. Piloting 3D printing technology to increase access to
    prosthetic devices 177
    Matt Ratto

23. Opportunities and challenges in the HELIOS project   183
    Martijn Blansjaar

24. The Tao of extreme making   189
    Brad Halsey

25. Field Ready: Transforming aid worldwide   193
    Tessa Fixsen-Lavdiotis

Part V: Summary and challenges for the future

26. Q&A with experts in humanitarian innovation   201

27. Concluding thoughts on humanitarian innovation   209
    Eric James and Abigail Taylor

Useful tools and techniques for humanitarian innovation   213

Annexes

1. The principles for ethical humanitarian innovation   233

2. UNICEF's principles for innovation and technology
   in development   235

3. Technology readiness levels: This is ready … or is it?   237

4. Measuring creativity   239

5. Innovation-management readiness assessment   241

6. Useful links and websites   243

Glossary   245

Index   249

List of Tables, Figures, and Photos

Tables

4.1	Characteristics of abundance and scarcity mindsets	32
4.2	The MINDSPACE framework – a checklist of influences on people's behaviour for use when making policy	40
7.1	Linear and dynamic mindsets	64
8.1	Paradigmatic characteristics of neo-Newtonian practice and adaptive pluralism	70
13.1	Stakeholder groups: Problem importance and level of control	114
A.1	Useful tools and techniques	213
A.2	Blueprint	227
A.3	Word associations	239
A.4	Innovation-management readiness assessment	241

Figures

2.1	The Ansoff matrix	16
4.1	Concepts, characteristics, and responses in linear and non-linear systems	29
4.2	The complete innovation process	33
4.3	The double-diamond model of design	35
4.4	Elements of field-ready innovations	39
6.1	The ill-defined missing middle	55
6.2	Unpacking innovation's missing middle	55
7.1	The Cynefin framework	63
9.1	Strategies for humanitarian innovation	83
13.1	Perceived importance and control in prioritizing	113
14.1	Additive manufacturing paths and value framework	119
14.2	Aid across the additive manufacturing framework	120
25.1	Engineering measuring hardware	195
A.1	Theory of change	225
A.2	Business-model canvas	229
A.3	Promise and potential map	230
A.4	Torrance test of creative thinking	240

Acronyms

ALNAP	Active Learning Network for Accountability and Performance in Humanitarian Action
AM	Additive manufacturing
BINGO	Big international NGO
BMC	Business-model canvas
CAD	Computer-aided design
CNC	Computer numeric control
CSR	Corporate social responsibility
DIY	Do-it-yourself
DFID	Department for International Development (UK)
DRR	Disaster risk reduction
FDM	Fused deposition modelling
FFF	Fused filament fabrication
FEMA	Federal Emergency Management Agency (US)
GAHI	Global Alliance for Humanitarian Innovation
GESI	Gender equity and social inclusion
HCD	Human-centred design
HIF	Humanitarian Innovation Fund
ICT	Information and communication technology
IFRC	International Federation of the Red Cross and Red Crescent Societies
LAN	Local area network
MEAL	Monitoring, evaluation, accountability, and learning
MVP	Minimum viable product
NGO	Non-Governmental Organisation
OCHA	Office for the Coordination of Humanitarian Affairs (UN)
OODA	Observe, orient, decide and act
OSAT	Open-source appropriate technology
PM	Participatory methods
R&D	Research and development
RCT	Randomised control trials
RUTF	Ready-to-use therapeutic food
SAM	Severe acute malnutrition
SCM	Supply-chain management
SEZ	Special Economic Zone
SMART	Specific, measurable, achievable, realistic, and time-bound

SMS	Short message service (text)
STEAM	Science, technology, engineering, art and mathematics
ToC	Theory of Change
TRIZ	Theory of the resolution of invention-related tasks
TRL	Technology readiness level
UNDP	United Nations Development Programme
UNHCR	United Nations High Commission for Refugees
WASH	Water, Sanitation and Hygiene promotion
WHO	World Health Organisation (UN)

Preface

'May you live in interesting times' is an old expression that we can easily and rightly say applies at this moment. The simple need to provide international aid is matched by the complex need to improve it. But where do we start? Take a vital but often overlooked element: supply chains. As much as 80 per cent of humanitarian aid is spent on logistics and shipping (Tatham and Pettit 2010).

The challenges facing humanitarian logistics are huge. Refugee camps present enormously challenging environments in which sudden spikes in demand, difficult-to-access locations, disruptions due to conflict or disasters, and normal supply-chain problems are commonplace. This means that orders for medical and other supplies can take weeks – sometimes months – to fulfil, severely impeding humanitarian operations. There is also a lack of, or slow, adoption of technology routinely used elsewhere. In addition, humanitarian logistics are expensive. When customs clearance, transportation, storage, middlemen, and administration are added in, the costs of basic items are often exorbitant. Innovation gives a pathway through this set of problems.

The aim of this book is to be a well-considered yet practical work for managing humanitarian innovation. We seek to share learning, spread ideas, and spark insight. Through its use of innovative projects, training workshops and action research, our hope is to improve existing international humanitarianism so it is better prepared to tackle the challenges faced. As noted at the start of *Managing Humanitarian Relief* (James, 2017), aid workers should be clear about their views, honest about their claims, and forthright in their approaches. This book is meant to help them do just that in this fascinating area of innovation.

To achieve these aims, this book presents new approaches that are beginning to transform the way humanitarian logistics are carried out. Innovation in logistics includes disrupting and improving supply chains through the use of technology, and engaging people to manage this approach. This book discusses what innovation is, and strategies for supporting it; it describes practical innovations and how they have been applied; and it outlines how innovation labs can be run. Finally, it covers how to fund innovation and suggests how humanitarian innovation might develop in the future.

In the process of putting this book together, we have tried to craft something that is engaging, helpful, and worth reading. To do so, it has been necessary to bridge the gaps between what is published in research and scholarly works, the practical and less formal writing of practitioners, and those with little more than a passing interest. As a result, there are different styles and voices, and we ask readers to accept and appreciate this: just as in our regular lives, we are all better off when we do.

Acknowledgements

As editors, we first and foremost thank all the writers who contributed to this joint effort. Without them, there would be no book. Where additional help was provided, it is acknowledged in the relevant chapters. A number of our reviewers, including John Bessant and Georg Hoehne, deserve appreciation. The staff at Practical Action Publishing, Field Ready and the Humanitarian Innovation Fund merit a great deal of thanks for their backing, insight, and forbearance while we prepared this volume. Finally, our closest friends and families (including Benjamin, who came into the world as the first contributions were reviewed) must be thanked for their patience and continual support.

Field Ready is supported by Elrha's Humanitarian Innovation Fund programme, a grant-making facility supporting organizations and individuals to identify, nurture and share innovative and scalable solutions to the most pressing challenges facing effective humanitarian assistance. <www.elrha.org/hif>

About the editors

Eric James, PhD, is the co-founder and executive director of Field Ready. He has over two decades of experience leading humanitarian relief programmes. He has been involved in several business start-ups, holds two patents, and was a fellow/advisor at Singularity University. Eric is an affiliated expert of the Harvard Humanitarian Initiative and an adjunct professor at the DePaul University's Refugee and Forced Migration Studies programme. He is author of *Managing Humanitarian Relief: An Operational Guide for NGOs* (Practical Action Publishing, 2nd Edition, 2017), among other publications.

Abigail Taylor is a strategic advisor for the consulting firm Spark Strategy. She has developed considerable experience in business development and partnership management in Europe, Africa, and, more recently, Asia. Abigail has worked for NGOs, social enterprises, and UNHCR. She has an MA in Conflict, Security and Development, a degree in Politics and has worked with the UK government in parliament and through government-focused institutions. She has particular interests in complexity theory, organizational systems, and managing scale-ups.

PART I
Setting the context

In humanitarian settings, context is everything and so setting the context is the best place to start. These contexts are distinguished by people's needs and their ability to cope. In situations that require life-saving measures, human suffering can be reduced and recovery and reconstruction are possible. In emergencies, simple poverty reduction is not enough. Less-developed countries are not the only places where these situations occur; a developed country can experience humanitarian need as the result of, for example, an acute disaster or refugee crisis. This part creates a foundation, providing:

- An overview of innovation and some brief definitions
- An exploration of innovation in the humanitarian space
- A definition of the complete humanitarian innovation process
- Some illustrative examples of humanitarian innovation in action
- A vision for the future

CHAPTER 1
Introduction: Key concepts and definitions

Eric James

Humanitarian innovation is an expansive topic so it is important to lay a clear foundation in terms of the context in which it occurs. In this chapter, time is spent defining innovation and the concept of humanitarian innovation before briefly considering why it is important and whether it can be 'managed'. The rest of this chapter defines other key terms used in the rest of the book.

Keywords: innovation, humanitarian, disasters, trends

Innovation in humanitarian contexts

The scale and impact of disasters and humanitarian emergencies is enormous. According to the Centre for Research on the Epidemiology of Disasters, between 2000 and 2015, disasters affected 3.1 billion people, caused US$1.8 trillion in damages and killed 1.4 million people. In 2015, 24 people were displaced from their homes every minute. Given current trends, the scale of human suffering is likely to continue at levels not seen since the end of the Second World War.

The four elements of volatility, uncertainty, complexity, and ambiguity wreak havoc on development processes and culminate in disasters. Hazards such as severe drought, desertification, flooding, and earthquakes can trigger a disaster and be amplified as social dimensions of vulnerability, poverty, and exclusion become more distinct. Simply put, those with the least resources – whether financial, human, social, or natural capital – are affected the most.

The challenges of climate change, economic crises, resource scarcity, increased urbanization and political marginalization add to ever-present violent conflict, whether in the form of chronic instability or new civil wars. Grafted onto this are inadequate (and sometimes corrosive) political governance, ineffective leadership, and bad decision-making which have a role in exacerbating the conditions in which disasters occur. Government, by far the largest donor to humanitarian issues, can scale back or even cut their funding altogether at a whim. So, while the reasons emergency situations occur may appear evident, a true understanding of the ramifications requires a deep appreciation of their complexity.

In a very real sense, disasters happen as a result of failures of development. Humanitarian relief, recovery, and reconstruction are the steps out of these

http://dx.doi.org/10.3362/9781780449531.001

situations of failure. Yet significant challenges remain. Examples include effective coordination, sufficient resource mobilization, astute management, and a keen understanding of the complexity of the environments in which events occur. To address these failures, improvements are needed at a basic level. This is why change needs to happen. One possible remedy is simple optimization. This is important but, for transformative change to occur, innovation is necessary.

Where there are big challenges, there are equally large opportunities. Several trends have emerged in recent years that give reason to believe massive positive change is possible.

First, there has been a reduction in poverty and an expansion in wealth worldwide. This has resulted in better access to health care and education and increased life spans. Importantly, experts in information and communication technology (ICT), engineering, and various technologies are not limited to key capitals but can now be found nearly across the planet. Partly due to a process of globalization, partly owing to successful development, this has resulted in what has been called the 'rise of the rest' (Zakaria, 2009).

Second, we are now living through an era of rapid technological change, which has ramifications that are still being studied and understood. Digital technology has accelerated a range of developments allowing us to do things that would have earlier been viewed as science fiction. The smartphone is the most ubiquitous illustration but examples exist in many other areas: additive manufacturing, artificial intelligence, autonomous vehicles, biotechnology, nanotechnology, the Internet of Things, and robotics. Together these form what is known as exponential technology, and this follows the law of accelerating returns in that its capacity, access, and cost-effectiveness increases at ever higher rates. To be sure, there are negative impacts of these trends such as disruptions to labour and capital markets (including job, business, and intellectual property loss), an increase in anxiety due to rapid change, and an unintended burden on the environment. But the potential upsides are huge.

Finally, there is a growing recognition that there are other ways to work and accomplish tasks. The do-it-yourself (DIY) culture that led to the global 'maker movement' has brought a level of self-reliance through hacking and tinkering which has influenced not just consumerism but also education, industry, and development. In many ways, this builds on the concept first advanced by Fritz Schumacher (1973), known as 'appropriate technology'. Such technology suits the socio-economic, cultural, and environmental contexts in which it is used, and promotes the self-sufficiency of those who use it. Examples include small-scale energy generation, various construction methods, different means of collecting and filtering water, and devices to increase mobility for those who have done without in the past.

There are numerous touchpoints between these different trends. Together, they have been described as a Fourth Industrial Revolution (Rifkin, 2014) and the Age of Abundance (Diamandis and Kolter, 2012). Tools and systems can be made not just stronger but even resilient to the point where they become stronger under stress, becoming what Nassim Taleb termed 'anti-fragile' (2012). Better understanding of how people work (e.g., 'results-based' management and a focus on happiness), although still not widespread, has also played a role in new ways of working. The intersection between participatory techniques, design thinking, and lean start-up methods is one example. Another is the rise of Open Source Appropriate Technology (OSAT), in which designs and instructions for different products and services are freely available on the internet.

These developments have not been entirely missed by those involved in providing international aid. As noted, information technologies have led to new and faster ways to share data and enhance communications. Mapping and aerial imagery, whether provided by satellites or drones, plays an increasingly important role in assessment, monitoring, and evaluation. Innovations using cash payments have been seen by many as revolutionary in their efficiency. Experimental 'labs' (described extensively later in this book) have been widely used by the UN and a range of NGOs (e.g., International Rescue Committee's Airbel Center). The space available in this book is insufficient to allow many of the examples found to be described.

Yet the aid community has been slow to adopt innovation across the diverse set of actors and areas with whom and in which it works. One recent study showed that, while 80 per cent of non-profit leaders felt that innovation is an urgent imperative, only 40 per cent believed their organizations were ready to do so (Sahni et al, 2017). More can be done, and indeed must be done, to cope with the challenges and opportunities now in front of us. In the forthcoming chapters, a range of models, examples, and practices are described that help make aid more efficient and effective in increasingly changing contexts.

Innovation defined

What is innovation?

There are a variety of ways to define and think about innovation and so having a sound grasp of its definitions can be helpful. The term originally comes to English from the Latin word *innovatus*, meaning 'to introduce,' 'renew', or 'restore'. Innovation is a concept that is deeply connected to creativity, invention, and entrepreneurship. The management expert, Peter Drucker (1985), noted that innovation is 'the means to exploit change as an opportunity ... [and] is capable of being presented as a discipline, capable of being learned, capable of being practiced'. Tidd and Bessant (2013: 18) observe that 'definitions of innovation may vary in their wording, but they all stress the need to complete the development and exploitation aspects of new knowledge, not just its invention'.

Whereas invention is about creating something new, innovation is concerned with improving – sometimes in profound ways – things that exist and can be useful. Seen this way, innovation is ultimately a process of change that leads to positive social impact. In speaking about innovation in the humanitarian sector, Ramalingam et al. (2009: 3) define innovations as 'dynamic processes which focus on the creation and implementation of new or improved products and services, processes, positions and paradigms [what are called the '4 Ps']. Successful innovations are those that result in improvements in efficiency, effectiveness, quality or social outcomes and impacts'.

What is humanitarian innovation?

Humanitarian innovation is a subfield of innovation that is still under development. For example, how preparing for and responding to disasters could serve as a source of innovation and even entrepreneurial opportunity is not well understood. Despite their undeniable impact on the socio-economic fabric of the affected populations, very few publications address the relationship between catastrophic events and entrepreneurial efforts (Monllor and Altay, 2016). Disruption of traditions and policies, and weakening of existing organizational structures after a catastrophic event, may create a favourable climate for innovation.

One possible explanation for this phenomenon is that 'disasters provide opportunities to update the capital stock and adopt new technologies' (Skidmore and Toya, 2002: 681). This idea embodies Schumpeter's theory of 'creative destruction', in which driving forces internal to the organization such as new products, new methods of production or transportation, or new markets, become the engine for innovation (Schumpeter, 1942). In our case, however, disasters are external forces which could also be considered disruptive processes of transformation. Schumpeter's process of creative destruction is therefore inverted in the face of external events as they act as the destructive force that creates opportunities for innovation (Noy and Vu, 2010).

For our purposes, the end goal of humanitarian innovation is to positively impact lives with high-quality products and services delivered to the right people, at the right location, at the right time, and at the right cost. This description is no different from the definition of logistics. Thus, it is not surprising to see logistics and supply-chain scholars showing great interest in humanitarian operations. Innovating 'hardware' is notoriously difficult and so gets special attention in this book.

Why innovate?

For those engaged in providing humanitarian aid, there are at least four reasons to innovate.

The first key reason to innovate is to improve significantly the performance of aid so that people's lives are saved and their suffering is lessened. Innovation can bring better practices that can improve disappointing performance. The result should be faster, less expensive and, by some measure, better than what currently exists.

Second, it is necessary to innovate to adapt to changing conditions. Contexts shift in ways that impact both people affected by disasters and those who try to help. This includes conflict that disrespects the norms of international law and practices, urbanization, and climate change. It also includes shifting demographics, shifts in policies, and emerging technologies which lead to new expectations and demands.

Third, innovation can be expected by various stakeholders, particularly donors. If there is a faster, less expensive, or better way to do something, it is reasonable to expect that this be incorporated into the practice of aid. Along with an increased amount of professionalism, calls for accountability and use of various business practices, some donors have specific requirements for a project to be 'innovative'.

Finally, innovation is needed to take advantage of new opportunities. The disposition of people affected by disasters has changed and will continue to change. Individuals are more mobile and connected than ever before. The nature of partnerships is changing and there are new ways of working with commercial entities, governments that were once recipients of aid, and a range of new types of non-profit organizations. Optimization or novelty are not enough for innovation to be deemed a success: there has to be a genuine transformation that is ultimately diffused, leading to widespread change.

Can innovation be managed?

Any process can be managed. Because innovation is a process, it can certainly be 'managed'. The context in which it often occurs – involving volatility, uncertainty, complexity, and ambiguity – can be mitigated and reduced and these are key roles of management. So innovation is 'more than just luck' (see Obrecht and Warner, 2016). This book outlines a range of ways to understand and inspire innovation from a management perspective.

Key concepts

Every sector has its own ways of doing things (standards and norms) and its own language (e.g., acronyms, slang, and technical terms) which are informed by key terms and concepts. Even when these 'terms of art' are contested and not fully agreed on, they still form a basis on which further discussion can be based and, in some cases, progress can be made. Here, we will introduce a number of important ideas that are touched on, and, in some cases, further elaborated on, in the rest of the book.

Abundance and acceleration

Abundance thinking is typified by a mindset that assumes there are enough resources to enable deep collaboration, an exploration of possibilities, risk-taking, and a welcoming of change together with the idea that still more positive outcomes are yet to come. It is contrasted with a scarcity mentality which holds that there are not enough resources and so competition is necessary, instead of sharing, and change is unwelcome. An example can be seen in the issue of access to water worldwide: although many people suffer from a scarcity of clean water, there is in fact an abundance of water when all water (including seawater) is considered, so it is a matter of finding the means of cleaning and providing access.

An idea allied to abundance is that key global trends accelerating now will continue to do so in the foreseeable future. A key notion behind the idea of acceleration is Moore's Law, which holds that the number of semiconductor circuits that can fit on a chip doubles every two years. Some recent technologies are said to be 'exponential' in the sense that their speed, cost-effectiveness, or overall 'power' is accelerating. These ideas are akin to a 'growth mindset', or holding the belief that positive traits such as capacities, including intelligence and leadership, can be developed with practise. This is often contrasted with having a 'fixed mindset', which refers to the idea that these traits and other characteristics are set at someone's birth.

Adaptive pluralism/experimentation

Adaptive pluralism is an approach to programme design and management that recognizes and embraces the complexity of the wider system. It is characterized by responsive (adaptive), multiple (pluralist), participatory methodologies. Adaptive pluralism has been developed as an approach over the last two decades by Robert Chambers (see Chambers, 2010).

Complexity

Complexity is a branch of science that provides a way to understand systems and change processes (Ramalingam et al. 2008). In simple or controlled contexts, it is possible to predict the response of part of a system (e.g. a knee-jerk reaction in a patellar reflex test). In contrast, a complex system is unpredictable, uncontrolled (but influenceable), non-linear, and the amount of change might not be in proportion to the intervention. Complexity is found where there are interconnected and interdependent parts but the unpredictable interaction between various parts of a system makes it impossible to always predict how it will respond to a single change. Complexity is found throughout nature, in networks and communities, and (during and after) disasters.

Design thinking

Design thinking is an approach to complex problems that focuses on solutions (particularly technology), actions, and users of the solutions. Using design thinking involves reasoning, creativity, and sharing to reach improved outcomes. Anyone can use design thinking to create, manage, and innovate solutions. Whereas analytical and critical thinking deconstructs to enable better understanding, design thinking attempts to explore and construct (build up) different solutions. Design uses experimentation, creation of models and prototypes, and adheres to general principles (as opposed to strict rules) to find what is both appealing and useful.

Human-centred design (HCD) focuses on the intended users and has as its starting point the mutual appreciation and compassion of designer and user. According to IDEO (2015), the 'mindsets' of HCD are empathy, optimism, iteration, creative confidence, making, embracing ambiguity, and learning from failure. Using many participatory techniques, HCD has been applied to a range of development concerns such as project implementation, education, mobility, health, and water, sanitation and hygiene (WASH) provision.

Lean start-up

Lean start-up is an approach to starting new businesses (start-ups) and launching new products. Recognizing that traditional business management approaches were ill-suited to entrepreneurship, Eric Ries (2011) and others formulated an approach that brought together scientific and 'lean' methods. Key aims of this method include an emphasis on quickly identifying people's preferences, having a tangible product to work with, and relying on data to drive decisions. It also recognizes that uncertainty is a common challenge and the approach is designed around organizations that have relatively scarce resources. To do so, it establishes basic hypotheses that are tested through the rubric 'build, test, measure'. For these reasons, many of its tenets are well-suited to humanitarian innovation.

Problems: simple, complex, and wicked

A simple (or tame) problem can be solved linearly and the problem and the solution can be readily identified. Complex problems are difficult to understand and their solutions require non-linear approaches (so traditional analysis and project management will fail), which can lead to new problems and unintended consequences. Where new environments and technology exist, so do complex problems. Wicked problems are a step beyond complex problems in that they are difficult or impossible to solve, as both the causes and their possible remedies are hard to recognize. First described by Rittel and Webber (1973), wicked problems arise because of incomplete, contradictory, and changing requirements which are resistant to being addressed.

References

Chambers, R. (2010) 'Paradigms, Poverty and Adaptive Pluralism', *Institute of Development Studies*, Working Paper 334.

Diamandis, P. and Kotler, S. (2012) *Abundance: The Future Is Better Than You Think*, Free Press, New York.

Drucker, P.F. (1985) *Innovation and Entrepreneurship Practices and Principles*, Harper and Row, New York.

IDEO (2015) *The Field Guide to Human-Centered Design*, IDEO, Palo Alto, CA.
Monllor, J. and Altay, N. (2016) 'Discovering Opportunities in Necessity: The Inverse Creative Destruction Effect', *Journal of Small Business and Enterprise Development*, 23(1), pp. 274–291.
Noy, I. and Vu, T.B. (2010) 'The economics of natural disasters in a developing country: The Case of Vietnam', *Journal of Asian Economics*, 21, pp. 345–354.
Obrecht, A. and Warner, A. (2016) 'More than just luck: Innovation in humanitarian action', *Humanitarian Innovation Fund*, ALNAP/ODI, London.
Ramalingam, B., Jones, H., Reba, T. and Young, J. (2008) 'Exploring the Science of Complexity: Ideas and Implications for Development and Humanitarian Efforts', *ODI Working Paper 285*.
Ramalingam, B., Scriven, K. and Foley, C. (2009) 'Innovations in International Humanitarian Action', in Ramalingam, B. et al., *ALNAP 8th Review of Humanitarian Action*, ALNAP, London.
Ries, E. (2011) *The Lean Start Up*, Random House, New York.
Rifkin, J. (2014) *The Zero Marginal Cost Society: The Internet of Things, The Collaborative Commons, and the Eclipse of Capitalism*, Palgrave Macmillan, New York.
Rittel, H. and Webber, M. (1973) 'Dilemmas in General Theory of Planning' *Policy Sciences*, 4, pp. 155–169.
Schumacher, F. (1973) *Small is Beautiful: A Study of Economics as if People Mattered*, Harper Collins, New York.
Schumpeter, J.A. (1942) *Capitalism, Socialism and Democracy*, Routledge, London.
Skidmore, M. and Toya, H. (2002) 'Do natural disasters promote long-run growth?', *Economic Inquiry*, 40(4), pp. 664–687.
Taleb, N. (2012) *Anti-Fragile: Things that Gain from Disorder*, Random House, New York.
Tidd, J. and Bessant, J. (2013) *Managing Innovation: Integrating Technological, Market and Organisational Change*, John Wiley and Sons, Chichester.
Zakaria, F. (2009) *Post-American World and the Rise of the Rest*, Penguin, London.

About the author

Eric James, PhD, is the co-founder and executive director of Field Ready. He has over two decades of experience leading humanitarian relief programmes. He has been involved in several business start-ups, holds two patents, and was a fellow/advisor at Singularity University. Eric is an affiliated expert of the Harvard Humanitarian Initiative and an adjunct professor at the DePaul University's Refugee and Forced Migration Studies programme. He is author of *Managing Humanitarian Relief: An Operational Guide for NGOs* (Practical Action Publishing, 2nd Edition, 2017) among other publications.

CHAPTER 2
A humanitarian innovation primer

Nezih Altay

To build a sound foundation for further examination of humanitarian innovation, this chapter examines several fundamental questions including 'what are the drivers of innovation?' and 'what are the different types of innovation?' In answering these questions, this chapter looks at a number of issues including partnerships and private-sector engagement. It presents a typology to explain the differences between cost innovation, good-enough innovation, and frugal innovation along with several case studies.

Keywords: humanitarian, innovation, partnerships, case studies

If there is really nothing certain in this world other than death and taxes, then individuals and organizations have to constantly innovate. Innovation is about change and finding smart, efficient, and effective ways to adapt to change. And change is inevitable. It is controlled by the first rule of thermodynamics, which says any system – if unchecked – will shift towards a disorderly state, one of greater entropy. That means the variability in a system will gradually increase if we do not attend to it. And variability creates cost. We build inventories, add redundancies, and throw more resources at it to be able to continue operating within our normal (expected) specifications. Consequently, any system we have is bound to become more expensive over time because we will use more and more money, time, and resources to keep it in line. Eventually our system will become so cumbersome to operate that we will not be able to afford it – unless we innovate and change the whole system.

The humanitarian system is one such example, although there is at least one important distinction in that its focus is on saving lives and reducing human suffering. Nonetheless, it faces unprecedented challenges and, therefore, the variability in the system is increasing rapidly. Climate change is affecting the timing, location, and intensity of weather-related events. Areas used to regular floods are experiencing drought, while some traditionally dry zones are frequently inundated. Warmer temperatures and humidity are increasing the intensity of storms (Emanuel, 2005). Besides natural disasters, long-term armed conflicts around the world add fuel to the fire. As a result, the world is experiencing the highest levels of displacement on record. A recent UNHCR report entitled *Global Trends: Forced Displacement in 2015* (UNHCR, 2016) indicates that an unprecedented 65.3 million people around the world have been forced from their homes. That means one in every 113 people on Earth is either an asylum-seeker, internally displaced, or a refugee, according to this report. While the displaced, whether their relocation is due to natural disasters or armed conflicts, stress the humanitarian system as it has never been stressed before, we should not forget another challenge: that presented by the more than 800 million people in the world who live on less than $1.25 per day (UNDP, 2015).

It is clear that the humanitarian system, squeezed from three sides – by climate change, refugee crisis and extreme poverty – is becoming very challenging to maintain. Although humanitarian donations have increased in the last decade, the funding available is still not enough to respond to all the humanitarian crises in the world. Moreover, according to UN OCHA (2017), regions such as Western, Central and Eastern Africa and the Middle East attract most of the humanitarian response money. The uneven distribution of these funds exacerbates the challenges in the humanitarian system and makes innovation inevitable.

This chapter will discuss the drivers for innovation and then present a typology for innovation with recent case studies.

What are the drivers of innovation?

When viewed broadly, the drivers of innovation come from a variety of sources. At the individual level, innovation can originate in the passion of people to problem-solve and improve their lives. It is sparked by creativity and ingenuity. At the organizational level, it can come about from pressures to improve efficiency, and effectiveness (which is often seen in the pursuit of doing things better, faster, and cheaper). In this context, innovation can be 'internal', in the sense that the impetus comes from management, or it can be external, brought about at the insistence of donors and other powerful stakeholders. At the systemic level, innovation can come about as a result of complexity and the persistence of different types of problems (classified as simple, complex and wicked elsewhere in this book).

The pressure to decrease costs is only one of the key factors driving innovation. Increased competition for donor funds, rising customer (beneficiary) and stakeholder expectations, economic, social, and demographic shifts across the world, stricter government regulations, and social concerns such as sustainability and accountability, all drive innovation and lead to new business models, products, and processes. Betts and Bloom (2014) argue that three other factors drive humanitarian innovation: private-sector engagement, partnerships, and technology development. Each of these is elaborated on below.

Private-sector engagement: Two significant trends lead the private sector to engage in humanitarian activities: the involvement of large corporations in corporate social responsibility (CSR) programmes, and the emergence of social entrepreneurship. CSR is a firm's engagement in actions that appear to further some social good, while social entrepreneurs form businesses in which the primary objective is to increase social welfare. Prahalad and Hammond (2002) called on the business world to see people living in extreme poverty as a large market of potential customers (in what are known as 'base-of-the-pyramid markets'). They argued that large corporations could greatly improve the lives of billions of people by stimulating commerce and development at the base of the pyramid.

Partnerships: The partnerships Betts and Bloom (2014) refer to are not simply collaborative efforts between two or more humanitarian organizations, but rather partnerships of humanitarian actors with groups and organizations from outside the sector. Humanitarian organizations may partner with large corporations to learn from them, get access to information technology, or tap into assets such as specialist software or heavy machinery. One such example is the agreement signed in 2002 between the World Food Programme and TNT Express. The two organizations agreed to collaborate on emergency response, logistics supply chains, transparency and accountability, school feeding support and private sector fundraising.

Another new actor in the humanitarian sector is academia. Since the beginning of this century, those studying supply chain management and logistics have developed an interest in humanitarian operations (Altay and Green, 2006; Van Wassenhove, 2006). As a result there are now graduate degrees, certificate programmes, and research centres dedicated to humanitarian logistics. Many humanitarian logistics scholars also work with humanitarian organizations to improve their operations. Some examples include the International Federation of Red Cross and Red Crescent Societies (IFRC) working with a team at INSEAD Business School and Indiana University to optimise the management of their fleet of four-by-four vehicles; the Federal Emergency Management Agency (FEMA) working with MIT researchers to develop an emergency management decision-support system, and an NGO in Liberia, Last Mile Health, working with a team from the University of Quebec in Montreal to design optimal delivery and inventory-management policies.

Technology Development: New information and communication technologies such as social networks, smartphones, Wi-Fi and local area networks (LANs) lead into new applications. For example, to map tribal violence based on reports and help Kenyan people protect themselves, a group of coders created a crowd-sourcing platform called Ushahidi. This open-source platform allows anyone to create maps based on reports coming from the field. Ushahidi was utilized during the response to the Haiti earthquake to create needs maps based on text messages coming from survivors. Similarly, Crisis Mappers helped the humanitarian community with needs maps and real-time updates on road conditions after the 2010 Haiti earthquake and 2013 Typhoon Haiyan. Other examples are discussed later in this chapter.

What are the different types of innovation?

Different forms of innovation require different approaches and management methods, so understanding a range of typologies and cases is useful. Govindarajan (2016) divides innovations into two main types: **linear** (which improve the performance of current practices) and **non-linear**. Non-linear innovations are more dramatic and potentially transformative. They involve redefining who is targeted by the innovation, reinventing the value offered, 'and/or redesigning the end-to-end value-chain architecture by which you deliver the value' (Govindarajan, 2016: 18).

Using the definition of innovation given by Ramalingam et al. (2009) and mentioned earlier, a typology of innovations is evident in what is described as 'the four Ps' of innovation. These are:

- **Product** innovation, which refers to a brand new product or service.
- **Process** innovation, on the other hand, is about how a product/service is created and delivered and mainly entails innovative production systems and creative reconfiguration of supply chain systems.
- **Position** innovation is about changing the context in which a product/service is being used; the underlying product or service does not change or changes very little.
- **Paradigm** innovation refers to changing the mental and business models used in the sector.

Whether the opportunity to innovate comes from a new technology or from the necessity to alleviate human suffering, the degree of innovation in a new product or service can range from **incremental** to **radical**. Incremental innovation is basically a repackaged version of something that already exists but still requires creative input, resources, and funding. However, radical innovation is a game changer, a paradigm shifter. An innovation may fall at any point on this incremental to radical spectrum. As Arshi and Chugh (2013: 150) have noted, 'incremental innovation can be viewed as doing something better, while radical innovation can be viewed as something different. While the former involves strategies to exploit and explore, the later involves re-framing and redesigning of strategies'.

Maybe a better method to distinguish between different approaches to innovation is the **Ansoff matrix**. Ansoff (1965) was interested in finding out whether innovations were market extensions based on existing technologies, new product development activities for existing markets, or newly developed products for entirely new markets. He used this to develop a framework to classify innovations based on their technical and market novelty. Recently, Zeschky et al. (2014) have used the Ansoff matrix to explain the differences between cost innovation, good-enough innovation, and frugal innovation. All three of these concepts have a place within the humanitarian context because they represent high-value, low-cost, market-specific solutions.

Cost innovations do the same for less. In other words, they provide functionality similar to other products and services that already exist in the marketplace but are produced at much lower costs. They are cost-engineered solutions with low technological innovation. Their focus is on making an existing solution more affordable to resource-constrained customers by using standard components, smaller packaging, and local supplies.

Good-enough innovations are re-engineered to fit the specific requirements of a target market. They tend to include features and functions designed to meet a range of resource constraints beyond capital constraints (focus is on value rather than cost). They require some degree of product novelty such as increased robustness, ease of use, or manual rather than automated processing.

Frugal innovations ('new for less') are, arguably, the best fit for products and services developed for base-of-pyramid markets because they are specifically developed for resource-constrained customers in emerging markets. Innovations geared towards solving problems here need to fit markets that are dominated by informal governance mechanisms related to reputation, group norms such as shaming, and social power. In these markets, property rights have little protection or simply do not exist. Furthermore, public infrastructure either does not exist or is inadequate or undependable (Calton et al., 2013). Unlike good-enough innovations, the focus of frugal innovations is on specific applications in resource-constrained environments. Frugal innovations are tailored to environments with poor infrastructure and are usually based on new product architectures so they are often disruptive. Here is one example: by making a stationary product portable, a frugal innovation may reach an entirely new customer group – so penetrating new geographical areas and increasing diffusion (Zeschky et al., 2014). A variation of this is what is known as reverse (or 'trickle-up') innovation, where novel products and services created in developing countries find their way to developed markets.

The placement of an innovation on the Ansoff matrix presented in Figure 2.1 is clearly not an exact science. The technical and market novelty of an innovation can be a subjective measure. Therefore, the extent of the technical and/or market novelty of an innovation should be judged relative to other cases.

To demonstrate the mechanics of the matrix we now present five cases.

Case studies on humanitarian innovation

The Wello WaterWheel (wellowater.org)

Wello founder Cynthia Koenig watched women in a small village in India make numerous trips to the nearby creek to get water. They would carry the water back to their homes in terracotta jugs on their heads. Since there is no running water in their village, women would spend hours just bringing water to their homes. So, Koenig came up with the WaterWheel, a drum made from

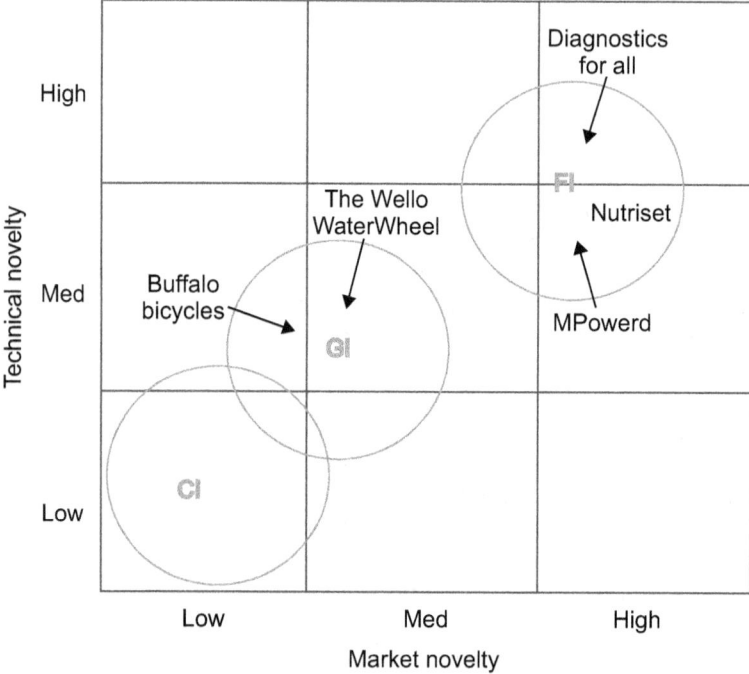

Figure 2.1 The Ansoff matrix

food-grade human-safe high-density polyethylene with a powder-coated mild steel handle that a person can roll behind them almost like a suitcase. The WaterWheel saves the villagers anywhere between two and five hours a day, depending on their usage. The product is produced in India and sold at an affordable price of $26. Unlike its African rival, the Hippo Water Roller, that sells for $100, Wello reduced costs by producing in high quantities. But that also meant selling a lot. The true innovation of the WaterWheel is mostly in the marketing. Wello partners with local non-profits, governments, and the Indian postal system to push its product. Because postal workers know everyone in a community, Wello encourages them to sell and distribute products. While a plastic drum is not a ground-breaking technological innovation, we can argue that the business model behind it is a relatively novel approach.

Buffalo bicycles (buffalobicycle.com)

World Bicycle Relief (WBR) is a Chicago-based international non-profit organization that brings mobility, in the form of a bicycle, to people living in extreme poverty. WBR was founded in 2005 by SRAM co-founder and executive vice president F.K. Day. SRAM is one of the largest high-end cycling component brands in the world. Through his experience and contacts in the high-end bicycle industry, Mr Day was able to create a synergy that resulted in an effective solution to the mobility problem in poor communities. SRAM engineers were involved in the design of the Buffalo, a bicycle specifically designed to withstand African road conditions and heavy usage. Buffalo Bicycles, a wholly owned, for-profit subsidiary of WBR, produces the bicycle components in China and Taiwan to control production costs. The components are then shipped to Africa and assembled locally in Angola, Kenya, Malawi, South Africa, Zambia, and Zimbabwe. WBR and Buffalo bicycles did not create a new product or market. It still produces and delivers a bicycle. However, the Buffalo is no ordinary bicycle: it is designed specifically for the market it is being sold in. Therefore, in this case, while market novelty is low, there is some technical novelty involved in the design and production of the Buffalo.

MPowerd (mpowerd.com)

New York City-based MPowerd created Luci Lights: ultra-lightweight, waterproof, and shatterproof, inflatable solar lanterns that are safer and brighter than their kerosene counterparts. Luci Lights use LEDs and are powered entirely by the sun with no need for additional batteries. They can produce up to 12 hours of bright light after charging with direct sunlight for seven hours. Although the company was originally formed in response to the 2010 Haiti earthquake, it quickly recognized that its innovative product is an affordable clean-energy solution that people could use in other situations such as camping or hiking. This bigger market (i.e., outdoor enthusiasts) allows MPowerd to operate a hybrid business model (the for-profit side financing the non-profit side of the business) and sell Luci Lights at deep discounts to people in need. There is nothing else like Luci Lights in the disaster relief or development-aid market, making it a novel product. From a technological perspective, we can argue that it falls in the medium category because LED light technology is not new but the use of it in a waterproof, collapsible, and inflatable housing is rather innovative.

Nutriset (thisbarsaveslives.com)

Plumpy'Nut is a peanut-based ready-to-use therapeutic food (RUTF) paste for the treatment of severe acute malnutrition (SAM). It is produced by Nutriset, an innovative French food manufacturer whose mission is to invent, produce, and make accessible solutions for the treatment and prevention of malnutrition in developing countries. Plumpy'Nut revolutionized the management of SAM around the world by removing the need for hospitalization and increasing the number of children receiving treatment. The result was a significantly improved recovery rate. Nutriset spent considerable funds and time developing Plumpy'Nut. Since it was the first RUTF of its kind, the technological novelty level of Plumpy'Nut on the Ansoff matrix is higher than that of the Buffalo bicycle and Luci Lights. Nutriset also created a whole new market for RUTFs placing itself in the high zone for market novelty.

Diagnostics for all (dfa.org)

Developed by chemistry professor George Whitesides and his team at Harvard University, paper diagnostics have the potential to change healthcare in the developing world. Paper-based tests, such as pregnancy tests, are not new, but Whitesides developed various tests that could be 'printed' on paper and delivered simply on site. Each test, most of which are based on a postage-stamp-sized piece of paper, consists of wax-based channels with a chemical at the end of the channel. The chemical interacts with particular indicators in a biological sample (e.g., blood, urine, or saliva) and changes colour. The colour patterns that appear on the test paper can be interpreted by looking in a catalogue. Paper is an inexpensive, readily available, portable, and disposable product that can reduce the cost of these diagnostic tests to pennies. Furthermore, paper diagnostics is a versatile tool that can be used on livestock or even to check food safety. Thus, the chemistry behind these tests and the fact that the DFA team created several new markets for them (e.g., food safety, livestock health) puts paper diagnostics in the upper right corner of the Ansoff matrix.

There are numerous other innovations we could have mentioned in this chapter. However, our objective here is not to analyse every single humanitarian innovation but rather provide a framework for analysis. Use of the Ansoff matrix is one such approach. To be able to categorize innovations in the humanitarian sector allows us to understand the nature of innovations in humanitarian aid.

References

Altay, N. and Green, W.G. (2006) 'OR/MS Research in Disaster Operations Management', *European Journal of Operational Research*, 175(1), pp. 475–493.

Ansoff, H.I. (1965) *Corporate Strategy*, McGraw-Hill, New York, NY.

Arshi, T. and Chugh, G. (2013) 'Strategizing for Innovation: An Empirical Investigation on Strategic Orientation and Innovation Types', *Business and Management Horizons*, 1(1).

Betts, A. and Bloom, L. (2014) 'Humanitarian Innovation: The State of the Art', *Occasional Policy Paper 009*, OCHA Policy and Studies Series.

Calton, J.M., Werhane, P.H., Hartman, L.P. and Bevan, D. (2013) 'Building Partnerships to Create Social and Economic Value at the Base of the Global Development Pyramid', *Journal of Business Ethics*, 117 (4), pp. 7217–33.

Emanuel, K. (2005) 'Increasing Destructiveness of Tropical Cyclones Over the Past 30 Years', *Nature*, 436, pp. 6866–88.

Govindarajan, V. (2016) *The Three Box Solution: A Strategy for Leading Innovation*, Harvard Business Review Press, Cambridge, MA.

Prahalad, C.K. and Hammond, A. (2002) 'Serving the World's Poor, Profitably', *Harvard Business Review*, 80(9), pp. 48–59.

Ramalingam, B., Scriven, K. and Foley, C. (2009) 'Innovations in International Humanitarian Action', in Ramalingam, B. et al., *ALNAP 8th Review of Humanitarian Action*, ALNAP, London.

UNDP (2015) *The Millennium Development Goals Report*, United Nations Development Programme <http://www.undp.org/content/undp/en/home/librarypage/mdg/the-millennium-development-goals-report-2015.html> [accessed on 19 September 2016].

UNHCR (2016) 'Global Tends: Forced Displacement in 2015' <http://www.unhcr.org/576408cd7.pdf> [accessed on 15 September 2017].

UN OCHA (2017) *June Status Report*, United Nations Office for the Coordination of Humanitarian Affairs, <http://interactive.unocha.org/publication/global humanitarianoverview/#documents> [accessed on 14 November 2017].

Van Wassenhove, L.N. (2006) 'Humanitarian Aid Logistics: Supply Chain Management in High Gear', *Journal of the Operational Research Society*, 57 pp. 4754–89.

Zeschky, M.B., Winterhalter, S. and Gassmann, O. (2014) 'From Cost to Frugal and Reverse Innovation: Mapping the Field and Implications for Global Competitiveness', *Research-Technology Management*, 57 (4), pp. 202–7.

About the author

Nezih Altay, PhD, is an associate professor of Operations Management at DePaul University. He is also a senior editor of *Production and Operations Management Journal's* Disaster Management department and a regional associate editor of the *Journal of Humanitarian Logistics and Supply Chain Management*.

CHAPTER 3
The potential of innovation: Relief aid of the future

Mickey McManus

Connectivity has the potential to crystallize a world-changing transition even for those who are impoverished, excluded, and vulnerable. In an age of complexity, we cannot afford to leave innovators who might have been born in destitute and marginalized areas to die of thirst. A lack of information flow deprives us all of their precious brains and creative passions. We can imagine a new future through helping people to learn the literacy of human-centred innovation; creating an 'Internet of Everything'; fostering connectivity and a worldwide community of billions of people; and refactoring the building blocks of manufacturing and computing into basic components that compute, store, sense, connect, and assemble. Combining this with a way to source local materials and fabrication resource sets to deploy with disaster-affected people will result in a new reality of 'massive small change', where locally-made gear can equalize the playing field and save lives in the process.

Keywords: innovation, disaster relief, complexity, futures

As the pervasive nature of the computing era comes into focus (trillions of computing devices connected to each other and to us), it is clear that connectivity has the potential to crystallize a world-changing transition even for those who are impoverished, excluded, and vulnerable.

We have no shortage of resilient, creative, and smart people in the world. By definition, the current generation of humans, even in the poorest places, represents the culmination of millions of years of survival of the fittest. We are here because we are survivors.

But, just as the lack of flowing water can drive a population to extinction, the lack of information flow in a population deprives us all of the precious brains and creative passions of those who are unconnected. We are literally sitting on a wellspring of innovation. Innovators can be found everywhere in the world and those from less well off areas deserve support.

There has been much celebration of the rapid advances made in the digital world. However, connectivity alone, while necessary, is not sufficient. Just as liquid flowing through a rocky, porous, inhospitable, and arid landscape will soon evaporate and leave us with little more than the residue of its passing, connectivity without a higher-order capacity for emergence and scale will not transform.

So what is missing? Call it a generative innovation which is capable of production and reproduction. It is a pattern of beautiful, rather than malignant, complexity and it is most recognisable in nature.

Two pathways: malignant and beautiful

Imagine that we give everyone a playing card and ask them to join the great flow of construction on our house of cards. Playing cards seem to have a lot of benefits: they are small, stackable, easily transported, and readily available. Each person painstakingly invests time and energy artfully placing their card on the house. It starts with two cards leaning against each other in a simple way. A linear plan is established to scale the construction, but things get more complex. Some people build round rooms, others build steeples. Soon a grand cathedral rises from our construction site. We stand proud of the collective ability of our innovators, but the joy is fleeting. A breeze ruffles the edges and soon a wind picks up. The house crashes down around us in a cascade of destruction. While it became ever-more complex in scale and design, a lurking danger reared its ugly head. It turns out that there were inherent design flaws and, most likely, errors in our thinking.

Now imagine a slightly different scenario. What if everyone were given a Lego building block? The flow of parts soon leads to a grand construction. This time arches and domes bubble up out of the creative crowd. Innovations follow innovations. Someone notices that the Lego framework is really just based on a connector made of one or more bumps that fit into corresponding sockets. People develop new mindsets that embrace concepts like adaptive pluralism, abundance, and dynamic thinking – even if they do not use those terms. Soon people are inventing new kinds of Lego components that can bridge gaps. Others make clear versions to shed light on the construction, still others make custom versions that look like people but have a bump on the top of the head and sockets for feet. People make single Lego bricks, others make snap-on wheels and axles, and soon an entire city, complete with vehicles and inhabitants, rises from the flow of people and blocks.

Both of these scenarios were about connectivity. Both fostered the flow of value and invention. But one of them was malignant and tended towards catastrophic failure, while the other was beautiful in its complexity.

Beautiful complexity

That same kind of beautiful complexity can be seen in nature: atoms make up molecules that make up cells that make up organs that make up systems that make up life on Earth. This is a generative pattern – one of process rather than form. It demonstrates the capacity of a framework or system to foster emergence by adhering to a set of simple rules (such as atoms make up molecules, sockets fit into plugs).

What we will need is not only 'connectivity for all', a right to be a part of the information flow, but also a way to cultivate new value from not just the information but also from making and sharing various forms of innovation. To do this, we need to harness leadership from informed supporters and champions of new mindsets and ways of working with the current trajectory of technology wherever vulnerable people are found.

Emerging future

Let's imagine the not-too-distant future. Imagine if a creative maker in a small village (or marginalized urban area) was given access to a generative framework – the organic ecosystem for production supported by a number of systems, institutions and organizations. There are a number of options for this group. Firstly, we could help them learn the literacy of human-centred innovation, based on rapid participatory techniques, so the inventor can sharpen their idea with a focus on unmet or unvoiced needs that are bubbling up.

Secondly, we can provide 'Internet of Everything' – authoring tools that embed economics directly into the fabric of every design – and supply the group with a way to reconstruct vitally important items through hyper-local manufacturing kits. They would be able to use supplies on the ground. This would help inventors from anywhere and on any economic footing. Finding and rewarding the value of the intellectual efforts they make will be critical.

Thirdly, we could foster connectivity and a worldwide community of billions of people.

Fourthly – and this one can be done in steps starting by repurposing existing smartphones and other connected devices – we could refactor the building blocks of manufacturing and computing into basic components that compute, store, sense, connect, and assemble. All this could be combined with a way to source local materials and fabrication resource sets that can be deployed with disaster-affected people wherever they may be.

The self-empowered inventor with her small team, supported in the right way, could solve immediate problems quickly. Solutions could be assembled from those bins of refactored computing 'raw material'. Maybe the product or service is built out of bamboo and twine, maybe from computation and storage, or maybe some sort of package is 3D printed from locally found refuse. Any sector – health, WASH, nutrition, shelter, education, and early recovery – can be transformed by these developments. Even search and rescue could benefit: currently, vital equipment used for finding and recovering people from collapsed buildings is expensive and unobtainable for many. Through experimentation, manufacturing, and training, the innovation of locally made gear can equalize the playing field and save lives in the process.

Further, those raw materials may be information devices that are sometimes hardware and sometimes software. Think of these devices as fungible (economics-speak for interchangeable): they might start out as software but, if someone can make a better one from hardware, the component can just be swapped out. Trained relief workers and those they help will be able to do these things in the future.

Back to our villager affected by disaster: She could make her product from local materials and equipment in her village makerspace. It might start out being handmade and, as she grows her business, she may build in some automated assembly to streamline manufacturing. Her creative, divergent thinking, nudged by the right kit and training, leads to the discovery of a differentiated product or service. Then she could publish the recipe as part of a worldwide 'internet of manufacturing' information commons. Think of it as a physical app store combined with an ever-growing how-things-work encyclopaedia. She will be emboldened not just through new tools and resources but, more crucially, new mindsets – a paradigm of innovation that embraces abundance, divergent thinking and adaptive pluralism.

If a villager on the other side of the planet needs a similar solution, he can download the recipe, use a machine-learning-generated substitution matrix to figure out what local materials can be used in manufacturing, and start selling it in his community. Because this is a generative system, the original inventor gets a small royalty for her work. If the derivative work gets used to build something more rich and complex, both the original inventor and the one who built on top of it share value. These might be fractions of a penny for bits of capability. But just about anything multiplied by a trillion turns into a big number. It would not be surprising if a developed economy stumbles on this sort of innovation, developed under extreme constraints by smart villagers, and turns it into a billion-dollar line of business. This resulting new reality will be massive small change.

Through connectivity coupled with a generative framework of atoms and bits, that original villager soon has investment capital to uplift her community. While developing economies may not have much in the way of tangible produced and exportable goods in the classic sense, every person, every community, every country is awash with insights from their natural human resources. Now, what if we could just harness that energy to power this future? I am excited to say that, in many ways, we are already seeing this happen. This book gives us a glimpse at what might be possible if we took these ideas seriously.

About the author

Mickey McManus is a research fellow in the office of the chief technology officer at Autodesk and is the chairman of MAYA Design. He co-authored *Trillions: Thriving in the Emerging Information Ecology* (Wiley 2012), and holds patents in connected products, vehicles and services.

PART II
Understanding humanitarian innovation and the challenges it raises

With an appreciation of the problems and the ameliorative potential covered in the first part, it is important to consider the options to 'do better' and 'do different' through innovation. A number of key elements are described including process of change, user engagement, fast failure/rapid prototyping, lean start-up/agile innovation, learning in context, and design thinking. This part covers:

- Change and the innovation process
- Innovating in challenging situations
- Innovation lifecycle and the 'Missing Middle'
- Complexity theory and adaptive pluralism

CHAPTER 4

How change happens and the process of humanitarian innovation

Eric James and Abigail Taylor

Innovation is all about change and understanding change processes is a key step in managing it. This chapter covers four key elements – context, complexity, creativity, and culture – that must be understood to effectively manage change and the process of humanitarian innovation. The innovation process is made up of a number of sequential steps including defining the challenge and identifying the opportunity, searching and selecting ideas, creating a prototype or starting a pilot, testing and using a viable solution, raising awareness about the innovation, and, finally, diffusion, which involves replicating the innovation outside its original setting. This chapter ends with a short discussion of innovation in other sectors.

Keywords: innovation, process, context, complexity, creativity, culture

Humanitarian relief workers need to appreciate the nature of change in order to understand the role they might play in creating change (both intentionally and unintentionally). In his contribution, Duncan Green (in Chapter 10 of this book) examines how change happens in more detail, including how change fits into the international aid sector and its structures, power dynamics, mindsets, and failures.

The four Cs of innovation

Before embracing change and starting on a process of innovation, it can be helpful to consider 'the four Cs': context, complexity, creativity, and culture.

Context

Context is simply the setting, environment, or set of circumstances in which an event happens. In humanitarian situations, context is the emergency that happens as a result of the failure of development. It is where a hazard triggers a catastrophic event that leads to human suffering and further vulnerability. Elements of history, economics, politics, environment, geography, culture, and so on all contribute to context. Context can often refer to a specific country or part of a country, or, conversely, a set of countries, region,

http://dx.doi.org/10.3362/9781780449531.004

or type of area (e.g., urban or rural). Appreciating context is key to effective humanitarian innovation. Understanding context is, however, not simple. The complexity of humanitarian response means that while challenges may appear similar across different responses, the root causes and contributing factors are never exactly the same. The specifics and nuances of each context must, therefore, be understood in depth if an appropriate solution is to be found. The importance of understanding the context and shaping solutions to it underpins the contributions of a number of authors to this book and, in Chapter 6, Ian Gray examines the implications of context for scaling humanitarian innovations.

Complexity

Complexity science provides a way to better explain and describe systems and change processes in the world around us (Ramalingam et al., 2008: 1). A complex system is characterized by:

- interconnected and interdependent parts;
- interaction between those parts, which shapes how change happens within the system;
- behaviour that is usually unpredictable and that, as a result of interaction between the parts, can produce an effect that is greater than the sum of those caused by the parts.

Thus, the unpredictable interaction between parts of a system (e.g., a community) makes it impossible to reliably predict how the system will respond to a single change. In a complex system, prediction is near impossible, change may not be proportional to the intervention, and behaviour cannot be controlled (though it can be influenced). By contrast, in controlled contexts (e.g., a car), we are able to predict the response of the system to simple interventions.

Taking context into account is a vital skill for innovators if they are to work effectively within complex systems. It is characterized by flexible, adaptive, and dynamic responses and the ability to sense and respond to different contexts – as opposed to using only pre-planned processes and systems (Overland, 2012; Snowden and Boon, 2007). It is a skill that comes naturally to many humanitarian relief workers.

Complexity theory does not describe a single set of circumstances. Rather, there are multiple models and concepts associated with the theory. Linear systems tend to be simple, ordered, process-driven, and reliant on control and compliance. These are some of the central ideas characterizing 'neo-Newtonian' conceptions of reality. By contrast, non-linear systems can be complex, chaotic or disordered, and reliant on dynamic, adaptable, and agile thinking. These are some of the central ideas of 'adaptive pluralism'. Figure 4.1 shows where some of the most commonly used concepts lie in relation to the linear and non-linear domains. These themes recur throughout this book and Robert Chambers, in particular, discusses them further (see Chapter 8).

Complexity can manifest itself clearly when it clashes with established processes and systems, especially in large organizations where standardization (compliance and other measures used to 'de-risk' operations) can take precedence. The following three examples identify situations where this struggle can be experienced on a day-to-day basis in humanitarian organizations.

Case study 1 - Funding: Traditional funders usually require organizations seeking grants to quantify expected outcomes in their applications, implicitly favouring proposals that promise to reach the greatest number of beneficiaries at the lowest cost or provide other such indicators. Funders are inclined to favour predictable programmes with quantifiable outputs. Often, donors apply a linear system to a complex reality. This tendency exists for numerous reasons: success is easier to communicate; it is assumed that such measures allow organizations to be held to account more readily; and programmes can be monitored through standardized mechanisms. For programmes that extend beyond the simple provision of supplies and services,

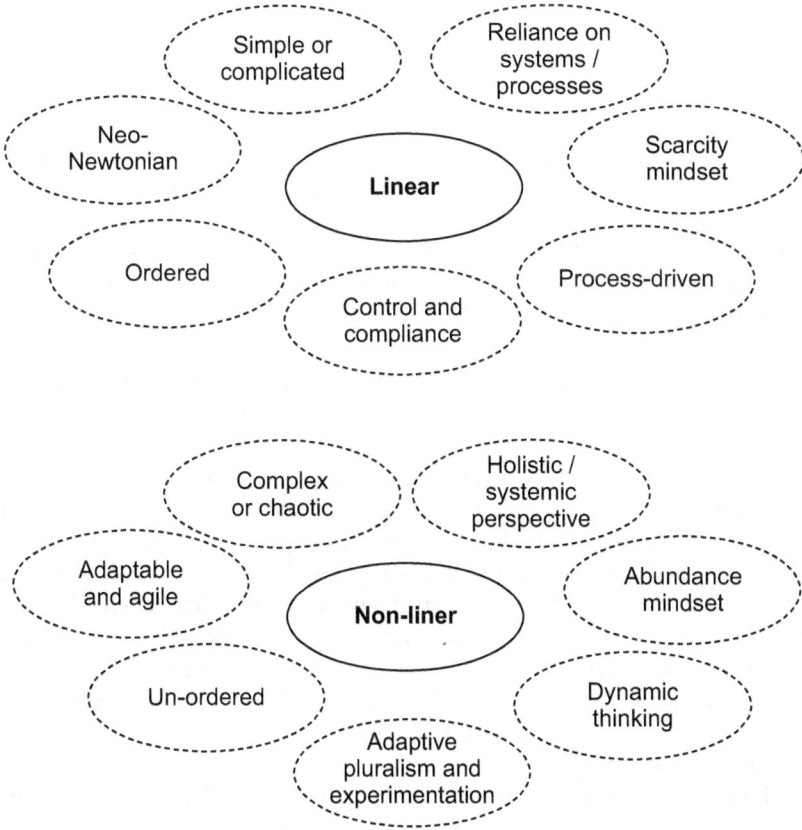

Figure 4.1 Concepts, characteristics, and responses in linear and non-linear systems

the complexity of the impacts mean that traditional fundraising campaigns and applications are unlikely to capture the full scope of the programme. This is particularly true when innovation is applied. The full impacts of an innovative programme are unlikely to be entirely predictable, quantifiable, immediate, or direct. The same programme will not have an identical impact in any two settings. This can frustrate attempts to experiment with multiple approaches, or to tailor and adapt programmes on the ground. In this way, the funding system clashes with the reality of humanitarian programmes.

Case study 2 - Monitoring and evaluation: Established approaches to monitoring and evaluation can create frustration because of their limited capacity to capture the full impact of programmes. The desire to create simple and standard processes to monitor projects originates from the practical intentions to:

- make it easier for management and other staff to understand the outcomes of a large number of programmes at a glance in consistent internal reports
- make it straightforward for programme staff to monitor progress as processes do not need to be re-invented for every new programme
- fulfil donor requirements.

However, many programmes cannot be effectively evaluated by relying on predetermined, quantifiable metrics. Innovation requires feedback, iteration, and an openness to failure. Helpful monitoring is therefore not oriented towards proving that targets have been met, but rather at capturing successes, failures, and areas for improvement. As an ongoing process, programme management should include mechanisms to learn from the findings of frequent programme iteration. In this way, relief workers are able to identify and respond to complex outcomes as they emerge, resulting in more effective programmes and innovations.

Case study 3 - Recruitment: Much recruitment in the innovation space does not happen through 'normal' recruitment channels. Innovation requires passionate leaders and advocates, and people with creativity who are able to see connections others may not, so the emphasis is on cultural fit (for example, seeking individuals with abundance mindsets) and on the ability of recruits to navigate uncharted territory and to build relationships that can contribute to changing the status quo. It can be difficult to identify these skills through traditional recruitment processes, such as creating a list of skills required and checking these against an applicant's CV or résumé. Traditional approaches to recruitment can draw out good candidates but to get great candidates non-traditional approaches are helpful. Prioritizing skills and attributes that are hard to evidence by simply looking at a person's credentials necessarily requires personal connection and deeper understanding of a candidate's experience and mindset. Recruitment through individual networks and relying on instinct can, therefore, be a more effective way to find outstanding candidates. Despite this reality, the latter approach can draw criticism as being less rigorous or less objective than established formal processes. Candidates can also be disappointed when told that they may not 'fit'. The ability to recognize complex and linear domains, and to identify the appropriate response to both, has been identified as a vital skill for those leading and working in humanitarian response.

Creativity

Creativity is central to innovation because it is from this that insight and new ideas are generated. Creativity is the ability to come up with novel solutions to problems. Ellis Paul Torrance defined creativity this way: 'a process of becoming sensitive to problems, deficiencies, gaps in knowledge, missing elements, disharmonies, and so on; identifying the difficulty; searching for solutions, making guesses, or formulating hypotheses about the deficiencies; testing and retesting these hypotheses and possibly modifying and retesting them; and finally communicating the results' (Torrance, 1966: 6). Creativity stems from the ability to harness original thinking, curiosity, and connections and to tolerate ambiguity. It is also linked to having the confidence and space to exercise these abilities. Creativity enables innovators to develop new solutions to problems, or to reimagine existing solutions in new contexts to address different challenges. The results of creativity can be tangible (e.g., hardware) or intangible (e.g., new ideas or funding opportunities).

Culture

Here, 'culture' refers to the mindsets found in organizations seeking to drive innovation and keep it open to change. It is the ethos (i.e., characteristic or spirit) and is found in the people within an organization and its teams. In a group or organization, the culture that develops can have a scarcity mindset or an abundance mindset. Embracing abundance thinking is one approach to fostering an innovative culture. Abundance thinking is typified by a mindset that there are enough resources to enable deep collaboration, explore possibilities, take risks, and allow an openness to different possibilities. It welcomes change with the idea that more positive outcomes are yet to come. An abundance mindset is commonly found in individuals who adopt different behaviours or strategies to find better solutions (known as 'positive deviants').

Organizations can build an abundance mentality into their ethos, and this can be instrumental in unlocking opportunities and removing barriers to change. By contrast, scarcity mindsets can kill abundance mindsets, stifling innovation and creating barriers to change. Table 4.1 contrasts the characteristics of abundance and scarcity mindsets. The ability to identify different mindsets can help leaders attract the right people. Such people will reinforce the organization's culture. Additionally, understanding the mindsets of individuals outside the team can enable entrepreneurs and

Table 4.1 Characteristics of abundance and scarcity mindsets

	Abundance mindset	Scarcity mindset
Relationships	Collaboration Open Generous with knowledge, contacts and compassion Trusts other and builds rapport Finds answers together with others I win / you win Convergence of interest	Competition Closed Stingy with knowledge, contacts and compassion Defaults to scepticism and suspicion Has all the answers I win / you lose Conflict of interest
Perspective	Optimistic about the future Thinks big Bold and embraces risk Thankful, reflective, and confident Everything is permitted unless explicitly forbidden	Pessimistic about the future Thinks small (though not necessarily always small-minded) Cautious and risk-averse Entitled and fearful Everything is forbidden unless explicitly permitted
Action	Focus on what can be done with available resources Focus on opportunities to attract more resources for everyone	Problem-focused Focused on scarcity of resources to attract more resources for themselves

positive deviants to position themselves more effectively to influence and work together with others.

The innovation process explained

Innovation produces something transformative by helping to reveal insights, produce 'eureka' moments, and increase serendipity through a deliberate process. There are many ways to explain what the process looks like. One widely known model is described by Tidd and Bessant (2013). This four-step innovation process is generally influenced by the organization's strategy as well as its culture. This model consists of four parts:

1. **Search**: problem identification and alternative solution generation. How can we find opportunities for innovation?
2. **Select**: selecting the most feasible solution. What are we going to do and why?
3. **Implement**: implementing this solution. How are we going to make it happen?
4. **Capture**: evaluating the solutions that create value. How are we going to get the benefits from it?

The common characteristic of the models is that they begin by identifying issues and work through the innovation process towards a new product or service. They are most often described in a linear or step-by-step (i.e., 1, 2, 3)

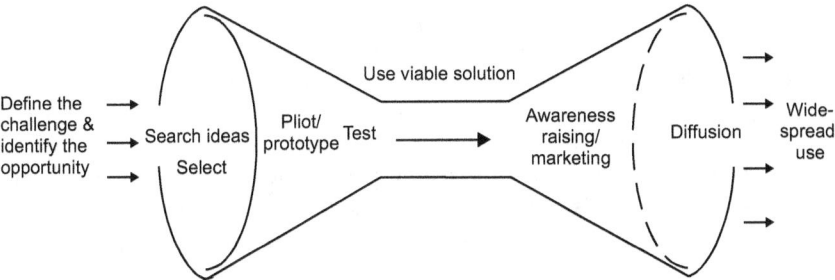

Figure 4.2 The complete innovation process

fashion but, in reality, the process is far more iterative, filled with starts and stops and occasional unexpected pivots and improvisations.

For humanitarian innovation, a comprehensive model that takes this complexity and non-linearity into account is needed. From our perspective, the double-ended funnel shown in Figure 4.2 represents the most useful understanding of the process of innovation. The steps it contains are closely linked and dynamic activities. As such, it is represented, described, and practised in terms of a general direction with many pauses, iterations, and feedback loops. While controlling each eventuality during the process may be impossible, planning and preparing a trajectory can help manage an innovation, taking it from idea to widespread use. The rest of this chapter is used to describe this model and concludes with a brief discussion of innovation in other sectors.

Define the challenge and identify the opportunity

In any humanitarian context, there are seemingly endless problems. Yet, for any innovation to have an impact, there needs to be focus. Innovation needs to start with understanding the scope of what can be done by narrowing the effort and identifying a specific problem. The problem identified needs to have some urgency (if it is not solved, it may, for example, cause extra work, waste resources or directly contribute to pain or suffering) and be solvable in some way (see 'use the viable solution' below).

The more precise the understanding of the problem, the better. This challenge may be related to a process or address a paradigm, but it may also be an opportunity to improve an existing product by applying technology either invented or borrowed from another field. The inspiration (i.e., the spark of an idea) for a solution should flow from the problem itself. With a problem identified, its remedy may appear within reach.

Developing an effective problem statement is one way to get started. It creates a necessary pause before plunging forward with a supposedly great idea, creates common understanding, and provides an end point on which to focus (and refocus when off-track) throughout the innovation process. The only effective way to create a problem statement is to know the people and the problem. In international aid, this is typically called an 'assessment'; in the commercial sector it is called 'market research', and in the *Lean Start Up* Ries (2011) calls it 'getting out of the building'. This problem statement covers five Ws (who, what, where, when, and why) and is SMART (specific, measurable, achievable, realistic and time-bound). 'Useful tools and techniques' at the end of this book provides a number of useful tools and techniques to help create it. When starting with a focus on the problem itself, it helps to begin with the end in mind.

Search ideas

With a problem identified, the search for possible solutions becomes more refined, easy and ultimately fruitful. During this stage, creativity is important, as is an openness to new ideas. Without these, potential breakthroughs may be missed. The pressure to conform to business-like requirements of meeting deadlines and ensuring accountability may present obstacles and make it more difficult to look at things differently and with fresh perspectives. Those involved in innovation need creative confidence, the 'quality ... [of] making leaps, trusting their intuition, and chasing solutions that they have not totally figured out yet' (IDEO, 2015: 19). Effective leadership may help increase creative confidence while reducing the pressure to conform to business-as-usual expectations.

Innovative ideas can come from virtually anywhere. The search for ideas may start with basic information gathering: while this is most likely to be desk-based or online, other sources, such as talking to potential end users, should be considered, depending on what is available locally. Inspiration and nascent new ideas may reveal themselves while considering a challenge from a different perspective. Other fields and phenomena can also provide new ideas. Nature (through what is called biomimicry), innovative companies (e.g., Tesla), and government agencies (e.g., NASA) might provide insight, but small ideas borrowed across sectors can be especially enlightening. For instance, surgeons in the UK observed the effectiveness of race-car pit crews and developed new ways of organizing the transition of patients from the operating theatre to post-op recovery. An effective innovation process provides opportunities to gain insight and fosters 'ah-ha' moments wherever they may come from.

The key question at this stage is not simply whether the innovation can be created, but whether it should be in the first place. In other words, it may be possible to create something new but, if it does not solve the problem, it is not worth pursuing. It is also important to realize that there are a lot of solutions out there looking for problems. This is the reason for the existence of so many unsuccessful consumer products, never-used smartphone apps, and 'development solutions' that are not used in the field. Each year, the US patent office receives well over 600,000 utility applications, most of which never become a commercial product.

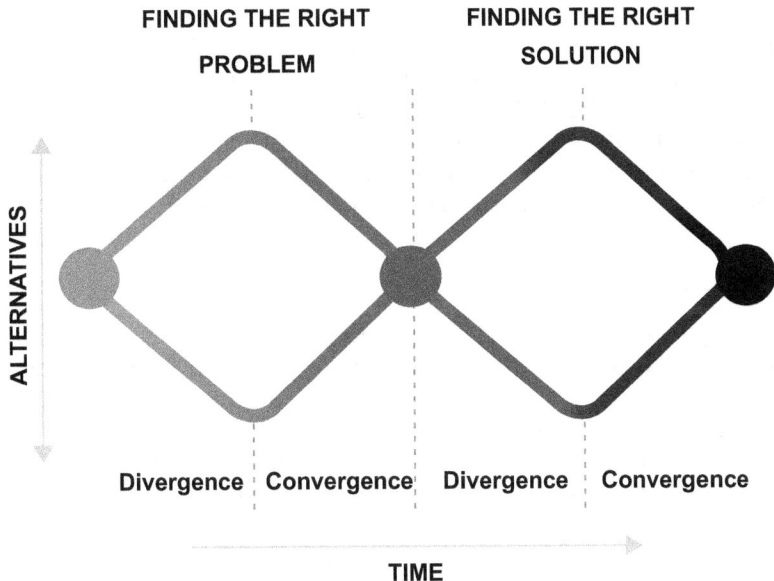

Figure 4.3 The double-diamond model of design (Design Council, 2005)

A thoughtful model that links the first element in the innovation process ('define the challenge or identify the opportunity') with the second ('search ideas') is found in the 'double-diamond' model of design shown in Figure 4.3 (Design Council, 2005). In this model, a problem is identified and then researched by examining users (in our case, aid workers and affected people), existing and available options, and then managing the information. The needs as well as the assets and capabilities of potential users should be considered. With the problem clearly established, research is creatively expanded, using divergent thinking, to include other fundamental issues (Norman, 2013: 220) to generate many possible solutions or outcomes. A range of considerations can then be taken into account. Convergent thinking is used to narrow in on a single, real and viable solution. When searching ideas, a similar pattern is followed: a wide range of options is considered (using divergent thinking) before converging on those elements that seem most desirable, feasible, and viable (IDEO, 2015).

Select

The aim of this stage in the innovation process is to reduce uncertainty and minimize risk before going forward with further development. Before each prototype is created or each pilot undertaken, the results expected need to be evaluated and the key features of the solution which will address (and ideally resolve) the identified problem need to be selected. This should not be seen as a conclusive step but as one that will require further adaptation, development, and evaluation as the innovation process continues.

While each part of the process of innovation relies on continual back-and-forth – eliciting constructive criticism, feedback, and advice – it is especially crucial during the selection phase. Feedback seeks the opinion of others to ensure learning and that the innovation remains focused on the problem that was identified at the start. In this way, the process remains sufficiently human-centred to be successful when adopted more widely. 'Useful tools and techniques' at the end of this book, provides a number of ways to obtain feedback.

Prototype/pilot

Once a potentially viable solution is identified, it is important to make something that shows the ideas generated so far. Words are not enough; an idea needs to be translated into something tangible. It is important to build something: a prototype. The word prototype derives from a Greek term meaning 'primitive form'. Creating a prototype involves building a model of a solution that approximates its appearance and behaviour. This is often done quickly because refinement can wait until further along in the process. The prototype can take many forms, from a very rudimentary model of clay, cardboard and tape to more sophisticated 3D printed mock-ups. The key thing is that the prototype can be learned from. Receiving feedback, particularly from people who are seeing the prototype for the first time, is crucial.

Good design – the plan for the creation of a useful item, system, or way in which people can be engaged to save lives and reduce human suffering – is an essential element of prototyping. Basic principles that can be kept in mind from the start include how people will use the innovation, aesthetics, functionality, and simplicity. Good design considers factors such as colour, shape, texture, and use of space (as in scale, balance and harmony). Human-centred design is intended to ensure these principles are part and parcel of an innovation by taking people's context, needs, and assets into account and taking an empathetic approach.

Because it is nearly impossible for a solution to 'hit the bull's-eye' on the first try, it is common to generate numerous prototypes. It is important to manage expectations by beginning with the mindset that a series of prototypes will be produced. In lean start-up methods, this involves the development of a minimum viable product (MVP) which includes the basic features that will satisfy the initial users (see the 'innovators' described in the section on Diffusion below). An MVP can be a drawing, a video, a mock-up of outside packaging, a brochure, a datasheet, or anything else that conveys a sense of the innovative solution. It does not have to be a fully functioning prototype. This allows learning to take place as quickly as possible, and for failures to occur without having to end the entire effort. 'Useful tools and techniques' at the end of this book, provides a number of ways prototypes can be created.

For the purposes of humanitarian innovation, a pilot is a trial phase done in the field, often over a predetermined period of time. In a pilot, the innovation is used with potential end users or in a situation that mimics a site of intended use. During a pilot, variables such as feasibility, unintended consequences, time, and cost can be evaluated prior to scaling the innovation (i.e., putting it into wide use). Both quantitative and qualitative elements can be measured to determine if the solution is an improvement over current practice. Feedback should be sought from end users as well as experts. It is a test of not only the technology but also the systems and human factors around the innovation, and this provides a way to learn. If the innovation involves a technology, this process corresponds to technology readiness levels (TRL) of 7 and 8 (See Annex 3).

It is important to be mindful of unintended consequences and uses. Ethical requirements and other considerations (e.g., resource constraints) are likely to curtail innovations that pilots show may be harmful, unnecessary, or a waste of time. At the same time, there can be positive, yet unplanned and inadvertent, outputs at this stage. The lessons learned during this stage may lead to other breakthroughs and new innovations. History is filled with instances of accidental discoveries leading to things that are better and more novel: stainless steel, plastic, cornflakes, Post-it notes and superglue are all examples.

Test

Testing is an essential step for learning and for confirming assumptions. It can be done at planned intervals but is often better as a continual process. Some find it helpful to first use new innovations within an organization (a practice informally known as 'dogfooding'). Before testing, the requirements and parameters of an innovation should be outlined so that the data collected can be the right type and the analysis measures the intended result. There are many methods of testing, and examining these is beyond our purpose here, but three are worth noting:

> *Functionality testing*: This type of testing ensures that the innovation works as intended. For instance, in electrical products, it may start with a simple test to determine if the on/off button works and then go far beyond this to determine trouble-shooting requirements. Destruction testing, which checks the robustness of hardware in the face of realistic scenarios exploring everything from wear and tear to issues of long-term durability, falls into this category. It can also include performance tests that measure, for example, a material's tensile strength and breaking point.
>
> *Software testing*: In software development, a 'box' approach is often used to ensure the coding that comprise programmes and applications operate as intended. Tests fall into one of three colour boxes – white, black, or grey – depending on the perspective engineers take to designing them. White-box testing examines the software's internal structure and components (code and algorithms). Black-box testing looks at the functionality of the software without considering the individual

components. Grey-box testing combines white- and black-box testing; i.e., testers know the state of internal data structures while testing the functionality.

Usability testing: This type of testing surveys end users to see how easy a product or service is to use. Users may be asked to complete tasks using the product itself to determine if they encounter problems or experience confusion. Similarly, acceptance testing ensures that a product or service meets the requirements of the intended end user before it is released or shipped.

In this testing stage, effective measurement and data-management are important. The analysis should reveal what happened and how basic assumptions have been addressed. Ideally, a mix of quantitative and qualitative data will be used to drive the process forward. The data should be organized and presented in a way that makes it engaging and easy to understand. It should grab people's attention and be persuasive. In particular, people who will champion the idea should feel compelled to tell others about it.

Openness to failure is an important element of effective innovation, particularly at this stage. Traditionally, organizations and management have attempted to avoid failure and responded to it with shame. Failure is most often associated with the pain of missed targets and dashed expectations. Yet the variables of innovation are too extensive to eliminate completely. When approached with an innovator's mindset, failure is part of the process, something to be expected, and even a catalyst for further innvation. Expressions common among inventors and entrepreneurs are 'fail forward' and 'fail fast' (meaning to 'fail' in a constructive way that captures the lessons learned and applies them to the innovation's next iteration). Having the professional maturity to be open to failure may not be easy in practice, but it is essential for innovative leaders. See Annex 5, which provides a measure that can be used to determine the degree to which management is open to the risks of innovation.

Use the viable solution

At this stage, the innovation has been tested and is ready to use. To be 'field-ready', the innovation should meet three basic requirements. First, it should be urgently 'desired' by the intended users. In other words, it should solve the problem initially identified by the people it will affect and who will use it. It should make a difference to their work and lives. If not, funding it will be difficult to obtain and end users will not use it. Second, the technology used should be 'feasible': it should have undergone testing and indeed work as intended. How long it will take to bring the innovation to fruition and what is needed to make it happen should also have been considered. Finally, it should be 'viable' from different organizational perspectives such as procurement, monitoring and evaluation

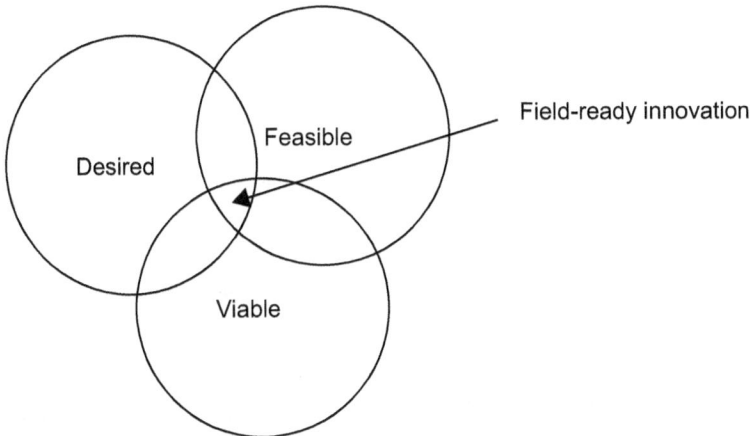

Figure 4.4 Elements of field-ready innovations

(M&E), and programme delivery. (If it is a commercial innovation, it should also be able to generate a profit.) This model is represented in Figure 4.4. If these three criteria are met, the solution will likely possess a number of characteristics including ease of use, robustness, repeatability and checked for quality and safety.

Awareness-raising and marketing

For the innovation to be ultimately successful, there must be awareness-raising and marketing. Marketing is the active promotion of the innovation. Awareness-raising simply involves ensuring an increasingly wide number of potential users 'hear about' the innovation; marketing involves providing them with the possibility of using it. There are a wide range of marketing activities, such as making the product appealing to a sufficient number of users. When done well, marketing takes into account the needs of the user and tries to satisfy their needs.

Marketing may not initially seem like a necessary step in the non-profit or humanitarian context. However, a range of innovations have failed to be used widely because marketing was not undertaken to the extent needed. A cycle has developed where someone has what they assume is a great idea, the work is done to create a prototype and get the initial users, but then no one adopts the innovation. Part of the problem may be basic awareness, but a lack of marketing is also likely to blame.

At this stage in the innovation process, appearance matters. Marketing is about building appeal and attracting people. As in any technical area, specialists are needed to ensure the right marketing approach is employed. If a new technology is being used, for example, they should be able to convey the 'magic' behind it in a way that humanizes it and makes it easily

Table 4.2 The MINDSPACE framework – a checklist of influences on people's behaviour for use when making policy

Messenger	We are heavily influenced by who communicates information
Incentives	Our responses to incentives are shaped by predictable mental shortcuts such as strongly avoiding losses
Norms	We are strongly influenced by what others do
Defaults	We go with the flow of pre-set options
Salience	Our attention is drawn to what is novel and seems relevant to us
Priming	Our acts are often influenced by sub-conscious cues
Affect	Our emotional associations can powerfully shape our actions
Commitments	We seek to be consistent with our public promises, and reciprocate acts
Ego	We act in ways that make us feel better about ourselves

understood. There are artful ways to provide a vision and show how an innovation can make a difference. The well-known marketer, Seth Godin (2006), sees it this way: 'In a world with too many choices and too little time, most consumers will just ignore stuff. You have to be remarkable to get noticed. People will ignore a regular cow but notice a purple cow'. So make sure people see your innovation as a 'purple cow' and give them a chance to approach it.

Taking behavioural insights (e.g., about factors that affect decision-making) into account throughout the innovation process can have a significant impact on the adoption of the solution. The MINDSPACE framework (Table 4.2) was developed by the Behavioural Insights Team and the Institute for Government in the UK to help policy makers understand what might influence people's behaviour (Dolan et al., 2010). The tool can be helpful in ensuring that an innovation is framed in a way which draws people in, encouraging potential users to change their behaviour and adopt the innovation.

Diffusion

Diffusion is when the new innovation goes into wider use. An innovation is diffused when it is replicated and adopted outside its original setting. The greater the adoption (i.e., the more users of the innovation), the higher the level of diffusion. This is the process of scaling-out.

Diffusion takes place over a period of time, not all at once. For example, 3D printing was invented in the 1980s by Charles Hull, and the origins of virtual reality can be traced to the work of Morton Heilig in the 1950s. Both technologies are only now becoming widely used, although they remain little-used in the development and relief sectors. Diffusion happens as the earliest users adapt, share their knowledge with others, and so on. Opinion leaders and change agents ('champions') play an important role in this diffusion process.

The users of an innovation can be categorized into distinct groups which form a bell-curve (Rogers, 1983). The first group is known as innovators. They are highly experimental and risk-tolerant, and may also have resources that others do not. The next group, early adopters, have some of the same characteristics as innovators but, if their use of the innovation proves fruitful, they are in a good position to share their opinions. Following the early adopters is the early majority. Those in this group are slower to adopt an innovation but still take it on faster than average.

Many innovations fail to scale to cover the gap between early adopters and the early majority. This is part of the 'missing middle' problem described by Ian Gray (see Chapter 6 of this book): good ideas die because of a lack of diffusion and failure to scale. It is therefore vital that everything be done to ensure that there is sufficient momentum once there is a useable viable solution. After the initial users/customers have been acquired, the marketing message needs to shift to one of 'social proof' (i.e., that others use it and so it is no longer risky) (Wosinska et al., 2001).

On the centre-right of the bell-curve, the late majority are doubtful about innovations and may only adopt because of social pressure or economic necessity. Finally are the laggards, who are the last to adopt an innovation because they do not find the innovation necessary, perhaps because they are traditionalists or lack the resources. They may also be distrustful of others. As diffusion progresses, there can initially be a high level of excitement (some see this as hype) followed by a trough of disillusionment that can take years to escape before a widely diffused productivity is reached (Basiliere and Shanler, 2014).

This pattern of diffusion applies well to social innovations (both development and humanitarian): just because an idea is a good one or an invention great, it does not mean that people will use it or organizations will allocate precious resources to buy, hire, or rent it. So, for diffusion to be successful (i.e., for scale to be realized), wider numbers of people need to adopt (i.e., use) the innovation to move it from one category of user to the next. Diffusion depends on awareness-building: people need to know about the innovation. This can be done through personal interaction and social influence, but marketing is needed for an innovative product or service to be successful.

Innovation in other sectors

Innovation is something found in every sector. The hard sciences, engineering, and other areas, including the creative arts, thrive on it. For some, the area in California known as Silicon Valley is the leader in many aspects of innovation. Innovations can be found in most sectors, primarily thanks to advances made in computing. These include both software and hardware, and are perhaps typified by the nearly ubiquitous smartphone. Many similar developments are now winding their way through different sectors and in different areas of the world.

Given this scale and pace of change, it is worthwhile briefly assessing the contributions and ideas that may be relevant to the field of humanitarian relief. The acceleration of technology is surely one of most positive changes. Every effort benefits from improvements in computing power, telecommunications, and technological changes in other areas. There have also been contributions to humanitarian programmes from a consideration of how technology can impact social change and the global nature of some organizations. Finally, there are some concepts and tools that lend themselves to other sectors, particularly in the process of innovation (e.g., lean start-up methods described below).

The focus on profit has generated enormous surpluses of wealth. The accompanying belief in the invisible hand of the market and its power to solve problems has led to a reliance, or at least an emphasis, on technological fixes and other quick hacks. As a result, human issues (e.g., resistance to change, entrenched mindsets, and power relationships) are often underestimated in ways that make major challenges (such as supplying sufficient energy or water and sustaining the environment) more intractable.

References

Basiliere, P. and Shanler, M. (2014) *Hype Cycle for 3D Printing*, Gartner Research Paper <https://www.gartner.com/doc/2803426> [accessed 15 September 2017].

Design Council (2005) *A study of the design process*. British Design Council, London, UK. http://www.designcouncil.org.uk/sites/default/files/asset/document/ElevenLessons_Design_Council%20(2).pdf [accessed 15 September 2017].

Dolan, P., Hallsworth, M., Halpern, D., King, D. and Vlaev, I. (2010) 'MINDSPACE: Influencing Behaviour Through Public Policy', *Cabinet Office/Behavioural Insights Team*.

Godin, S. (2006) *Purple Cow: Transform Your Business by Being Remarkable*, Penguin, London.

IDEO (2015) *The Field Guide to Human-Centered Design*, IDEO, Palo Alto, CA.

Norman, D. (2013) *The Design of Everyday Things*, Basic Books, New York.

Overland, S. (2012) 'World Vision Emergency Response Development', commissioned by World Vision Australia.

Ramalingam, B., Jones, H., Reba, T. and Young, J. (2008) 'Exploring the Science of Complexity: Ideas and Implications for Development and Humanitarian Efforts', *ODI Working Paper 285*.

Ries, E. (2011) *The Lean Start Up*, Random House, New York.

Rogers, E., (1983) *Diffusion of Innovation*. Free Press, New York.

Snowden, D. and Boone, E. (2007) 'A Leader's Framework for Decision Making', *Harvard Business Review*, November 2007, pp. 68–76.

Tidd, J. and Bessant, J. (2013) *Managing Innovation: Integrating Technological, Market and Organizational Change*, John Wiley and Sons, Chichester.

Torrance, P. (1966) *Verbal Tests. Forms A and B-Figural Tests, Forms A and B, The Torrance Tests of Creative Thinking-Norms-Technical Manual Research Edition*, Personnel Press, New Jersey.

Wosinska, W., Cialdini, R., Barrett, D. and Reyhowski, J. (eds.) (2001) *The Practice of Social Influence in Multiple Cultures*, Lawrence Erlbaum Associates Publishers, Mahwah, NJ.

About the authors

Eric James, PhD, is the co-founder and executive director of Field Ready. He has over two decades of experience leading humanitarian relief programmes. He has been involved in several business start-ups, holds two patents and was a fellow/advisor at Singularity University. Eric is an affiliated expert of the Harvard Humanitarian Initiative and an adjunct professor at the DePaul University's Refugee and Forced Migration Studies programme. He is author of *Managing Humanitarian Relief: An Operational Guide for NGOs* (Practical Action Publishing, 2nd Edition, 2017) among other publications.

Abigail Taylor is a strategic advisor for the consulting firm Spark Strategy. She has developed considerable experience in business development and partnership management in Europe, Africa, and, more recently, Asia. Abigail has worked for NGOs, social enterprises, and UNHCR. She has an MA in Conflict, Security, and Development, a degree in Politics, and has worked with the UK government in parliament and through government-focused institutions. She has particular interests in complexity theory, organizational systems, and managing scale-ups.

CHAPTER 5
Problems and potential

John Bessant

Humanitarian innovation is about trying not only to innovate under severe resource constraints but also to find new ways out of situations where the mainstream innovation trajectory may be blocked. There are growing efforts to make the humanitarian innovation system more effective by learning lessons from the past, from across the sector, and, crucially, from wider innovation-management experience. This includes the engagement of experienced mainstream organizations and offering them a laboratory for exploring and deploying new solutions at the edge of where they would normally work.

Keywords: innovation processes, humanitarianism, challenges, learning

When disaster strikes, we need innovation and we need it fast. But often the mainstream solution pathways are blocked so we have to invent radical alternatives. We need to improvise. Think about an earthquake and the problem of moving food and medicine around. It becomes massively more complex when the roads are unrecognisable lumps of rock separated by gaping fissures. How do you handle water and sanitation when pipes are broken and smashed? How do you communicate when your phone lines are down? How can you provide healthcare when the hospital is in ruins? How do you house thousands of people whose homes are part of the wreckage? Under these conditions we need as much creativity as we can get.

The good news is that there are some impressive examples of innovation in this context – you can read about some of them in this book. And the underlying *process* is one we would recognise – taking knowledge and configuring it to create value to end users. Sometimes it is the result of novel R&D, for example using drones to carry relief supplies over damaged terrain, or Big Data to help in the management and logistics of large temporary settlements like refugee camps. But much of the time it is adapting and configuring existing knowledge to new purposes; sometimes it is borrowing a single idea from elsewhere, sometimes it is about creating a platform on which many variations can evolve.

Sadly, the continuing ability of disaster to surprise us, and the scale of misery which it brings, mean that humanitarian innovation capacity is at a premium. Fortunately there are growing efforts to make the humanitarian innovation system not only more efficient (via better solutions and infrastructure) but also more effective by learning lessons from the past, from across the sector and, crucially, from wider innovation-management experience. For example the UK's Department for International Development (DFID) recently commissioned a review of the humanitarian innovation ecosystem, and discussion of the theme formed a major part of the United Nations' World Humanitarian Summit in 2016 that led to the setting up of the Global Alliance for Humanitarian Innovation (GAHI).

Strengthening the humanitarian innovation capability means finding ways to deal with a number of key challenges, including the following:

- **The 'heart vs. head' challenge**: By its very nature, humanitarian innovation attracts people with a strong desire to do good, to make the world a better place. Unfortunately, whilst they may be rich in goodwill they often lack some of the core entrepreneurial skills needed to turn an idea into something which creates real and sustainable social value. This is not just the challenge of learning about *the* discipline of innovation and how to manage it; it is also about doing so under particularly difficult conditions with limited resources, lack of control, and an urgent need to build and work with diverse networks.
- **The 'fuzzy front end' challenge**: Humanitarian innovation is often a matter of finding novel solutions to old problems – but the kind of experimentation and prototyping we might recommend based on lean start-up and other agile innovation practices is hard to pull off in a context which is strongly risk-averse. In the humanitarian innovation case this is not simply the problem of a slow-moving organization with a strong immune system – there are powerful forces at work to restrain uncontrolled experimentation. Most of the financial and other resources are donated and so there is a strong sense of stewardship, being careful about the projects on which these resources are spent. And there are also powerful ethical considerations – trying out minimum viable products and experimenting with prototypes amongst suffering populations is neither practical nor desirable. So the resource-allocation system for innovation is strongly biased towards backing safe bets and proven ideas.
- **The 'user engagement' challenge**: One of the dangers in humanitarian innovation is that well-intentioned providers make assumptions about what end users actually need and what will work in their context. Inappropriate solutions provided with the best of intentions litter the sites of disasters – complex equipment which cannot be maintained, supplies used for different purposes. For example, researchers from the (now closed) Humanitarian Innovation Project at the University of Oxford found that people in Ugandan refugee camps were using emergency mosquito nets not as an anti-malarial aid but as a source of rope with which to build the shelters they felt were a more urgent need.

Underpinning this is an assumption that solutions can be designed far from the context in which they are to be implemented. What is needed is a recognition of the importance of user perspectives – for example, how people actually behave under crisis conditions, how they prioritize their emergency needs, how best they can support themselves, and the like.

Empowered users are a rich source of ideas – many important humanitarian innovations arose in this bottom-up fashion. For example, the crisis-mapping app Ushahidi emerged from users mashing-up Twitter and other social media feeds to help provide a reliable information platform during the post-election violence in Kenya. The app has subsequently been used all around the world, including during the Brisbane floods and the Fukushima nuclear disaster.

- **The 'mad mavericks' challenge**: A key characteristic of crisis conditions is that old, established solutions may not work: there's an urgent need for radical thinking. Agility, risk-taking, experimentation, and fast learning are key skills in this context – precisely the kind of environment in which entrepreneurs thrive. But the lean start-up model of experimenting and failing fast may not be appropriate under conditions where there may be the ethical consideration of playing with people's lives. Even if that were acceptable, the organizational context – using public money and with rigorous rules and procedures for careful control – militates against doing anything different. The result is that, whilst many humanitarian innovation ideas come from entrepreneurs, they are often seen as mavericks working below the radar, operating undercover, bootlegging their way. The big question for the humanitarian sector is how to internalize and institutionalize such players – how to create a context for innovation.

   An example is the case of cash programming, a radical change in the business model associated with providing food assistance. The original entrepreneurial experiments took place back in the mid-1980s but it took a further two decades before this powerful approach became accepted as a legitimate mainstream model.

- **The 'missing middle' challenge**: Humanitarian innovation involves multiple experiments carried out in a 'crisis laboratory'. Many of these lead to interesting and relevant solutions which have a positive impact in a local context; the challenge is how these can be made to scale. Dan McClure and Ian Gray (2015) call this the challenge of the missing middle, and it runs right across the spectrum of humanitarian innovation. Part of the problem comes from the nature of the humanitarian innovation process itself, which often acts as a brake on moving rapidly to scale. Reliant on donor money, there are many checks to ensure that such money is well-spent and this builds in a concern for careful evaluation, and expansion only when it can be based on solid evidence. Allied to this are important ethical concerns which may require cautious look-before-you-leap approaches, again slowing the spread of ideas until they have been fully explored and demonstrated their ethical credibility. And the sector is also characterized by political activity with different strategic agendas associated with major players.

Learning for humanitarian innovation ...

These are familiar themes to anyone working in innovation management – and that is good news for the humanitarian innovation sector in terms of adapting recipes already proven elsewhere. This is beginning to happen. As an example, consider the growing use of entrepreneur-labs and similar spaces to allow early stage exploration and prototyping. Or the provision of specialist funding streams which offer advice and guidance as well as finance – such as the mentoring available within the Humanitarian Innovation Fund. Then there are the efforts to emulate the kind of 'ambidextrous' solutions used in the corporate venturing activities of large organizations.

... and learning from it?

Managing humanitarian innovation is not a different art form so much as a variation on a core theme – essentially, how to manage innovation under crisis conditions. So there is also an opportunity to learn *from* the humanitarian innovation 'laboratory', to gain new insights by looking at the ways in which the humanitarian sector innovates – the routines by which it can convert ideas into value. At its heart, humanitarian innovation is not only about trying to innovate under severe resource constraints but also about trying to find new ways out of situations where the mainstream innovation trajectory may be blocked. It involves different versions of the innovation routines search, select, and implement, and some key characteristics of these include:

- **Ends rather than means drive innovation**: The presence of a challenging task – a crisis – compels innovation, even if the ways of reaching the goal are unclear.
- **Identification with the vision builds a creative community**: Users and change agents are united by a common cause, and build a shared sense of community identity and purpose.
- **User engagement and input takes centre stage**: As we saw earlier, there is a risk in humanitarian innovation that inappropriate solutions are developed at a distance from the end user. A powerful alternative approach is to recruit user insights at the earliest stages, not only increasing idea-sourcing but also building in compatibility (and thus enabling downstream diffusion) at the outset.
- **Extensive search**: Because normal pathways may be blocked, the search for solutions pushes out into new and unfamiliar territory.

Two mechanisms are important here. The first is a version of what Karim Lakhani (2006) and others have called 'broadcast search', in which problems are opened up to 'the crowd' to seek alternative perspectives and new lines of enquiry.

A second strategy for extending the search space is to reframe the problem, working at a higher level of abstraction to find common elements between this problem and other contexts in which it may have been solved. Recombinant innovation of this kind – to use Andrew Hargadon's (2003) term – has a long history in innovation, building bridges between different worlds to find solutions to similar problems.

- **Creatively combining**: Improvising solutions from what is available, often in novel configurations. The French word *bricolage* helpfully describes this process – one of the core elements in the entrepreneur's mind-set; as Baker and Nelson (2005) explain, this involves 'making do by applying combinations of the resources at hand to new problems and opportunities'.
- **Experimental learning**: Improvising and building on what emerges, learning fast from early prototyping. This agile approach is being adapted to meet the concerns of the humanitarian sector for rigorous evaluation and a strong evidence base. By using tools emerging from approaches like lean start-up (Ries, 2011), controlled experiments and fast data-gathering become possible and help convince mainstream organizations of the potential relevance of radical options.
- **Tolerance of imperfection**: Rather than planning the innovation from the outset, the journey is one of stepping-stone jumps, improving as the design takes shape and often building key elements of the user experience into the process. This agile model relies on prototypes – minimum viable product versions of a solution that are created quickly to engage users and get feedback about key design features that can be improved.
- **Importance of boundary spanning**: Several features of innovation under crisis conditions (for example, creative combination of inputs, extensive search across different worlds, and mobilising networked resources) depend on entrepreneurs acting as boundary-spanning agents. Their success depends in part on being able to link different fields and bring together a diverse community.

We are still learning about how to manage humanitarian innovation. Although it has been around a long time (the origins of agencies like the Red Cross, who spend their time innovating, go back at least 150 years), it is only in the last ten years that we have really started to look at humanitarian innovation as a specific topic. There are rich opportunities to climb fast up the learning curve by piggy-backing on the hard-won lessons of players trying to innovate in other sectors. But there is also a powerful source of new thinking for the mainstream innovation community.

Humanitarian crises thrust the innovation challenge – how to quickly create and deploy often-novel solutions that work – into sharp focus. And they meet the challenge in ways which fit an unfamiliar user context, working with limited resources against the clock, and trying to scale fast. In essence, they represent an extreme stage on which the key elements of today's innovation management drama – the search for agility, frugal solutions, design thinking, open innovation, working out of the box – play out on a daily basis.

What appears to be emerging from this crucible is a model for working with innovation which may have wider relevance. Engagement of experienced mainstream organizations from the commercial world in this activity is not just good corporate social responsibility – it also offers them a laboratory for exploring and deploying new solutions at the edge of where they would normally work.

References

Baker, T. and Nelson, R.E. (2005) 'Creating something from Nothing: Resource Construction through Entrepreneurial Bricolage', *Administrative Science Quarterly*, 50(3), pp. 3293–66.

Hargadon, A. (2003) *The Surprising Truth About How Companies Innovate*, Harvard Business School Press, Boston MA.

Lakhani, K. (2006) 'Broadcast Search in Problem Solving: Attracting Solutions from the Periphery', Conference Paper, *Technology Management for the Global Future*.

McClure, D. and Gray, I. (2015) 'Scaling: Innovation's Missing Middle', *ThoughtWorks*, <https://www.thoughtworks.com/insights/blog/scaling-innovations-missing-middle> [accessed 15 September 2017].

Ries, E. (2011) *The Lean Start Up*, Random House, New York, NY.

About the author

John Bessant, PhD, is Chair in Innovation and Entrepreneurship at Exeter University where he is also research director. Originally a chemical engineer, John has been active in research, teaching and consultancy in technology and innovation management for over 25 years. He is the author of over 20 books and numerous other publications. His most recent books include *Managing Innovation* (with Joe Tidd, 5th edition, Wiley, 2015) and *High-Involvement Innovation* (Wiley, 2003).

CHAPTER 6

Innovation lifecycle and the missing middle

Ian Gray and Dan McClure

Despite enthusiasm for small-scale investment in piloting new innovations, there appears to be a broad failure in the humanitarian sector's ability to scale up and scale out successful ideas. This creates a need to understand and address the neglected elements of the innovation cycle that lie between the conclusion of a pilot programme and the ultimate wide-scale operation and optimization of an established programme. This is innovation's 'missing middle'. It is a complex space that needs much more attention if an ever-growing number of pilot-programme investments are to 'grow up' and deliver meaningful value. This contribution seeks to provide a framework for thinking about barriers to scaling and how to technically progress from proven idea to broad-based operation.

Keywords: scaling, innovation, failure, diffusion

The problem: failing to scale good ideas

In the humanitarian sector, there is good reason for optimism. There have been high-profile wins transforming our approach to relief and development, such as the use of cash transfers to replace physical aid deliveries. Another trend that highlights the desire to innovate within the aid industry is the number of positions and teams focused on innovation that organizations have developed over the past few years. This shows that organizations are putting resources behind their innovation rhetoric. The donor community has attempted to provide new funding models to stimulate innovation. Funds such as the Humanitarian Innovation Fund (HIF) are evidence of a focus that is stimulating the development of numerous pilot products and programmes.

The industry appears to be building on its strengths of solution-finding and driving innovation, often field-led, at a small scale. However, there is a growing sense that there is a systemic problem with our ability to scale these successful innovations. Even as the number of pilot programmes continues to multiply, and skill at managing a portfolio of new ideas matures, there are few examples of great ideas that have been deployed at scale, impacting large populations and serving needs in varying environments.

When carrying out the research for this chapter, leaders in the humanitarian innovation space struggled to identify more than two or three innovations that they felt had truly gone to scale. In semi-structured interviews, these leaders repeatedly cited the same small set of success stories. Community-managed acute malnutrition and cash transfers were consistently cited as examples of innovation that have been taken to scale. There was a clear theme: pilot programmes were proliferating, but there was little evidence of them going to scale. The following issues emerged from the interviews as underlying challenges to the scaling of new ideas:

Preference for new over scale: There seems to be an obsession with new, 'shiny', and bespoke solutions. When good solutions that needed longer-term investment in order to scale already existed, the backing of new pilots continued to be the dominant innovation strategy.

Legacies supported by misaligned incentives: Outdated legacy organizations, departments, and systems were sustained due to misaligned incentives in the industry. Despite progress being made in accountability and measuring effectiveness in some agencies, the lack of consumer and citizen power over post-disaster products and service provision in many disaster-affected communities means that entrenched legacies continue to exist, blocking the adoption and scaling of new ways of doing things.

Investment size and time: Funders and decision-makers showed a lack of understanding of the real costs of taking an innovation to scale and ensuring that it is maintained and updated. Achieving scale takes significant time and financial investment, in both the private and not-for-profit sectors. In some ways, this is confirmed by the fact that the two prime examples of innovations at scale were actually pilot programmes over a decade ago.

Risk-aversion: Embracing small pilot programmes has been an important step for a humanitarian sector that can be deeply risk-averse. The risks of pilot programmes are now widely seen as acceptable since they are relatively cheap and limited in scope. However, taking an idea to scale is a far more expensive and drawn-out process. At this level of investment, the risk of picking the wrong pilot to scale can paralyse decision-making.

Measures of success: Risk-aversion is made worse when there is a lack of understanding of what constitutes success. For example, do 40–50,000 deployments of Ushahidi across 159 countries, or Frontline SMS being downloaded 200,000 times across 130 countries, constitute scale?[1] Does the widespread adoption of an innovation within large INGOs who can afford it, such as Oxfam and Save the Children, amount to scaling?

Building/finding new skills: Many traditional humanitarian organizations are innovating outside their core competencies. To develop new competencies to scale effectively they often need to look outside of their own organization and build partnerships with organizations that have diverse new skills.

Unpacking the innovation lifecycle

Why don't successful pilots consistently go to scale? A large part of the problem is likely rooted in a failure to recognize the deep differences that exist between the stages of the innovation lifecycle.

There is a natural tendency to see scaling as simply the last stage of a successful pilot programme. The intuitive idea here is that an innovator's key responsibilities have been checked off at the end of a successful pilot. Ideas have been tested and validated on a small scale, so it is now appropriate to just 'roll it out' like a well-established programme.

The apparent failure of this strategy needs a systemic explanation that accounts for persistent challenges across many fields and programmes. The authors believe that the heart of this problem is a failure to recognize four substantially distinct stages of innovation.

Stage one: invent – exploring ideas

Invention model using 'lean innovation': fail fast, learn and iterate quickly

Invent is possibly the most common first stage of the innovation lifecycle. This is where prototypes and pilot programmes are widely used. Eric Ries' *Lean Start Up* (2011) popularized the build-test-learn model, where small investments are used to validate new ideas by actually doing work in the field. As new information arises during the pilot, the best response is to remain flexible, pivoting the direction of the pilot quickly and often.

This is a lightweight system that tests ideas cheaply in terms of both key human resources and financial investment. To promote speed, retain flexibility, and enable as many different responses as possible, most rules and dependencies are suspended.

It leads to a difficult and unpredictable journey. Top-down control is seldom effective, so daily collaborative problem-solving replaces formal reporting and, because passion, personal energy, and individual commitment drive the effort, members of the team cannot be viewed as interchangeable cogs. The innovations themselves are often what is known as the 'minimum viable product' (MVP), held together by the proverbial duct tape and requiring a special set of circumstances to work.

Stage four: optimize – continuous improvement

Small changes to robust existing processes

At the other end of the innovation lifecycle, ideas are mature and have already been widely adopted. A very different system is at work. Ironically, it also embraces simplicity as an organizing principle, but for entirely different purposes and with a much different execution strategy.

This stage focuses on making complex things better. In a factory, for example, this would mean capturing intricate factory operations to create detailed standards and processes. With this done, it becomes possible to routinely measure performance against expected standards.

In using this approach, a frontline practitioner can make changes at the local level, innovations as it were, without a full appreciation or concern for the underlying complexity. There are still many moving parts, but a worker on the factory line does not need to worry about this messiness when proposing an innovative adjustment, as the change can be contained.

On the surface, simplicity fosters a culture of incremental improvement – but it comes with a trade-off. Whereas simplicity was used in the invent stage to promote flexibility, the optimization stage's ability to 'bound' the innovative change within the complex system creates a barrier to deeper change and radical innovation.

The missing middle

Since they have such radically different approaches, it is difficult to make the transition between these two stages. They are fundamentally different systems for creating value, with little alignment between their approaches or goals.

A deep transformation must occur between the initial invent stage and the ultimate optimize stage of the innovation lifecycle. This missing middle, shown in Figure 6.1, has received much less attention and lacks the established practices and framing models that have benefited innovators working to invent and optimize.

Many ideas for dealing with the perceived scaling challenges have emerged. The author believes much of this messiness can be attributed to a general failure to appropriately unpack the challenges and journeys that occur in the missing middle. Dividing the scaling process into two distinct stages as shown in Figure 6.2 helps unpack these differences.

The goal of stage two in the innovation lifecycle is to scale up, serving many people in the existing context using a solution that is sustainable over time. This begins with a successful pilot, an idea that has been validated, but is hardly ready for prime time.

During the pilots of the invent stage, many compromises will have been made. In almost every case, the project will be too simple to expand and serve a large number of beneficiaries, even when limited to its current context. Supply chains, legal compliance, ongoing staffing, and business models are just a few of the areas likely to have been given little consideration as the invent team explored a new idea. A sustainable solution cannot be based upon duct tape and heroic efforts to keep it working. It must deliver value over time to many people within a single context, using sustainably available resources.

Stage three looks to scale out the innovation by deploying it in additional locations. To achieve large-scale impact, innovations need to be able to work in more than one context. To justify the heavy investment in an idea, the solution must be made to perform satisfactorily in multiple locations and, in most cases, be able to be delivered by multiple organizations. Furthermore, these varied deployments and operations must be made at a price that can be sustained at scale.

The need is therefore to remove or hide complexity that permeates the earlier sustainable solution. This cannot be done by simply discarding difficulties, the way that fast-moving insurgents do in a pilot programme. Rather, in the scale-out stage, the innovator must make hard choices between outcomes, cost, and flexibility.

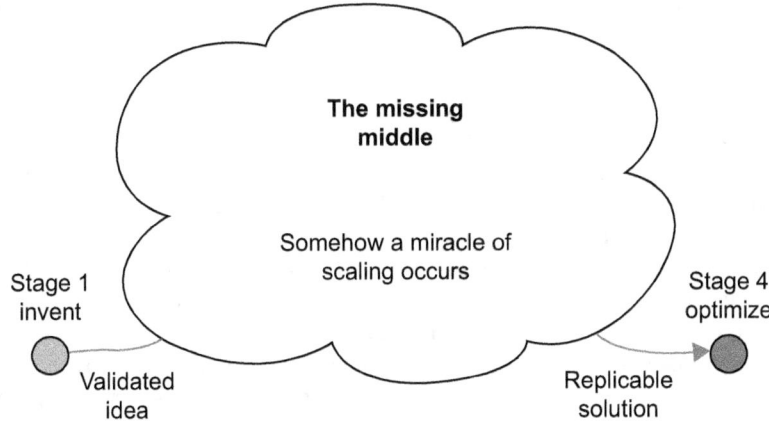

Figure 6.1 The ill-defined missing middle

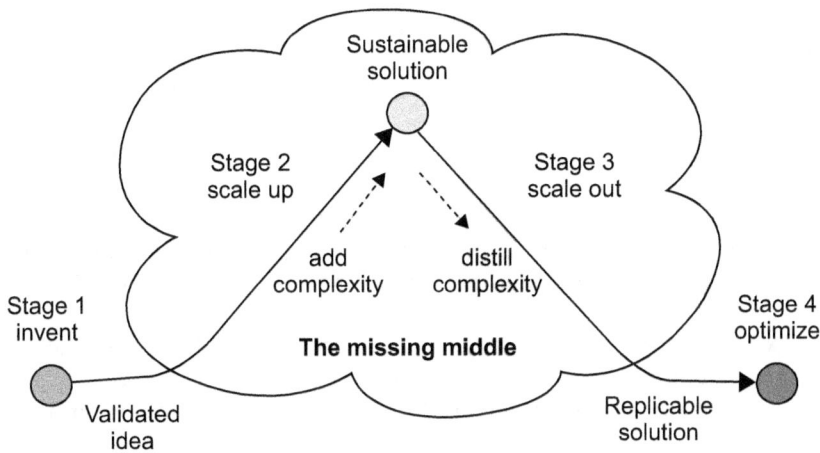

Figure 6.2 Unpacking innovation's missing middle

The journey through the missing middle connects invest and optimize along a path that is rather like climbing a mountain of complexity. Complexity is added to the pilot programme to create a sustainable solution, and then is selectively distilled out again to produce a system that can be replicated at scale and, ultimately, optimized in many contexts.

Stage two: scale up – climbing the mountain

Develop a sustainable solution for a single context/country and across a single organization

The initial invent stage of innovation is designed to allow rapid exploration and learning. However, once an idea has been validated it is necessary to shift the innovator's strategy and develop a system for value creation that works in the real world without the pilot's special attention and allowances. Best practices in the invent stage encourage pragmatic simplifications that need to be addressed. To achieve a sustainable solution, the innovation must ensure completeness, compromise, and connection.

Completeness: Best practices in lean product innovation specifically encourage the creation of an MVP (Ries, 2011), and this is what people intuitively do with complex problems: They pick key bits to ignore or simplify. Such factors include sustainable business models; long-term maintenance and support services; training; administrative processes; quality control; and security. In most cases, the omitted elements must be added back into the pilot in order to create a sustainable solution.

Compromise: A second form of simplification does not go as far as omitting a key function, but involves cutting corners by making compromises in the approach. Excess expertise is often leveraged to help speed pilot programmes forward, learn from experiments, and respond to unexpected problems. Having a smart and resourceful person on the spot makes all this easier. However, really smart people don't scale well. This compromise needs to be replaced with the more complex and more difficult approach of drawing on the pool of resources that are actually available.

Passion is often in great supply during a pilot programme, with highly motivated and driven individuals intensely focused on making things work. They can be more than a little surprised to discover that their successors are more conventionally motivated. A realistic model of rewards aligned with individual goals and needs must eventually replace the evangelical energy of the inventor.

Fixing a compromise can be frustrating because, unlike in the challenge of completeness, there is something that works already. The aspect of the solution that has been made possible by compromises simply cannot be taken to scale.

Connection: Most pilots are developed in something of a bubble. In contrast to this, the real-life context of any meaningful innovation is made up of a web of systems. If we want the innovation to function within the other parts of a complex world, we need to determine how to plug into, for example, accounting systems and supply chains. Each point of integration establishes a set of constraints on the solution, takes time to set up, and limits the ability to pivot. Just as importantly, during the pilot phase, the owners of the surrounding systems are (rightfully) sceptical about demands on their time from a tiny initiative. Integration is, therefore, often justly deferred during the pilot, but the solution cannot remain in a bubble once it moves up to scale.

When the stage two sustainable solution is complete, there is a complex system that is well integrated into the immediate context. It can scale up and deliver value to a large audience which falls within its unique set of circumstances. This is a meritorious one-off success, but it does not directly enable the kind of replicable improvement that so many investors in innovation hope to create. For some innovations and innovators, this scaling up is sufficient, but those seeking to achieve large-scale impact need to embark upon the journey of scaling out.

Stage three: scale out – descending the mountain

Make the sustainable solution replicable for additional contexts/markets

To make the idea replicable, much of the complexity added in the scale-up stage must now be hidden. In effect, another transformation is needed, going down the mountain of complexity.

Why replication is hard

At the heart of the problem is context. Situations which superficially resemble each other are seldom actually the same in all their important attributes. These differences manifest themselves in multiple ways, but all can contribute to the failure of a 'proven' solution.

Assumptions: Key assumptions that underlie a programme's design in the original context are altered or even false in the new context. At this point, an answer can be right in one context and wrong in another, and no amount of good work in the original design will seamlessly account for potential variations in context.

Change over time: Assumptions that operated perfectly at one point in time can become useless when conditions on the ground change.

Integration: At every point of integration with the local environment there are potential difficulties. There is a broad class of problems around establishing standards and driving conformance with them.

Context dependencies: Even if there is agreement on standards, these standards come with their own context dependencies. Everyone may agree to use a particular standard for a particular purpose, but that does not mean the standard supports the actual needs of others further out in the ecosystem.

Making trade-offs

There is seldom a single elegant solution to this challenge of replication in diverse and changing environments. The innovator must choose which of the competing factors is the most important and on which ones compromises can be made. Replicable systems have to take some portion of the complexity from the sustainable solution and package it in a way that allows it to be adopted by different stakeholders in a world that refuses to remain static.

The reality is that the innovator must make trade-offs among the multiple dimensions at play:

- Complexity (How many moving parts and exposed elements can we accept?)
- Customisation (How much tailoring of the solution are we willing to do to meet unique local conditions and needs?)
- Change (How much change over time do we expect to have to support?)
- Conformance (How much agreement with our approach and standards do we expect from others?)
- Capacity (What kind of resources do we expect to be available? What skills? What funding?)
- Consistency (What level of performance must we achieve? How uniform do results need to be?)

Ideally, these trade-offs are made intentionally; for example, trading off an ability to customize solutions against the reality of limited resource capacity may be entirely justified in some situations, but a foolish choice in others.

Systems for distilling complexity

A closer look at commonly used deployment strategies reveals that they differ in which priorities they implement. They all hide complexity from the initial sustainable solution, but they manage the distillation of complexity differently. Each makes trade-offs in a different way. An innovator working to scale out their solution can choose the approach that makes the best compromises for their goal.

- **Custom deployment**: Move to a new context by doing the same thing the scale-up team did in the original environment, tailoring functionality and connections to the local conditions. This approach keeps all the complexity from the original solution, a strategy that requires unique high-value people, substantial time, and large budgets to replicate in each new environment. Ironically, the process of custom creation can encounter unexpected pitfalls so, despite the investment, the consistency of the outcome is uncertain.
- **Packaged solution**: Distil the basics of the solution into a set of rote instructions and replicate the approach in production-line fashion. The innovator hides complexity and limits customization. This can be affordable and easy to adopt in environments with limited resource capacity. However, the forced consistency often fails when confronted with local differences that really do matter.
- **Platform**: The platform approach takes a position mid-way between these extremes, packaging together a suite of elements with very tightly defined interfaces and standards. Complexity is hidden and conformance with the outside world is enforced. However, the platform is not the whole solution. It is designed as the foundation for independent

innovation, with creative additions being built on top of the core black box. Examples include open-data kit-based survey tools or micro-cash transfers using mobile phones.
- **Tool kit**: Tool kits are similar to a platform in the sense that they have components that are tested and include well-defined interfaces to connect with other tools. Elements are relatively autonomous and can be assembled in different ways to meet local conditions.
- **Standards**: Create standards and constraints that bind all the players in a space. This aligns other innovators to a validated approach and enables multiple solutions to work together. Standards are quite powerful in that they can impact a broad range of innovations, but they are notoriously difficult to create, adopt, and enforce. They are also particularly vulnerable to change.

Managing scale up and scale out

There is no one right way to manage an innovation across the entire lifecycle. Over the past few years there has been a period of cultural adjustment within the humanitarian community. 'Fail-friendly' innovation management models have been increasingly accepted as a practice in support of the invent stage of innovation. A similar shift in management strategies needs to occur as innovations move from invent to scaling.

Innovations that are scaling up must focus on complex programme architecture and engineering. Demands beyond the talents of the original invent teams are piled onto the initiative. The nature of risk shifts too: leadership priorities shift from managing uncertainty and risk of unexpected failure to dealing with organizational engineering problems that are complex and hard. Finally, there are many problems of different types (e.g., complex and wicked), and issues without clearly defined answers that often come with messy and complex social dynamics.

A number of management changes come out of this shift:

- **Measuring progress to end state**: Measures must be introduced that reflect the progress the programme has made towards becoming a sustainable solution.
- **Passionate owners**: The path to engineering a complex system requires a big-picture vision of the end state. This holistic view is used to knit together the various elements and to make sure there are no key gaps. In the authors' experience, this cannot be delegated to a committee or captured in a pre-planned report. An active and passionate architect, with a holistic view of the initiative, is needed to guide the creation of the sustainable solution and, eventually, distil complexity to create a replicable solution.
- **Time and investment**: The creation of complex sustainable systems is a long journey that can easily require more time and money than the original pilot. Substantial investment can be required to simply distil

a complete, sustainable, and replicable solution that can be deployed elsewhere. Time frames may well extend beyond the short-term attention span of most grant-funded efforts.

By understanding the different requirements and challenges of the scaling journey, the humanitarian sector will start to be able to deliver truly scaled solutions that impact large numbers of people. Mastering the art and science of scaling up and scaling out is key to completing this journey.

Note

1. Number of deployments of these platforms at the time of the original research.

Reference

Ries, E. (2011) *The Lean Start Up*, Random House, New York.

About the author

Ian Gray is founder and managing director of Gray Dot Catalyst, a strategy and innovation consultancy. He set up Gray Dot Catalyst after fifteen years as an innovator and leader in the humanitarian, development, and advocacy sectors.

Dan McClure is innovation design lead at ThoughtWorks. He has over thirty years of experience in designing, leading, and advising on innovations in private, public, and social organizations.

CHAPTER 7
Complexity theory and humanitarian relief

Jenny MacCann

Understanding complexity is key to understanding the context in which humanitarian aid and innovation occur. This chapter is divided into two parts. The first looks at complexity, adaptive strategy, and the difference between linear and dynamic mindsets. The second presents ten principles for emergency management, covering issues such as experimentation, risk, feedback, learning, coordination, and decision-making.

Keywords: complexity, humanitarianism, decision-making, cynefin framework

Whether they have a slow or rapid onset, emergencies trigger a unique shift from a long-term, often strategically linear, step-by-step mindset to a chaotic environment requiring dynamic thinking and action. Humanitarian work is too often simplified to fit a linear model that does not recognise the complexity of aid contexts. The literature cited in this chapter characterizes emergency management as a complex sector with complicated correlations and patterns. Instead of applying linear thinking, humanitarian leadership requires an adaptive and dynamic approach. As is noted in *Humanitarian Horizons* (Feinstein International Center, 2010: 46): 'The future will require organizations to be far more adept at handling uncertainty and far more willing to be administratively and programmatically more flexible'.

Emergencies as complex events and the theory behind adaptive strategy

For the past three hundred years, the dominant view of organizations has been that they operate like predictable machines in which managers can control and understand all the relevant parts (e.g., people, institutions, and culture) and that there are replicable solutions to any problem across an organization (Wheatley and Kellner-Rogers, 1998). More recently, organizations have been better described as living systems where emergencies are difficult to define, in unstable, socially complex contexts, and that are interdependent with a number of other complex systems such as culture, environment, and politics (Ramalingam, 2012). In complex environments such as emergencies, organizations and individuals must use different ways of functioning to handle the complexity. There is now a body of research and knowledge recognising that, as no two emergencies are the same, effective emergency management must allow for a flexible, dynamic, and adaptive response (Overland, 2012).

The Cynefin Framework (pronounced *ku-nev-in*) is a tool that clarifies how to function at different levels of uncertainty. First developed by IBM, it has since been applied in a number of fields. It is composed of five domains: simple, complicated, complex, chaotic, and disordered (see Figure 7.1). Each context requires a different set of actions. For example, in a simple context we only need to sense the problem, find the process/best practice and apply it. In this domain, it is possible to sense > categorize > respond. However, in a complex context we probe the problem to further investigate a range of solutions, sense what is happening as we apply different tactics, and respond when we find a pattern that is succeeding. Here the appropriate tactic is to probe > sense > respond. The fifth domain, disorder, is difficult to recognize. The appropriate response is to break down the situation and assign each of its constituent parts to one of the other four realms.

The simple and complicated domains assume an ordered context, where cause and effect are knowable and right answers are determined on the basis of on facts. Complex and chaotic contexts (where emergencies undoubtedly lie) have a level of disorder where there is no obvious relationship between cause and effect as events unfold, and the way forward is found by sensing and responding to the context (Snowden and Boon, 2007).

The importance of handling complex contexts appropriately is highlighted in ALNAP's report *Leadership in Action* (Buchanan-Smith and Scriven, 2011). Key leadership qualities identified in it include:

- The ability to judge when particular skills and approaches are relevant and desirable in a given context.
- Recognising the importance of context, and knowing where and how to focus efforts.
- The ability to make decisions rapidly when needed, according to the situation on the ground.
- Investing in contextual analysis, listening, and the ability to learn and to be adaptable.

Adaptive strategy

An adaptive strategy is a harmonious combination of deliberate and emergent strategy approaches (with strategy encompassing planning and implementation). A deliberate (or linear) strategy is carefully planned and controlled by the organization. Emergent strategies have no preconceived plan but instead emerge from a context. An adaptive strategy involves continuous planning, but provides the flexibility of sensing and responding

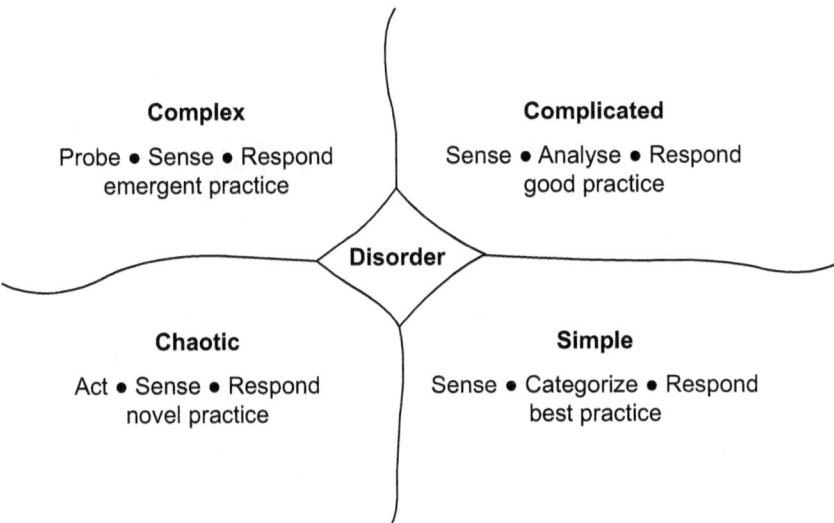

Figure 7.1 The Cynefin framework

to a context to meet changing contextual needs. It is partially planned and partially unplanned. Unplanned aspects of strategy should not be random or reactive, but have parameters or boundary conditions (such as organizational purpose or capacity) that allow effort directed to respond to the context. Adaptive strategy creates a cycle of trying something, receiving feedback, and learning or adapting to the context. The more complex the context, the more adaptive an organization needs to be (Mintzberg and Waters, 1985; Hart, 2010).

Adaptive organizations

Haeckels (1999) explains that if an organization starts with an underlying assumption of predictable change, then the goal is to become efficient, strategy is linear, and the organization can be guided by its policies and processes. If the organizational assumption is of unpredictable change, then the goal is to become adaptive to its context and to sense and respond to its environment. Consequently, the organization must have a clear vision, and focus on principles which lead staff without restricting them through rules. The distinction is further delineated in Table 7.1.

Ten principles for emergency management

A key finding of research is that emergency responses cannot be run using linear mindsets with associated processes and rules; they must be led using principles which allow flexibility, creativity, and adaptation to dynamic and

Table 7.1 Linear and dynamic mindsets

Category	Linear mindset: Replicate and implement	Dynamic mindset: Sense and respond
Management style	Administers, focuses on systems, relies on control, asks how and when, eye on the bottom line, imitates, accepts status quo.	Innovates, focuses on people, inspires trust, asks what and why, eye on the horizon, originates, challenges the status quo.
Mindset behind strategic intent	Organization is an efficient mechanism for implementing projects for well-defined issues that have predictable needs.	Organization is an adaptive system for responding to unanticipated requests in unpredictable environments.
Know-how	Expertise is embedded in products.	Expertise is embedded in people.
Process	Mass-production.	Customized responses defined by need.
Organizational priority	Invest in efficiency and predictability, repeatable procedures, and replication.	Invest in system and staff competencies to enable rapid and dynamic response capabilities.
Focus	Programme management, increase scale of programme.	Successful contextual programme, meeting contextual needs.
Operational concept and governance	Functional and sequential activity, central planning, predefined hierarchy.	Networked and parallel activity, dynamically formed teams, decentralized decisions.
	Unified view and plan.	Unified vision and purpose.
Strategy	Strategy as plan.	Strategy as adaptive design.

fast-changing contexts. Part 2 will assemble ten principles for working in complex environments from diverse fields. The first five principles relate to organizational behaviours, and the second five emphasise the importance of relying on people over process.

1. **Try new things**: Encourage new ideas and actions and ensure your organization is fundamentally open and willing to try new approaches. Scale up actions which are successful and scale down the unsuccessful. Ensure the organization learns new principles for success from the unsuccessful. New ideas/actions should be trialled within the general boundary conditions of an organization (such as technical capacity or purpose), which assist by acting as a filter to select which new ideas can and should be trialled, and which others may be useful in different contexts or organizations (Harford, 2011).
2. **Decentralize**: Decentralized organizations allow rapid, contextually appropriate responses as they provide flexible and rapid action to a changing emergency environment. It is difficult (and often impossible) for those leading outside the physical operating environment (the field) to make appropriate contextual decisions. It is better to operate through decentralized teams which are supported, coordinated, and resourced

through a centralized oversight mechanism. Decentralization can be increased or decreased depending on the capacity of staff on the ground and the changing context and levels of complexity. Empowering employees assists decentralization by providing them with the space and trust to lead, rewarding risk-taking, and supporting staff leadership (Leonard, Baker and Snider, 2010).

3. **Manage risk**: In a linear, compliant mindset there is the assumption that risk can be controlled. Conversely, in a complex context, risk is fluid and can only be managed. This means risk is inherent in context and cannot be planned out or dealt with through processes. Compliance, then, supports basic accountability, and managing risk must be made a part of the organizational culture through principles such as decoupling risk, planning for the worst, and keeping communication lines open (Harford, 2011). ALNAP (Buchanan-Smith and Scriven, 2011) highlights 'a mature and balanced approach to risk-taking, prepared to innovate, yet quickly learning from and correcting mistakes' as a key emergency-leadership quality.

4. **Seek out feedback and learn from mistakes**: The key to solving challenging problems is to adapt to the relevant context and its complexities as quickly as possible. To adapt, it is critical to try new things, improve actions that feedback shows are working, and learn from mistakes. To adapt as quickly and appropriately as possible, an organization must create tight feedback loops (between research and practice, and between feedback and action), admit failures/mistakes and use them to create successful actions (Overland, 2012; Renaud, 2012; Leonard et al., 2012). Barder (2010: 15) suggests that 'as change makers we should not try to design a better world, we should make better feedback loops'.

5. **Coordinate with a range of actors**: In emergencies, relationships, coordination, and interaction are important because, in an emergency, it is beyond the ability of a single person or organization to make sense of what is happening. Effective emergency response relies on strong pre-existing networks involving a range of actors (such as media, NGOs, academics, private-sector bodies, and others), a refusal to tolerate silo mentalities in teams and organizations, building teams that work across the organization and feel comfortable networking outside the organization, and being creative to ensure coordination continues even when there are few staff and little time (Ramalingam, 2012; Hart, 2010).

6. **Use practical wisdom**: Practical wisdom is about doing the right thing in the right place at the right time. Practical wisdom allows us to identify and judge a situation, and gives us the flexibility to bend rules to take the right action. Rules and processes are static: they do not change according to circumstance, and, in complex contexts, they can restrict our ability to do the right thing. Wisdom and judgement are

of a particular time and place and allow us to navigate the intricacies and complexities of a difficult decision. The emphasis is, then, not on learning a set of rules or processes and following them perfectly, but rather on focusing on the principles of work and adapting these to the context. Here rules become aids, allies, guides, and checks to ensure the right action (Swartz and Sharpe, 2010).

7. **Get the right experience for the job**: Only with relevant experience do the maturity, judgement, and intuition which are essential to handling emergencies develop. Experience gives a leader credibility and respect, allowing others to have confidence in their knowledge and chosen approach. For humanitarian personnel, it is just as important to acknowledge limitations due to lack of experience, and delegate to those who have the right experience. Also, particularly in emergencies, a variety of diverse experiences is extremely important (Buchanan-Smith and Scriven, 2011).

8. **Build good mental models**: 90% of critical decisions are made through a process of recognising parallels with past experiences stored in the brain as mental models (highlighting both a situation and a suggested action). When a difficult situation occurs, our mind flips through these mental models (stored past experiences) and chooses a match to create action. These intuitive skills help to us spot potential problems, manage uncertainty, and size up situations to make tough decisions quickly. Most importantly, we can build good mental models (like we build muscle) through decision-making exercises, simulations, reviewing past decisions and experiences, and gaining feedback (Klein, 2004).

9. **Ensure action**: Effective, and often rapid, decision-making is key to success in complex emergencies. Although at times leaders need to hold off on decision-making, in complex contexts rapid decision-making is a clear (sometimes the only) way to move forward and build momentum. Key decision-making skills for leaders in emergencies include making decisions without resorting to an organizational blueprint; making decisions on the basis of incomplete, unreliable, and contradictory information; and the flexibility to change decisions as the situation changes. Three critical requirements are knowing when to allow for consensus and when to make a decision, ensuring leaders are experienced decision-makers, and keeping decisions at the right level (Buchanan-Smith and Scriven, 2011; Renaud, 2012).

10. **Learn to improvise**: Every context is different and needs creative and coordinated action within boundaries. At times during extreme or chaotic events, the rules no longer relate to what is happening on the ground. It is at these times that improvisation and creativity are critical. Improvisation allows organizations with a shared framework or principles to adapt to the context, with individuals implementing, communicating, and responding to each other to make sense of what is happening around them (Barder, 2010).

Conclusion

The literature on emergency management describes a complex sector which requires a dynamic mindset and principled behaviour to navigate complexity. This chapter's analysis finds the need to build humanitarian leadership able to handle complex challenges, rather than managerialism based on compliance. Humanitarian leadership is, then, realizing the level of complexity in an emergency through sensing and responding to the context, creating tight feedback loops to allow adaptation, and enhancing actions that are seen to be working while scaling back those that are not. Furthermore, emergency systems will only work if there is investment in people's ability to navigate them appropriately. Since adaptive organizations function using different competencies and skills to those of linear organizations, it is imperative to build the capacity of all humanitarian personnel, both short- and long-term.

References

Barder, O. (2010) 'What Can Development Policy Learn from Evolution', *Owen Abroad* <http://www.owen.org/blog/4018> [accessed 5 September 2012].

Buchanan-Smith, M. and Scriven, K. (2011) *Leadership in Action: Leading Effectively in Humanitarian Operations*, ALNAP/Overseas Development Institute, London <http://www.alnap.org/resource/6118.aspx> [accessed 15 September 2017].

Feinstein International Center (2010) 'Humanitarian Horizons: A Practitioners' Guide to the Future', Humanitarian Futures Programme and Feindtein International Center <http://euhap.eu/upload/2014/06/hfp-humanitarian-horizons-jan-2010.pdf> [accessed 15 September 2017].

Haeckels, S. (1999) *Adaptive Enterprise: Creating and Leading Sense and Respond Organisations*, 1st edition, Harvard Business School Press, Boston, MA.

Harford, T (2011) *Adapt: Why Success Always Starts with Failure*, Farrar, Straus and Giroux, London.

Hart, P. (2010), 'Organising for Effective Emergency Management', *Royal Commission on the Victorian Bushfires*, Australian National University, <http://www.royalcommission.vic.gov.au/getdoc/84dc72b7-9939-4acd-b761-678e40e55db4/EXP.3031.001.0001> [accessed 15 September 2017].

Klein, G. (2004) *The Power of Intuition*, 1st edition, Random House, New York, NY.

Leonard, H., Baker, G. and Snider, E. (2010) 'Organising Response to Extreme Emergencies', *Victorian Bushfires Royal Commission*, Harvard University. <http://www.hks.harvard.edu/var/ezp_site/storage/fckeditor/file/Leonard_2010%20Bushfires%20Testimony.pdf>.

Leonard, H. and Howitt, A (2010). "Organising Response to Extreme Emergencies: The Victorian Bushfires of 2009", *Australian Journal of Public Administration*, 69(4): 372–386.

Mintzberg, H. and Waters, J. (1985) 'Of Strategies, Deliberate and Emergent', *Strategic Management Journal*, 6(3), pp. 257–272.

Overland, S. (2012) 'World Vision Emergency Response Development', commissioned by World Vision Australia.

Ramalingam, B. (2012) 'Complex System and Aid', USAID presentation in Washington, USA.

Renaud, C. (2012) 'The Missing Piece of NIMS: Teaching Incident Commanders How to Function in the Edge of Chaos', *Homeland Security Affairs*, 8(8), pp. 1–19, <http://www.hsaj.org/?article=8.1.8> [accessed 15 September 2017].

Snowden, D. and Boone, E. (2007) 'A Leader's Framework for Decision Making', *Harvard Business Review*, pp. 68–76.

Swartz, B. and Sharpe, K. (2010) *Practical Wisdom: The Right Way To Do The Right Thing*, First edition, Penguin Books, New York, NY.

Wheatley, M. and Kellner-Rogers, M. (1998) 'Bringing Life to Organisational Change', *Journal for Strategic Performance Measurement*, <http://www.margaretwheatley.com/articles/life.html> [accessed 15 September 2017].

About the author

Jenny MacCann is the director of the Response Innovation Lab. She has extensive experience in humanitarian programming having led World Vision's Nepal earthquake response and held leadership roles in the responses to Typhoon Haiyan and the Haiti earthquake. She has also worked in West, East, and Southern Africa and Palestine.

CHAPTER 8

Knowing for the twenty-first century: Reflexivity and rigour

Robert Chambers

In this chapter, two contrasting schools of thought are explained. Traditional thought and management practice is dominated by a neo-Newtonian paradigm which is characterized by linear thinking and a focus on things, not people. A different, more flexible paradigm of adaptive pluralism is characterized by complexity thinking and fits with the domain of people. The argument is made here that the latter paradigm recognizes responsiveness, adaptability, participation, local ownership, and plural approaches and so is better suited to the contexts in which humanitarian innovation occur. To help aid workers to embrace adaptive pluralism, two key dispositions – reflexivity and rigour – are examined.

Keywords: humanitarianism, neo-Newtonian, adaptive pluralism, reflexivity, rigour

The paradigms of things and people

Two paradigms can be identified in the thought and practice of the aid sector: the neo-Newtonian paradigm and the paradigm of adaptive pluralism. The neo-Newtonian paradigm is characterized by linear thinking and fits with the domain of physical things. What I call the paradigm of adaptive pluralism is characterized by complexity thinking and fits with the domain of people.

The challenge and opportunity presented by this distinction is to understand and bridge the two domains to improve humanitarian outcomes. Recognising the characteristic elements of each domain and understanding the value of different actions, processes, or mindsets in different contexts can enable aid workers to better navigate the complex environment of humanitarian relief.

This chapter examines the domains of neo-Newtonian practice and adaptive pluralism before considering two key dispositions that can help aid workers to embrace adaptive pluralism: reflexivity and rigour. In adopting these dispositions, one embraces a creative, innovative mindset, laying the groundwork for better decision-making, programme design and implementation.

The word paradigm is used to mean a mutually reinforcing system of concepts, values, methods, and procedures, behaviours, relationships, and mindsets. Table 8.1 contrasts characteristics of the two paradigms.

http://dx.doi.org/10.3362/9781780449531.008

Table 8.1 Paradigmatic characteristics of neo-Newtonian practice and adaptive pluralism

Paradigm of	Neo-Newtonian practice	Adaptive pluralism
Ontological origins and assumptions	Things, the physical world Newtonian science Order Laws of nature Linearity	People, the social world Complexity science Edge of chaos Emergence Non-linearity
Pervasive concepts	Universality Uniformity Stability Equilibrium Controllability Predictability	Local specificity Diversity Dynamism Emergence Uncontrollability Unpredictability
Methods, procedures, processes	Standardized Sequential routines Fixed menu Manuals Best practices	Pluralist Iterative adaptation A la carte and combinations Repertoires Fitting practices
Embodying and expressing	Comprehensive rules to regulate Conventions, conformity	Parsimonious rules to enable Originality, inventiveness
Roles and behaviours	Supervising Auditing Controlling Conforming, complying	Facilitating Coaching Empowering Performing, improvising
Favoured and prevailing approaches and methods include	Questionnaires Randomized control trials Log frames	Participatory methodologies ICT Participatory reviews and reflections etc.
Valuing and relying for quality	Conventional rigour – best practices: specialization standardized regulation measurement precision statistical analysis	Complexity rigour – fitting practices: versatility, adaptive pluralist, eclecticism, facilitation, alertness, surprises, relevance, triangulation, successive approximation
Relationships	Vertical Hierarchical Impersonal Unidirectional	Lateral and 360-degree Democratic Personal Reciprocal
Goals, design and indicators	Planned, pre-set, fixed	Negotiated, evolving, emergent

Source: Chambers 2010

In the 1990s, concepts, values, and methods that align with the paradigm of adaptive pluralism dominated aid work. Thought and practice centred around people; people living in poverty and marginalized groups were placed at the centre of aid work. Participation and empowerment characterized rhetoric.

Over the last two decades, neo-Newtonian practice has become prevalent. Donors and lenders triggered a shift in practice towards a linear, more control-oriented, upward accountability through the introduction of results-based management, log frames and 'rigorous' impact assessments. However, as an environment characterized by a reality of creativity, complexity, and emergence, aid work demands responsiveness, adaptability, participation, local ownership, and plural approaches. Effective aid work more appropriately lies within the paradigm of adaptive pluralism.

The remainder of this chapter will examine dispositions that are integral to aid work – reflexivity and rigour– using the paradigmatic lens to help understand ways in which we can increase the effectiveness of aid.

Reflexivity and rigour

Reflexivity is deep, critical reflection on our own mindsets, professional conditioning, and personal predispositions. These reveal themselves in our work and relationships. The ability to constantly adapt and use a plurality of approaches is important when engaging with complex (non-linear) communities, contexts and systems.

The World Bank 2015 World Development Report, *Mind, Society and Behaviour*, explores the importance and impact of mindsets and biases in the aid sector. A key sentence from the report concludes that 'development professionals can be susceptible to a host of cognitive biases, can be influenced by their social tendencies and social environments, and can use deeply ingrained mindsets when making choices' (World Bank, 2015: 180). Exercising personal reflexivity can enable aid workers to adequately recognize changes in the sector and in the environments in which they work, and to respond effectively to these changes and the reality of the environment.

In a similar vein, the language we use betrays the mindsets we have. The pervasion of the word 'deliver' over the last decade is just one example of the neo-Newtonian disposition creeping not only into thought and practice, but also into sector parlance. The word is associated with linear, managed processes. The word 'reflexivity' is associated with agile, creative processes. The important thing for the manager of innovation is to excel at the paradigms of both neo-Newtonian practice and adaptive pluralism. This should not be underestimated: language frames our lives and, if the language changes, then so too does the way we see things.

The complex and unpredictable nature of aid work demands that practitioners embrace inclusive rigour at all stages of their work. Counter to this, the type of rigour demanded by donors in planning and impact assessment is invariably reductionist.

Randomized control trials (RCTs) are possibly the most frequently cited example of reductionist practice. Used in the context of, say, medical research, RCTs have a clear value, where there are very similar units (people's bodies) and highly standardized inputs (medical treatments).

However, aid work happens in a complex, uncontrolled environment with multiple and indeterminate causation and unpredictable emergence. In such contexts, RCTs are limiting, costly, slow, and inconclusive. For many humanitarian interventions, running multiple parallel experiments instead is likely to produce richer and more valuable information on the efficacy of the project.

A second example of the pervasive control orientation of the 1990s is the log frame (see e.g. Wallace et al., 2006). An approach of adaptive iteration (or 'adaptive programming', see World Development Report 2015, chapter 11) would allow aid programmes to be much more responsive to the reality in the field which cannot be fully understood and predicted at the planning stage.

These neo-Newtonian tools have been widely applied, at the demand of donors, to the uncontrollable, unpredictable, and less measurable (i.e., complex) paradigm of people and processes that is aid work. Because of the power relationship between donors and recipients, these constraining shifts are largely unremarked upon and unchallenged by recipients. The limitations and shortcomings of the control orientation leaves NGOs and aid workers in a position where they can do less, and they do it less well.

Environments of unforeseeable and unpredictable flux and change, the domain of complexity, are much better served by inclusive rigour which embraces:

- Eclectic methodological pluralism (employing a range of approaches rather than a singular approach)
- Adaptive iteration (responding to the context and change)
- Improvisation and innovation
- Triangulation (checking and cross-checking, doubting evidence)
- Plural perspectives
- Being open, alert, inquisitive, reflexive, and nimble.

This is not to say that neo-Newtonian practices, those which emphasize standardization, have no place in aid work. Rather, it is to say that the application of neo-Newtonian approaches should be thoughtful and used alongside more holistic, responsive, and participatory tools that characterize the paradigm of adaptive pluralism.

Ways forward

The final part of this chapter will outline four potential ways forward – though there are many different possibilities.

Offsetting biases and exploring blind spots

Referring back to the 2015 World Development Report, 'because the decisions of development professionals often can have large effects on other people's lives, it is especially important that mechanisms be in place to check and correct for their biases and blind spots' (World Development Report, 2015: 180).

Biases and blind spots can be created by countless factors, including bias towards measurability. Those conditions which are easy to measure will commonly gain greater attention than those which are difficult to measure. For example, research into under-nutrition is heavily focused on diarrhoea (which is easy to measure) despite the fact that strong evidence points to environmental enteropathy (which is extremely difficult to measure) as a more significant cause of under-nutrition. This creates a blind spot in targeting the best potential interventions to addressing the problem of under-nutrition.

Employing participatory methodologies and embracing complexity

The lives that poor people lead are very often difficult for them to control, and much more complex than development professionals often think. Participatory methodologies have the great virtue that they enable poor people, or they can enable poor people, to express their realities. Participatory methodologies can therefore enable aid workers to develop a true understanding of the complex, diverse, dynamic, uncontrollable, and unpredictable local realities of the environment in which they are working and the experience of many poor people. What comes out of participatory processes is very often surprising to the outside professional. Two examples are considered below.

Participatory statistics have proven themselves to be very powerful, very insightful and generally more reliable than other methods (see Holland, 2013). However, despite having been proven over the last two decades, participatory statistics are not used as a matter of routine and are not on university curricula.

Reality checks are immersion and listening studies, which can be employed to gain an insight into communities, change over time, and the impact of policies and interventions. The methodology is simple. Researchers stay with a family in a rural village for a week, participating in and learning about ordinary life. At the end of the week, researchers gather and share experiences from different parts of the country, creating a picture of the country from the perspective of the people living there.

Developing mechanisms for rapid action learning and sharing

The factors underlying a problem are multiple and often unexpected. To begin to truly understand the problem you are trying to solve, it is necessary to become involved with policy and its implementation in the field. Developing mechanisms for rapid action learning and sharing – finding and convening pioneers and innovators in the field – is vital here.

In India, for example, Rapid Action Learning Units have been proposed, and processes of rapid action learning adopted, with the aim of finding effective ways to tackle the challenge of rural sanitation – the most intertwined and wicked problem India has ever encountered in rural development. Rapid action learning searches for, and seeks to learn from, promising grassroots innovations, and to initiate trials, undertake research, and share experience and practical lessons.

Enhancing professional reflexivity

Education curricula, organizational culture, and professional development must change dramatically to foster the skill and practice of reflexivity. For example, university courses should promote regular critical reflection on what students have learned and what effect the learning has on the way they see the world, and how differently people on different disciplinary courses see the world. The effects of this could be quite dramatic in terms of generating a broader and more realistic view of the world, and also enable us to become more critically aware of our biases and predispositions.

Aid workers must be equipped to recognize the interconnectedness and unpredictability of the environments in which they work. Adopting certain dispositions and approaches (just a handful of which are explored here) can enable aid workers to navigate this complexity by embracing the domain of adaptive (and participatory) pluralism. This is a domain that, by its very nature, must continuously evolve as the sector learns and adapts to constant change.

References

Chambers, R. (2010) 'Paradigms, Poverty and Adaptive Pluralism', *Institute of Development Studies*, Working Paper 334 <https://doi.org/10.1111/j.2040-0209.2010.00344_1.x>.

Holland, J. (2013) *Who Counts? The Power of Participatory Statistics*, Practical Action Publishing, Rugby <https://doi.org/10.3362/9781780447711>

Wallace, T. with Bornstein, L. and Chapman, J. (2006) *The Aid Chain: Coercion and Commitment in Development NGOs*, ITDG Publishing, Rugby <https://doi.org/10.3362/9781780440019>

World Bank (2015) *World Development Report 2015: Mind, Behaviour and Society*, World Bank, Washington DC.

About the author

Robert Chambers is a research associate and emeritus professor of the Institute of Development Studies, University of Sussex. A prolific writer and thought leader in International Development, his current interests include rigour for complexity, epistemology, and rural sanitation.

PART III
Organizing humanitarian innovation

There are numerous dynamics to navigate in managing innovation. This part highlights the ways in which innovation can be organized and managed in the sector. To help individuals and organizations prepare and implement innovation, this part covers elements such as leadership, organizational change, ethical concerns and partnerships by considering:

- Leadership and management
- Understanding change
- Ethical and gender considerations
- Building and sustaining partnerships
- Influencing innovation adoption

CHAPTER 9

The leadership and management of innovation

Eric James

The leadership and management of innovation in humanitarian relief can be a significant challenge. An innovative leader is able to navigate through and around the resistance normally encountered, finding new and better ways to support innovation. Luckily, many of the tools and techniques that help propel people, teams, and organizations can be optimized for innovation. Being a truly effective leader, however, involves a series of steps that are captured in the INSPIRE framework, described in this chapter. This involves working from the inside out (i.e., innovative leaders know that excellence starts with themselves), knowing the context, being able to effectively strategize, preparation, generating and integrating good ideas, re-examining the approach, and executing plans effectively.

Keywords: leadership, management, innovation, strategy, implementation

Innovating in the area of humanitarian aid presents a number of challenges. For starters, the contexts in which we work are complex, the organizations we work for are not always supportive of change, and even our mindsets and basic tools might not be up to the task at hand, let alone well-suited for creative and novel problem-solving. Anyone who has worked in the field long enough has run across a myriad of 'people problems' such as lack of trust and accountability, unrecognized and underused talent, and inadequate prioritisation. This is often what drives staff to seek new employment with other organizations and, eventually, leave the sector altogether. Even more importantly, this situation generates missed opportunities for positive change.

Leadership and management often determine the outcome of a project. Management involves ensuring compliance and is distinguished from leadership with its focus on vision and direction. Peter Drucker (2008: 18), the management expert, described it this way: 'Management is doing things right, leadership is doing the right thing'. Therefore, leadership is often recognized as a key ingredient in innovation because of its purpose of sparking new ideas and allowing for creativity that leads to transformation. Using trains as an analogy, first the tracks need to be laid in the right direction (as determined by leadership) and then the trains need to run on time (through good management). In practice, the right balance of leadership and management are needed to create the space and support for innovation to take place.

Innovation is a key competence of effective leadership and management that drive change. Resistance to change in general, and innovation specifically, is normal. Some people may feel that innovation is a luxury that needs to be put off until the 'basics' are done, yet the opposite is often true. Certainly if people's lives and suffering are at stake, and the only option is inactivity, management is essential (the trains need to run on time, after all). Even in emergencies, there is more often than not the time to find better, more innovative, ways to work and achieve results. In these cases, the train might end up running faster, better, and cheaper. An innovative leader is able to navigate through and around the normal resistance to change, finding new and better ways to support innovation. For these reasons, being an innovative leader involves having the right skillset and the right mindset. To help steer a way through this complex set of issues, the following framework can be used to INSPIRE innovation:

Inside out: Start with you
k**N**ow the context
Strategize
Prepare: Put first things first
Ideate and integrate
Re-examine
Execute

This chapter develops this seven-part framework. Rather than a straight checklist of management practices, these are instead mindsets, methods, and tools that innovative leaders use to make their efforts a success.

Inside out: start with you

Before starting on a journey to solve problems innovatively, it is important to recognize that this is not just a set of practical tools and tips; it is more about having the right frame of mind, working from the inside out. The greatest change is achieved through paradigm shifts. A paradigm is a way of thinking, a pattern, or theory; it is a model or mindset through which the world is viewed. Once a person sees his or her world from a new perspective, their behaviour will change significantly.

By understanding that change happens from the inside out, change becomes possible. Therefore, by extension, knowing and mastering yourself becomes the first critical step in leadership. This follows long-established wisdom, found at least as far back as the Ancient Greeks and the famous dictum: 'Know thyself'. Only after mastering oneself is it possible to lead other people. Once other people are led well in a small team, it is possible to have superior outcomes.

Several key ideas are essential in order to follow this inside out model. One needs a degree of personal and professional maturity to attain this mindset. This can be developed in numerous ways such as by conditioning and through experience but, for this behaviour to be lasting, key habits need to be practised. As Aristotle noted centuries ago: 'We are what we repeatedly do. Excellence, then, is not an act, but a habit'. With continued practice, characteristics like determination, flexibility, and confidence will establish themselves. When a challenge is encountered, confidence can be maintained even while ideas and practices are questioned. From this questioning (and, by extension, re-examining, testing, and reworking), genuine and transformative change can be pursued.

Effective leadership has to be built on a foundation of good habits; otherwise, ineffective practices will surface, hypocrisy becomes evident, and little can be achieved because all time is spent trying to build consensus and influence others. Examples of self-mastery include taking care of personal mental and physical wellbeing, balancing work/life responsibilities, and taking time to plan and prepare. Ethics flow from these habits (starting with the near universal golden rule of treating others as you treat yourself) and into the practices of leadership, management, and innovation.

Formation of new positive habits takes deliberate practice for at least several weeks, if not longer. Habits may be focused on competence (your ability to achieve results) or on personal character (mental and moral qualities), and have a personal or professional end in mind but, often, these overlap. It is more effective to replace unwanted behaviours with new positive habits instead of trying to replace old or 'bad' habits. Try doing this in small, incremental steps. Legendary US basketball coach, John Wooden, described this process: 'When you improve a little each day, eventually big things occur. When you improve conditioning a little each day, eventually you have a big improvement in conditioning. Not tomorrow, not the next day, but eventually a big gain is made. Don't look for the big, quick improvement. Seek the small improvement one day at a time. That's the only way it happens — and when it happens, it lasts' (Wooden and Jamison, 1997). To put this into practice, and work toward becoming an innovative leader, try the following five practices – asking yourself the associated questions – for the next month:

1. **Be honest with yourself**: Consider a few key questions such as: 'Do I really know as much as I should to be innovative?' and 'Am I really open to new ideas or ways of working?'
2. **Show gratitude**: Are you able to hear – and say thank you for – constructive criticism?
3. **Know your thinking and learning style**: Do you know how you learn best: whether you are a visual, aural, reading/writing, or kinaesthetic learner? (See Annex for a website giving more information about a VARK analysis tool.)

4. **Set regular goals**: Do you plan and prepare daily, weekly, and monthly? Do you regularly set specific and realistic personal and professional goals (e.g., being on time, eating properly, or exercising, being loyal to the absent, effectively linking big ideas with small actions)?
5. **Reach for occasional stretch goals**: How often do you set and achieve goals that take you out of your comfort zone and broaden your horizons (e.g., learning a new skill, travel, reaching an educational milestone or producing/contributing to new knowledge)?

When the Internet company, Google, studied their internal organizational management, they found a number of indicators related to culture, commitment to change, and learning that pointed to a good manager (Garvin, 2013). They determined that this is one who:

- is a good coach
- empowers the team and does not micromanage
- expresses interest in and concern for team members' success and personal wellbeing
- is productive and results-oriented
- is a good communicator who listens and shares information
- helps with career development
- has a clear vision and strategy for the team
- has key technical skills that help him or her advise the team.

Annex 5 provides an innovation management readiness assessment.

kNow the context

An innovative leader is able to understand the organization they work for, as well as the context in which they operate, and make the most of both for positive change. Getting to know the organization starts when a job application is first sent in and continues throughout one's tenure. An organization grows and changes over time, adapting to the situation, and is reliant on its leaders and influencers. An innovative leader is able to gauge their organization's ripeness for change and use their influence to promote innovation by connecting with channels and champions who may be supportive.

In places that are undergoing rapid change – especially those experiencing humanitarian emergencies – context is everything. It determines the path to be taken, influences a myriad of decisions, and can cause the unexpected to happen. An ability to detect and understand weak signals can make a significant difference in leading and managing innovation.

Appreciating emergent events is a good place to start. This can occur when new, unplanned, or unexpected behaviours appear. Given that the future is filled with such complexity, it is impossible to accurately calculate probabilities and take into account all the different possibilities that may come about. In such cases, it may help to think broadly and creatively. Building off the work of Nassim Taleb's concept of the Black Swan (2012), Sardar and Sweeney (2016) propose the following typology:

> *Black swans*: High-impact events that appear out of the blue (e.g., a meteor strike). An innovative leader will ask: 'What do other people think will never happen?'
>
> *Black elephants*: High-impact events that are visible to everyone yet may not get the attention they deserve (e.g., refugee crises and climate change). An innovative leader will ask: 'What are most people missing or not seeing?'
>
> *Jellyfish*: Small events that can escalate (like a jellyfish bloom) into high-impact events (e.g., riots that lead to revolutions). An innovative leader will ask: 'What can or might lead to chaos?'

Standard desk-based research – using a wide variety of sources – is a good place to start. It may be possible to use personal and professional networks. Most often, the best way to gain a good understanding of context is simply to be open to the new context, ask people questions, and listen carefully. Part of this is gaining a personal understanding of the context, developing what is sometimes called situational awareness. A simple tool such as the observe, orient, decide, and act (OODA) loop can help in understanding not just surroundings but new and complex situations (in relief as opposed to research) where certain outcomes are expected.

To understand organizations and contexts with the right mindset, it can be helpful to approach people and challenges expecting complexity, with abundance thinking, and with the right tools. An innovative leader needs to be able to think abstractly about innovation and then ground their thinking in the realities of their current context. They must be able to connect the big with the small by applying current technology and openness to what might be possible to their observations of the, often tiny, details found in humanitarian situations.

An example includes the founders of the Embrace baby warmer. They recognized the need for a baby warmer in a village health centre. This equipment is normally prohibitively expensive and so out of reach for many. Connecting this context with an understanding that certain substances (known as phase change materials) remain at a constant temperature for long periods of time led to an innovative breakthrough and the development of a low-cost warmer now used in numerous countries.

Strategize

A strategy is the plan for achieving an aim or set of objectives and, hence, to strategize is the act of creating a strategy. Formulating a strategy can be no small task at times. Strategy may seem like a paradoxical element: humanitarian innovation may appear to be fast-paced, non-linear, short-term, and based at least in part on improvisation whereas strategy involves long-term planning. The pressure to strategize may come from several fronts including resource constraints, the demands of donors, and common mindsets that dislike free-flowing experimentation. A number of strategic tensions along these lines have been noted by De-Wit and Meyer (2004). They include 'logic versus creativity' and 'planned versus emergent' tendencies which reveal themselves in discussions about strategy. In strategizing for innovation, it is therefore helpful to think about it as an investment in the future whose benefits take time to realize.

As a starting point, considering the overlap of three areas can be helpful. The foundations of practical action and the management of structure and process can be found in the first: relief aid. There is a tendency to look to other fields, particularly business management, for best practice. However, the practice of management itself is agnostic to the specifics of any particular sector of endeavour. As noted by Jim Collins (2001), examples of good management come from various sectors including religion and the military, as well as non-profits and the business sector. A range of large and small organizations – including Oxfam, MSF and the International Rescue Committee – epitomize these characteristics.

The second area, design, lends important factors such as adaptability and perspective that go far beyond aesthetics. In recent years, a key contribution from this area, human-centred design, has been adopted by numerous sectors, and its similarity to the participatory techniques of the development sector is striking. Companies such as IDEO have become well-known design specialists.

The last area, business start-up, contributes a number of useful methodologies including lean and agile practices. Examples of good practice can be found in commercial firms including Apple, Dropbox, and Zappos.

Each of these components has its flaws and can be subjected to criticism. Together, however, they engender an approach, a mindset, and contribute a number of tools that can help the innovative leader strategize. Where contributions from these three areas overlap (as shown in Figure 9.1), there are several common characteristics. These are:

Focus on people: When working on difficult problems, particularly when technological fixes are involved, affected people can be forgotten in the rush to provide a solution. These areas provide tools to centre and establish empathy with others.

Dealing with ambiguity: Disaster relief inherently involves many unknowns, and managing innovation in this context can add further uncertainty. Each of these areas offers ways to deal with the ambiguity, including an openness to change, and ways to break large problems into manageable bits.

Speed: Responding to disasters and their aftermath must be done quickly. With time at a premium, a mindset – along with appropriate systems and tools – that produces results is a must. Approaches including reduced administration and streamlining bureaucratic rules enable humanitarian innovation.

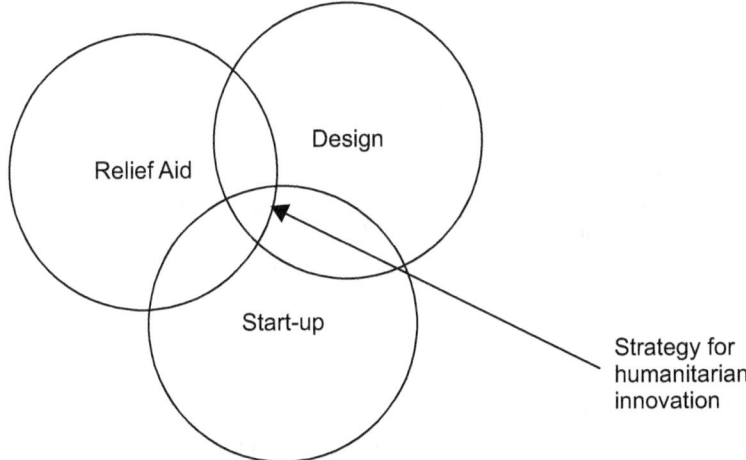

Figure 9.1 Strategies for humanitarian innovation

Flexibility: While demanding compliance with standards can be an asset in stable situations, it can be detrimental in situations of rapid change. Having an approach that is designed to be adaptable and malleable is an important enabling factor.

Learning: There is a common perception that learning is time-consuming, but the right methodologies can speed this process. When done properly, new and improved products and services can be trialled and deployed in the field through using the right learning systems. This may involve failing fast and pivoting to more effective ways of doing things than traditional approaches.

Innovative leaders find it is helpful not to develop a detailed strategic plan but to have a road map that provides a common and realistic vision, identifies what resources (including talent) are needed, and aligns systems with the end state in mind. This focuses an organization's innovative efforts while keeping other tasks functioning. This is supported by the three box mode of Govindarajan (2016), which identifies the importance of having some staff working on the present (in effect, keeping the trains running on time) while others focus on the future by creating and implementing innovative solutions.

Prepare: put first things first

This part of the INSPIRE framework is based on the adage: 'Unless you know where you are going then you won't know how to get there'. In other words, once a direction is determined, a key element in any endeavour is preparation. Innovative leaders prepare by putting first things first, and this has a number of implications.

First, start with the end in mind. Stephen Covey (2004), noted that every human creation is actually created twice: a mental creation precedes every action and physical creation. Just as having a clear blueprint helps build a well-constructed house, an organization needs to have a clear plan for how it will achieve its goals. This is what Gugelev and Stern (2015) describe as the 'endgame'. They suggest that any social innovation should have a clearly articulated situation in which it culminates. This enables all efforts to be directed toward reaching that outcome from the start. They outline five possible endgames for a product, service or, indeed, an organization. It may be:

- an open-source solution
- replicated by others
- able to be adopted by government or commercial entities
- achieved outright (e.g., finding a durable solution to a specific population's displacement or other finalization of a relief situation)
- providing a sustained service through ongoing support.

If the endgame is understood across an organization and is easily communicated, the strategy and preparation become more effective.

Second, follow the Scout's motto: 'Be Prepared'. Preparation involves getting ready – taking time to think, study, rehearse, practice, confer, and verify information – before actually doing anything. Preparation reduces, but does not eliminate, failure. Successful people know that, without it, most efforts will fall short of their intended outcome. Being prepared gives space for experimentation and the ability to place small bets on new projects. In so doing, an innovative leader makes it safe to fail early on and treats failure as a learning opportunity. So, while being prepared really is the best way of preventing failure, approaching failure with the right mindset helps to deal with it when it happens. As Borrud and Gliege (see Chapter 17 in this book) point out, it is the effort that matters. This is echoed in the Japanese proverb: 'Fall seven times, stand up eight'.

Finally, prioritise by planning to succeed. By having a clear end in mind, preparing to reach that goal and prioritising the right things will make success more likely. As Covey (2004: 154) asked, 'What one thing could you do in your personal and professional life that, if you did on a regular basis, would make a tremendous positive difference in your life?' For those working in humanitarian assistance, this can be a real challenge when faced with so many challenges and competing priorities.

There is no easy way to deal with these challenges but the decision matrix developed by former US president, Dwight Eisenhower, can help. By separating those tasks and responsibilities that are important but not urgent (e.g., planning, preparation, study, and relationship-building) from the truly urgent and important (e.g., genuine crises and deadlines), there is less stress and burnout. By focusing on the important but not urgent, more time can be spent on deep thought, renewal, and recognising new opportunities and connections: all activities that are important to innovative leaders.

Integration

For an innovative leader, integration involves bringing together elements of an idea, plan, team, organization, and ecosystem (i.e., the community and stakeholders) to make an innovation successful. This means being both driven and creative while building consensus. Creativity, using imagination and generating original ideas, can be learned and cultivated. There are a range of theories that explain the methods and sources of creativity. Divergent thinking can help when it is tapped into. Dyer, Christensen and Gregersen (2011) recognize key behaviours that optimize the creative impulse in people:

- **Associating:** drawing connections between questions, problems, or ideas from unrelated fields.
- **Questioning:** posing queries that challenge common wisdom.
- **Observing:** scrutinising the behaviour of customers, suppliers, and competitors to identify new ways of doing things.
- **Networking:** meeting people with different ideas and perspectives.
- **Experimenting:** constructing interactive experiences and provoking unorthodox responses to see what insights emerge.

Striking the right balance between creativity and the tasks of management may be a challenge. If working at a global level, consider mainstreaming the innovation process from the start. The term 'mainstreaming' means that innovation is part of everyone's mindset and extends into everyday activities. It is the opposite of a siloed approach where 'labs' are placed outside of the main activities and areas. If the new product or service is mainstreamed, buy-in by those within an organization not directly involved may be more likely. Doing this will likely involve abundance thinking, with its emphasis on expanding the pie in a social sense.

Re-examine

It is possible for obstacles (whether minor hurdles or major roadblocks) to arise in the effort to create positive and innovative change. Questioning the direction of an innovative project and the assumptions that underpin the effort can be an important exercise. Moreover, with staff turnover and the realities of the demands of management, it is not unusual to be brought into an effort that is already underway. In such cases, it important to consider redefining the problem and rethinking the limits of the tasks at hand. This is what Levitt and Dabner (2014) describe as thinking 'like a freak'.

An example of thinking like a manager focused on optimising a supply chain is: 'Q: How can we make our supply chain faster? A: With the right ICT'. An innovative leader would answer the same question with: 'We will make the problem of a slow supply chain less relevant if we move manufacturing to where supplies are needed'. An ineffective leader might say that 'there is no other way', or 'there's nothing we can do'. An innovative leader, by contrast, is likely to have the habit of considering alternatives that produces a more effective way of thinking. They are likely to say, 'perhaps we need to talk to someone else', or ask 'have we considered all the alternatives?' As Albert Einstein noted, 'We can't solve problems by using the same kind of thinking we used when we created them'.

Part of the 'freak' approach includes remaining child-like when encountering challenges (Levitt and Dabner, 2014). The Zen Buddhist concept of *shoshin*, meaning beginner's mind, also conveys this idea. Having this mindset means being eager, open, and having a lack of bias. The concept applies equally to those who know a problem, subject, or context very well: the point is to take a beginner's approach so that discovery and learning can be maximized.

People are inherently social and collaborative when knowledge is shared. This is especially true in the increasingly specialized areas that have developed during the process of professionalization of humanitarianism. So the importance of measurement, done through monitoring and evaluation, is now a recognized element of most aid projects. This helps produce a level of data-driven decision-making that would not have been possible without the energy, learning, and resources that have been put behind it.

At the same time, there are a number of pitfalls that the innovative leader should be aware of. These pitfalls are the result of various types of bias, and the unintended consequences of policies and measurement. When a metric becomes a target for social change, it stops being useful because of the likelihood that users and monitors will focus on it to achieve a better result. This is known variably as Campbell's Law (1979) or Goodhart's Law (1975). In the field of humanitarian response there are various illustrations of the cobra effect, where an attempted solution actually makes the problem worse, such as aid contributing to the continuation of violence.

According to research carried out by Sloman and Fernbach (2017), people typically believe they have more knowledge than they actually do (this is revealed when people are asked to explain in detail such things how a toilet or bicycle works). When it comes to policy or complex social phenomena, this 'illusion of knowledge' leads to incorrect assumptions that are reinforced by bias encountered when people are isolated (physically) or remain within small communities (e.g., on social media).

Execute

This last part of the INSPIRE framework, which involves moving an initial idea through the idea funnel of the innovation process to a successful product or service, requires a shift in focus that depends on the needs of the team and the innovation under development. Such an approach has been called a contingency model of management (Fiedler and Garcia, 1987). Communicating clearly and consistently, attention to detail, and encouragement can all contribute to the innovative process.

To make an innovation scale and be sustainable, it is important to have a bias toward action. Some fall into a trap of 'analysis paralysis', spending too much time thinking about a problem, instead of actually solving it. It is worth remembering that there is no such thing as perfect. As Voltaire is believed to have said, do not 'let perfect be the enemy of good'. Often, an 80 per cent solution will be good enough (particularly where learning and further development are needed) so setting limits and making small changes can beneficial. Try following the Japanese concept of *kaizen* or continual improvement, a technique used to ensure quality in the workplace. This practice humanizes the workplace by encouraging participation and teaches people how to perform experiments to eliminate waste and needlessly difficult tasks. Employing the most appropriate project-management tools and techniques can help ensure that the innovative solution is ultimately successful.

Execution of an innovation, like the implementation of any project, can be frustrating. There are likely to be setbacks and times when the task might appear to be too difficult to even try. This is especially true in humanitarian assistance. One simple metaphor can help in times like this. Inventor Buckminster Fuller suggested that to influence or otherwise change a seemingly insurmountable challenge, remember the trim tab, a small device used to turn large ocean-going ships. A trim tab does not turn the ship but instead helps turn the large rudder by creating a space of low pressure. Innovative leaders, through their mindsets and actions, act as metaphorical trim tabs on big challenges.

A final note: be sure to thank each team member for their contribution, and to celebrate things that have been accomplished. Life is short and, if you are truly an innovative leader, you may have just helped change the world.

References

Campbell, D. (1979) 'Assessing the Impact of Planned Social Change', *Evaluation and Program Planning*, 2(1), pp. 67–90 <https://doi.org/10.1016/0149-7189(79)90048-X> [accessed 14 November 2017].

Collins, J. (2001) *Good to Great in the Social Sectors*, Harper Collins, New York, NY.

Covey, S. (2004) *The 7 Habits of Highly Effective People*, Free Press, New York, NY.

De-Wit, B. and Meyer, R. (2004) *Strategy Process, Content and Context*, third edition, Thomson Learning, London.

Drucker, P. (2008) *The Essential Drucker*, Harper Collins Business, New York, NY.

Dyer, J., Christensen, C. and Gregersen, H. (2011) *The Innovator's DNA: Mastering the Five Skills of Disruptive Innovators*, Harvard Business Review Press, Cambridge, MA.

Fiedler, F. E. and Garcia, J. E. (1987) *New Approaches to Leadership, Cognitive Resources and Organisational Performance*, John Wiley and Sons, New York, NY.

Garvin, D. (2013) 'How Google Sold its Engineers on Management', *Harvard Business Review* <https://hbr.org/2013/12/

how-google-sold-its-engineers-on-management> [accessed 20 September 2017].

Goodhart, C. A. E. (1975) 'Problems of Monetary Management: The U.K. Experience', *Papers in Monetary Economics*, Reserve Bank of Australia.

Govindarajan, V. (2016) *The Three-Box Solution: A Strategy for Leading Innovation*, Harvard Business Review Press, Cambridge, MA.

Gugelev, A. and Stern, A.(2015) 'What is Your Endgame?' *Stanford Social Innovation Review*, Winter, pp. 40–47.

Levitt, S. and Dabner, S. (2014) *Think Like a Freak*, William Morrow and Company, New York, NY.

Sardar, Z. and John A. Sweeney (2016) 'The Three Tomorrows of Postnormal Times', *Futures* 75, pp. 1–13.

Sloman, S. and Fernbach, P. (2017) *The Knowledge Illusion: Why We Never Think Alone*, Riverhead Books, New York, NY.

Taleb, N. (2012) *Anti-Fragile: Things that Gain from Disorder*, Random House, New York, NY.

Wooden, J. and Jamison, S. (1997) *Wooden*, McGraw Hill, New York, NY, p. 143.

About the author

Eric James, PhD, is the co-founder and executive director of Field Ready. He has over two decades of experience leading humanitarian relief programmes. He has been involved in several business start-ups, holds two patents and was a fellow/advisor at Singularity University. Eric is an affiliated expert of the Harvard Humanitarian Initiative and an adjunct professor at the DePaul University's Refugee and Forced Migration Studies programme. He is author of *Managing Humanitarian Relief: An Operational Guide for NGOs* (Practical Action Publishing, 2nd Edition, 2017) among other publications.

CHAPTER 10
Understanding change: How does change happen?

Duncan Green

Change is the essence of innovation, so an appreciation of how it happens is important. This chapter looks at a number of elements that are part of change including theory, agility, and failure. It is argued that change should be understood to happen internally within a given country or community. It should also be recognized that small changes often have significant impact. When this is properly understood, more impactful interventions can be implemented.

Keywords: change, theory of change, agility, failure

Change happens in many different ways, depending on the type of change you are aspiring to: for example, whether it is economic, social or political in nature. Aid professionals need to think more about how change happens endogenously; i.e., internally, within any given country or community. They should also recognize that contributions to change are often small, so it is important to first work out how change happens in a particular social or political system, then work out how this might fit in and contribute to change processes.

The nature of change in international aid

One way of understanding development is that economic, social, and political change takes place above all through shifts in an underlying force field, and that force field is power. Examples of power within the system include the ever-changing interplay between an international NGO and a local NGO, an employee and an employer, a civil rights activist and the rest of society, or an entrepreneur and big business. There is a constant interplay of power between people, and between the relative level of agency, capability, and opportunity they have to change things. In any system, a development intervention is about redistributing power – whether you pursue an accountability initiative, or seek better prices for producers in the market, you are rearranging power in a progressive (or regressive) way.

Theory of change: going in two incompatible directions

One way of approaching a theory of change is as a more complete version of the conventional approach to projects and programmes (using log frames, project plans, etc.). This approach should include a clear understanding of the intended change (impact), how the change will be achieved, and how the change will be measured. In theory, if this work is done in advance, an intervention can be delivered and the impact measured to see if change has been achieved. However, this linear understanding of change is often misguided, because we are operating in complex systems with so many feedback loops and connections that any intervention ripples through the system and has many impacts that are completely unpredictable.

In reality, a theory of change should be seen more as a compass than a map. This will allow you to initiate an intervention with the ability to adapt and change course in response to events. The key is to observe and respond to changes in the system, rather than committing to a fixed plan that may be replaced with a completely different fixed plan if the intended impact is not achieved.

Thinking differently

Currently, a very crude caricature of development and humanitarian aid is that you do all your 'thinking' in advance: undertaking analysis of the situation, deciding on an intervention to change the situation, then fundraising for the intervention. After the planning process is complete, the thinking is also complete, and the 'doing' commences; the plan is implemented, after which an evaluation is undertaken and continuation funding sought. If you are operating in an unpredictable (complex) system, this may be a flawed approach: your initial ideas will always have to be modified in light of experience – we learn by doing (and failing).

There is, of course, a balance to be struck. Too much thinking can prevent the doing (analysis paralysis), but if you just do without periodically standing back to consider whether the intervention is working, and whether any alterations are required, then interventions are more likely to fail (and are certainly less likely to achieve maximum impact). The key is building in the agility and the ability to respond to events. You are operating in a complex system, which means you're only as good as your feedback loops and your ability to respond to them. The measure of these might be, for example, the quality of your engagement with the community and your ability to adapt the programme to fit their needs.

Balancing agility with the realities of bureaucracy

People play a double game in all aid bureaucracies whether they are working in a government, donor organization, international organization, or NGO. People follow the process and learn to speak the language that is required of them by their funders and other stakeholders; but they also learn to improvise, respond to events and to 'make it up as they go along', because that is how aid programmes work in reality.

The question is, how do we combine these two worlds to make the planning relevant to reality? Answering this question will be essential to ensuring that NGOs are fit for purpose in the future. NGOs must operate less like supertankers and more like white-water rafts – able to negotiate the rapids of events and complex systems, and adjust quickly. This may require a greater number of independent units within BINGOs. It may require that BINGOs deliberately spin off innovations as start-ups that will either sink or swim. Either will feed more ideas into the system. The period of massive monocultures in development planning is over.

Embracing failure

The sector must recognize that, just as in markets or the evolution of species, a large proportion of innovations will fail. This mindset has been adopted in the private sector, and the private sector has enjoyed highly visible, massive impact through innovation.

Failure is good, but failure has to be fast. Fast failure means rapidly detecting when something is not working out as planned, then cutting your losses and moving resources into something else. *Slow* failure sucks the resources and energy out of an organization. The cost of innovation will be minimized by failing cheaply and quickly. NGOs must avoid the temptation to commit to innovations for a number of years before they have the chance to consider whether the innovation is failing.

Ultimately, good innovation processes imitate the most powerful change process in the word: evolution. Evolution works through variation, selection of the fit variants, and amplification of those fit variants.

Further Reading

Bowman, K., Chettleborough, J., Jeans, H. Rowlands, J. and Whitehead, J. (2015) *Systems Thinking: An Introduction for Oxfam Programme Staff*, Oxfam GB, Oxford.

Green, D. (2016) *How Change Happens*, Oxford University Press, Oxford.

Green, D. (2015) 'Fit for the Future? Development Trends and the Role of International NGOs', *Oxfam Discussion Paper*, Oxfam GB, Oxford.

Green, D. (2012) *From Poverty to Power: How Active Citizens and Effective States can Change the World*, secondedition, Oxfam, Oxford.

Meadows, D and Wright, D. (2009) *Thinking in Systems: A Primer*, Routledge, Abingdon.

Ramalingam, B. (2013) *Aid on the Edge of Chaos*, Oxford University Press, New York, NY.

Rowlands, J. (1997) *Questioning Empowerment: Working with Women in Honduras*, Oxfam UK and Ireland, Oxford.

About the author

Duncan Green is a senior strategic advisor at Oxfam GB and is also currently a professor in Practice at the London School of Economics. He is author of *How Change Happens* (Oxford University Press, 2016) and *From Poverty to Power: How Active Citizens and Effective States can Change the World* (Practical Action Publishing, 2nd edition, 2012). He also authors the *From Poverty to Power* blog.

CHAPTER 11
Ethical and responsible use of ICT

Nathaniel Raymond

Ethics are at the core of humanitarianism and are thus an essential consideration in innovation. This chapter argues that humanitarians are using ICT – just one form of many innovations entering the sector – without having yet gone through a process that allows the technologies to be used ethically. Ethical limitations for the use of technologies must be identified, standards set, and regulations put in place. In the process, a number of elements across the sector, such as responsibilities, transparency, and feedback loops, will need to be further developed.

Keywords: ethics, humanitarianism, information communication technologies, data

The adoption of the Ushahidi crowd-mapping platform during the Kenyan election violence in 2007–2008 initiated a Gartner hype cycle (Basiliere and Shanler, 2014) about the possibilities of digital data for humanitarian situational awareness. Current efforts to innovate the use of technology by the humanitarian sector are providing capabilities to responders that, even a decade ago, were thought to be out of reach for most organizations and are now commonplace.

However, humanitarian actors are struggling to update their ethical and technical standards to responsibly integrate and keep pace with these innovations, particularly the use of information communication technology (ICT). The sector is now entering a 'dissonance phase' in which the excitement that marked the initial phase of adoption has turned to frustration and re-examination based on the realization that these innovations have unintended consequences.

Some of the unintended consequences these technologies have raised in the humanitarian context are related to the following questions: What responsibilities do humanitarians have to protect the privacy of individual and demographic data collected by ICT? How does the use of ICT potentially change how crises unfold? Are information and data humanitarian needs equal to those such as food, water, shelter, and medicine that are supported by traditional types of aid?

Most technologies follow a cycle through which societies integrate innovations into normal use. The phases in this cycle are:

Phase one: initial adoption
Phase two: friction and adaptation
Phase three: negotiation of a compact about acceptable use
Phase four: integration and absorption

In the negotiation phase, society negotiates with the value proposition and the risk proposition around a technology and begins to form a compact through creating formal and informal regulations for appropriate deployment of the technology. The negotiation often continues throughout the integration phase of an innovation. In some cases, social compacts about the use of a technology may proceed initial adoption, as happened in the case of aviation.

Sometimes friction can show up unexpectedly in the midst of a well-established social compact. The impact of disasters such as Three Mile Island and Chernobyl in the nuclear energy sector are examples of this phenomenon. The cycle should be recognized as one which occurs continuously, even for commonly used technologies, and is sometimes out of order.

Three things must be established for a tech to be integrated and absorbed:

1. **Limitations**: Technical (what it can't do) and social (what it shouldn't do) limitations need to be set. The informal process of identifying limitations as part of social discourse and with experience of using the tech often leads to the establishment of standards and regulations.
2. **Standards**: Things that have to happen to help meet the limitations.
3. **Regulation mechanisms**: These introduce the capacity to enforce the standards.

Current humanitarian use of ICT has inverted this cycle. Humanitarians are continuing to integrate and absorb ICT without having yet gone through the process of negotiating a compact with crisis-affected populations about acceptable ways of using these technologies. Thus, limitations have not been identified and standards and regulations have not been established as part of the integration process.

The humanitarian sector has arrived at this point because it has prioritised assumptions and aspirations over limitation setting, translating past standards of humanitarian practice into this new area of operations, and agreeing whether and how regulation needs to occur. Some of the humanitarian sector's motivating assumptions appear to include the following:

- technology democratizes social systems it affects
- ICT can serve to protect vulnerable populations
- ICT use can elevate people economically.

Humanitarians have encoded these assumptions into the way the sector has decided to deploy these technologies; the assumptions are social software.

As of yet, humanitarians have no commonly accepted framework for the use of ICT and data in crises, and efforts to identify suitable approaches are only beginning (UNOCHA, 2016). While initial steps have been taken, in, for example, the *Signal Code: A Human Rights Approach to Information During Crisis* (Greenwood et al., 2017), there is no standard for ICT and data use. There is evidence that our use of ICT is actually causing disasters. In a recent report on data preparedness in humanitarian response, the Signal Program has identified four types of data disasters (Raymond and Al Achkar, 2016):

- **Data disparity**: Humanitarian actors may have incomplete, inaccurate, and/or insufficient data – because of a lack of a sharing relationship or because the data may not exist – to make informed decisions about the needs of affected people, which may lead to inaccurate or inequitable responses.
- **Data deluge**: The amount of data generated by responders and affected communities after a disaster may overwhelm a responder's ability to make sense of the large flows of information, negatively affecting the ability to make decisions. The lack of accepted protocols for verification and corroboration of data often leads to uncoordinated and uncontrolled sharing.
- **Data distortion**: Improper and inaccurate analysis of data can either inflate or minimize the severity of a disaster situation, making responses less effective and wasting limited humanitarian resources.
- **Data damage**: In certain cases, data that is not used in a responsible way and in compliance with data privacy and data protection laws, can cause, or be perceived to cause, harm to an organization, affected people, and their communities. Incidents where data causes damage to affected people can break trust between partners and affected communities.

A possible major cause of these data disasters may be that ICT generates a different type of data to those humanitarian ethical and technical standards were designed to regulate. This new type of data, unlike traditional forms of personally identifiable information (PII), can be referred to as demographically identifiable information (DII) (Raymond and Al Achkar, 2016). DII is primarily about communities and populations, rather than specific individuals.

Research also shows that technical limitations mean it is becoming less and less possible to ensure privacy or anonymization of DII. In large data sets, it is possible to track patterns which are unique, a phenomenon known as 'unicity'. Using the concept of unicity, it is possible to identify individuals from large datasets (de Montjoye et al., 2015). Conversely, it is also possible to use known personal information about an individual to identify that individual in a large dataset, a phenomena known as 'eccentricity' (Narayanan and Shmatikov, 2007).

Unicity and eccentricity, individually or together, can be exploited and extrapolated to identify supposedly anonymized individuals and demographic groups. To mitigate these new threats to populations as a result of ICT use in crisis response, UNOCHA (2016) identifies four principles to help build data responsibility into humanitarian action (UNOCHA, 2016: 12):

- **Responsibility as a process**: Responsible use of data is not simply a policy to be agreed in the initial phase. It is an integrated and iterative set of processes which require the necessary capacities to support them throughout a humanitarian operation. Trained personnel are required to design and implement how organizations will execute and evaluate them at every stage of a project. As a minimum, organizations should implement four steps in the data responsibility process: (1) evaluating context, (2) taking inventory of the data and how it is stored, (3) identifying risks and harms associated with the use of data, and (4) developing mitigation strategies.
- **Bright-line rules and red-button responses**: Organizations need the capacity to develop and adhere to 'bright-line' rules before they deploy data- and ICT-based interventions. Examples include clear restrictions on what data should not be collected, shared, or otherwise used. Groups also need the capacity to identify and plan to address 'red-button' moments that would require the immediate cessation of a project. Developing plans before these moments occur enables organizations to react effectively.
- **Transparency**: Few organizations submit their use of data to transparent public review and scrutiny. Groups deploying data-based interventions should intentionally capture and publicly share information about their own projects as well as critical incidents, such as when a specific population is harmed or infrastructure is compromised. Responsible data users also share their best practices with other organizations.
- **Feedback loops**: Organizations using data responsibly establish feedback loops with key stakeholders, in particular, affected populations and other organizations in a specific data ecosystem. Given that the tempo of data-related operations is often high, and that dynamics can change quickly, it is essential to establish feedback loops and the capacity to manage them before an activity begins. Organizations should also have internal feedback loops to monitor data practices throughout the project's lifecycle.

The principles above represent a starting point for data responsibility. While data responsibility should be fully integrated into organizational operations, a comprehensive ethical regime similar to the Sphere Standards is also required for humanitarian use of ICT.

For there to be true integration and absorption of ICT and the data it produces into humanitarian operations, the process of negotiation to agree a social compact with the populations humanitarians seek to serve must be developed. That process is, at present, only nascent. Successful completion of this process will not depend on technology and its use, per se. It will depend, instead, on the sector's renewal of its commitment to the ethics, legal foundations, and values which make humanitarians truly 'humanitarian' under international law and custom.

References

Basiliere, P. and Shanler, M. (2014) *Hype Cycle for 3D Printing*, Gartner Research Paper <https://www.gartner.com/doc/2803426> [accessed 24 September 2017].

Greenwood, F., Howarth, C., Escudero Poole, D., Raymond, N., Scarnecchia, D. (2017) 'Signal Code: A Human Rights Approach to Information During Crisis', *Harvard Humanitarian Institute*, <http://hhi.harvard.edu/publications/signal-code-human-rights-approach-information-during-crisis> [accessed 24 September 2017].

de Montjoye, Y.-A. de, Radaelli, L., Kumar Singh, V., Pentland, A. (2015) 'Unique in the Shopping Mall: On the Reidentifiability of Credit Card Metadata', *Science*, 347(6221), pp. 536-539 <http://science.sciencemag.org/content/347/6221/536> [accessed 24 September 2017].

Narayanan, A. and Shmatikov, V (2007) 'Robust De-anonymisation of Large Sparse Datasets', *University of Texas at Austin* <https://www.cs.utexas.edu/~shmat/shmat_oak08netflix.pdf> [accessed 24 September 2017].

Raymond, N. and Al Achkar, Z. (2016) 'Data Preparedness: Connecting Data, Decision Making and Humanitarian Response', *Harvard Humanitarian Institute* <http://hhi.harvard.edu/publications/data-preparedness-connecting-data-decision-making-and-humanitarian-response> [accessed 24 September 2017].

UNOCHA (2016) 'Building data responsibility into humanitarian action', <https://docs.unocha.org/sites/dms/Documents/TB18_Data%20Responsibility_Online.pdf> [accessed 24 September 2017].

About the author

Nathaniel Raymond is director of the Signal Program on Human Security and Technology at the Harvard Humanitarian Initiative (HHI). Raymond was previously director of the Campaign Against Torture at Physicians for Human Rights, and served in a variety of roles at Oxfam America, including as communications advisor for Humanitarian Response and interim coordinator for Tsunami Communications for Oxfam International.

CHAPTER 12

Building partners for innovation (and resilience)

Justin Henceroth and Ashley Thompson

Successful innovation has the ability to build the capacity of the actors involved, and so partnership is worth close examination. This chapter discusses the ecosystem of humanitarian innovation and defines the different roles of those involved. It then presents key principles and guidelines for navigating and developing partnerships that can help ensure more successful cooperation. Next, it describes indicators available for evaluating partnerships. Finally, the chapter considers gender and the inclusion of women in partnerships to ensure more lasting and equitable innovation.

Keywords: humanitarianism, innovation, partnership, resilience, gender

Introduction

Innovation tends to be more successful when done with an emphasis on partnerships with industry and innovation leaders pursuing collaborative relationships with local governments, organizations, and people. Effective partnerships ensure critical local knowledge is embedded into the process, provide sites and venues for testing and iterating prototypes, and build the community networks and buy-in that are essential for any successful scaling of a trialled innovation.

The value of partnering extends beyond the ability to localize and contextualize innovations. Partnerships can enhance the outcomes of the innovation process and deliver tangible benefits even if the innovation itself fails. A successful innovation process not only delivers something tangible but also builds the capacity of the actors involved.

Two goals that often guide humanitarian efforts are to build resilience and to foster gender inclusion and equality. Many innovations, therefore, are judged on their ability to deliver change that works towards these two goals. Research within both of these areas of concern highlights an important distinction between 'the product' and 'the process'. There are many tools and products that contribute to resilience and gender equity and deliver tangible change – such as improved building design and representation quotas in government. However, the process through which these kinds of actions are undertaken contributes to their impact on larger goals. Partnerships that actively enable all stakeholders, especially lower-power groups that are traditionally repressed or marginalized, deliver longer-term benefits in the form of improved capacity, stronger networks, and greater ability to learn and reorganize in the face of change.

Despite the benefits, innovating through partnerships is a challenge. The humanitarian sector brings global organizations and NGOs in direct contact with (often) remote, less developed and often-marginalized communities. Successful partnership in the humanitarian sector – even when implementing projects that an organization has significant experience with and capacity in – presents a number of challenges of language, culture, background, and understanding.

Roles for local partners

Local partners play important roles throughout the innovation process. From the initial ideation stage to the final review and scaling of successful innovations, local partners can lead or contribute in many different ways. Organizations hoping to manage innovation with local partners need to be able to identify the roles and contributions they expect. These roles will change depending on the context, the specific innovations being pursued, and the capacities of local partners.

Local organizations are capable of leading innovation processes themselves. Indeed, in many cases, local partners are better positioned to imagine, design, and create the types of break-through innovations that will contribute most significantly to improved disaster response and quality of life thereafter. As companies, organizations, and individuals embedded in communities, local partners have the key cultural and contextual knowledge to develop technologies, products, and processes that are useful locally. They also have insight into the unique local challenges faced when developing and implementing projects and ideas.

At the same time, when trying to bring in new technologies and advances developed elsewhere, local organizations also serve as partners to international organizations by grounding and contextualizing specific technologies and processes and testing these new innovations in situ. Throughout the innovation process, at least four different roles for local partners can contribute to more contextually appropriate and successful innovation.

Innovators: Local organizations can both generate and help refine ideas for innovations. In some cases, they may be able to see gaps, issues, or challenges that are specific to a local or country context that international aid partners may not be able to identify. These gaps can become the basis for developing and refining innovations. At the same time, as new technologies and processes are brought into the humanitarian sector, local partners can help identify ways in which those innovations can be modified, adapted, and applied to have the maximum effect locally.

Implementers: Local organizations are well positioned to support or conduct pilot and field tests of innovations. Their connections with communities and governments can help secure the institutional and social relationships required to conduct testing, and their ability to work and communicate with the people and organizations that are testing innovations will ensure that key feedback is communicated. Local organization staff often have specific knowledge of field sites and conditions that will greatly improve the efficacy of pilot testing.

Multipliers: After ideas have been successfully demonstrated, local partners and networks of local partners should be engaged to take those innovations to scale. This can include engaging local partners to manufacture new products in-country, build or install new innovations in a community, and train or educate communities in how to utilize innovations effectively. Multiplying or scaling innovations is a different process to carrying out smaller-scale pilot or field tests, and may, therefore, engage more and different kinds of partners.

Communicators: Local partners have networks extending far beyond aid agencies and international partners. Local partners can communicate project outcomes and successes through their networks in order to not only educate and deliver greater impact, but also to continue fuelling innovation and partnership by bringing more and more effective partners into the process. Over time, communication around the innovation process can help to fuel a culture of innovation, where actors and organizations share stories and knowledge of successes and failures in trying new things, thus spurring additional thinking, creativity, and innovation.

Types of local partner

The use of the singular term local partner, while emphasizing the importance of working with people who are from the area and understand the local context, obscures the diversity and range of potential partners. Partners could include almost any business, organization, institution, or individual with the ability to drive, support, engage in, contribute to, or benefit from innovation. Throughout the innovation process, different partners may be capable of performing different functions and filling diverse roles. Humanitarian agencies, international partners, and innovators should be both flexible and dedicated to working with all potential partners that exist in a given location. While there is a broad range of roles, there are archetypal partner types that are particularly likely to offer benefits to innovation processes.

Academic institutions: As centres of research, knowledge, and teaching, academic institutions bring significant intellectual strength and capacity to innovation processes. Academic institutions can support research and development at the early stages of innovation, develop methodologies for testing innovations, support monitoring and evaluation of testing processes, or provide people, in the form of professors, students, researchers, interns, or employees, to drive and manage innovation processes. Academic institutions are also often deeply embedded in or connected to local networks, governments, and institutions, and can help generate support for development, testing, and scaling of innovations.

Innovation labs, makerspaces, and community development centres: In recent years, across all sectors, numerous community spaces devoted to innovation and making have popped up in cities throughout the world. These centres, makerspaces, and innovation labs are bringing together smart people and innovative organizations to develop and test new ideas and products. These centres can serve as the source of innovative ideas, as a space to connect with highly skilled and innovative people, and as partners at any stage of the development process. Some of these centres also have a specific focus on social innovation, which may readily transfer, or be directly applicable to, humanitarian contexts. To the extent that these centres also serve as incubators and accelerators, they may play a key role in helping innovations scale in the local context.

Private companies: Private companies are often the vehicle for delivery of new technologies and ideas at scale. These companies have the knowledge of the newest technologies or products available in a given country, and the capacity to deliver them. They can provide valuable insight into local markets, supply chains, and delivery processes. They could be engaged to identify potential gaps in the market, new opportunities that have not yet been pursued, or verify whether there might be a market for a given innovation. They can also provide insight into developing innovations and serve as partners in efforts to scale up.

Trade associations: National trade associations with a focus on a specific sector will have connections to companies and skilled staff. These associations offer services such as education and capacity building that could be utilized, particularly in efforts to scale up processes through leveraging market forces. They may also have connections to specific government ministries and agencies that could help generate support for innovation products. In many developing countries, these trade associations have also worked with international donors in the past and so have experience serving as intermediaries between the humanitarians, innovators, and local companies.

Local and international NGOs: In many places, there is a thriving community of NGOs at both local and national level, and in developing countries there is often a high presence of international NGOs. These NGOs bring significant experience of working in poor and underserved communities and could be engaged in the innovation process to identify key issues. The networks and offices that NGOs have at the local level and in more remote places can also facilitate testing and scaling of innovations.

Government agencies: Many government agencies have mandates to provide services or benefits to people within a specific area and innovators may have to at least inform and acquire permission from relevant government agencies. However, opportunities exist to engage these agencies in a more productive way. Potential methods include utilizing government networks to promote innovation – for example, by linking efforts to scale up with existing subsidy programmes or by distributing innovations through government channels – and supporting government to delivering on its responsibilities – for example, by generating information and data to identify new ways to deliver services.

Households and villages: Ultimately, innovations in support of the poor and vulnerable will have to improve conditions at the household and village level. Therefore, all innovation projects should consider how they support and include households and villages in identifying, promoting, and utilizing any innovation.

International and local partnerships

One aim of the expanding interest in humanitarian innovation is to merge global advances in technology and processes with humanitarian work; thus, international organizations are key actors in this rapidly growing and intersectional field. As these international actors seek to develop, test, and scale innovations, partnerships with local organizations are critical to ensuring innovations are culturally and contextually appropriate. However, the interface between local partners and international partners has the potential to be fraught, with different languages, cultures, and ways of working presenting myriad opportunities for conflict and disagreement. Working through these conflicts requires communication, regular follow-up, and general commitment from all parties to authentic, rather than token, collaboration. However, there are some key principles and guidelines for navigating and developing these partnerships that can help ensure more successful cooperation, and, therefore, more successful innovation.

- **Build things for local context**: At the end of the day, humanitarian innovation processes are tasked with delivering tangible benefits to the people affected by disaster. All ventures and projects should intend to add direct value and benefit for local people and communities.
- **There are many kinds of expertise and knowledge**: Expertise and knowledge exist in multiple forms, ranging from technical and scientific know-how to local and cultural knowledge. Working successfully to bring innovation requires the application and integration of a range of knowledge types. Partners working on humanitarian innovation should recognize both the value and limitations of the knowledge they bring – as well as that of their partners – in order to ensure that ventures are both innovative and reflective of local contexts.
- **Communicate**: Innovation ventures and projects will require the engagement of multiple partners at different levels and times. In order to facilitate effective cooperation and collaboration, systems should be put in place to ensure clear and regular communication.
- **Respect**: All partnerships should be built upon mutual respect. The different backgrounds, skills, and knowledge types of partners will lead

to different methods and styles of working which could lead to tension, conflict, or miscommunication. Maintaining a position of mutual respect will allow partners to work through disagreement in ways that are mutually beneficial and lead to improved understanding.
- **Assume good intentions**: All partners engaged in innovation support the underlying goals and motives of improving the lives of people both locally and around the world. When there is tension or disagreement, all partners should assume that the other partners are approaching their work with good intentions and with their full capacity. Even when the activities of other partners may seem confusing, discussions addressing the issue should begin with an assumption that there is reason, rationale, and good intentions behind partner actions.
- **Fit within local culture and customs**: Innovations should seek to fit within the generally accepted spectrum of standards, customs, and mores of local culture. Local organizations and people are the best guides to ensuring that actions fit within this context, even when the innovation seeks to shift the status quo or affect cultural or social hierarchies. All innovation partners should rely on local guidance and cultural knowledge to ensure actions and projects are appropriate and appropriately targeted.

While the specific approaches and working relationships will need to be adapted from place to place and project to project, these principles serve as a framework for creating successful working relationships between multiple partners, particularly among partners from different countries and cultures.

Indicators of successful partnerships

In order to ensure successful partnerships, it is important to find ways in which to monitor, assess, and review how well the different partnering organizations are working together because this is itself a tangible outcome – one which, indeed, may significantly impact the result of the innovation itself, in both success and failure. Basic systems to monitor partnerships ensure partnerships are working well, are supporting overall objectives, and are proving beneficial to all stakeholders. An effective system for monitoring and reviewing partnerships should include both formal review processes and informal measures embedded in a culture that encourages members and affiliates to identify barriers, and discuss and resolve issues as they arise.

A key way to formalize a review process is to identify key points at which partners will engage in meetings or interviews specifically to discuss the partnership. These meetings should happen both before and after engagement within the partnership as well as at key points throughout the process. Interviews or meetings with a partner conducted before a project or engagement should focus on what each partner hopes to gain from the partnership. Interviews after a project should include reflections on what a partner gained from participating, reflections on the partnership, including what worked well and what did not work well, and a discussion of future opportunities to continue or expand engagement. Periodic one-on-one meetings with partners throughout a project also ensure that different organizations have the opportunity to provide feedback and receive guidance before the conclusion of the project. These one-on-ones could be scheduled at regular intervals, such as once per quarter, or at key times, such as the beginning of each new stage of the innovation process.

A second important element to formalize is a communication process that enables conflicts, complaints, and other issues to be submitted, managed, and resolved. A defined and clearly articulated process for raising and resolving issues will ensure any challenges partners face can be brought up in a professional manner and dealt with through mutually established mechanisms. This can help partners feel that they are working in a dynamic venue and have a voice enabling them to shape the partnership and their engagement in a way that is beneficial to them. As a result of all partners being able to trust standing processes, over time, a level of trust will develop that supports communication, commitment, and cooperation across all aspects of a project.

In reviewing innovation processes, there are key indicators of success. Many of these indicators will be specific to the needs and objectives of an innovation process; however, some indicators of successful partnerships are common across processes and contexts. Successful partnerships will be those ensuring that project goals and objectives are achieved, while also contributing to growth and development of the individual partners – particularly local partners. Successful partnerships will generally exhibit the following characteristics:

- **Partners are communicating effectively**: There are systems in place to ensure consistent and regular communication, and all partners feel that they are receiving information, feedback, and guidance in a timely and clear manner.
- **Innovation is successfully tested**: The partnership ensures the project successfully develops, tests, and monitors innovations in the field. Successfully testing innovations will require all local and international partners to fulfil their roles within the partnership.
- **Local partner capacity is built**: Local partners develop new skills, knowledge, and capacity, enabling them to continue working in the field and to consider ways they could introduce innovation or entrepreneurialism into their operating models.
- **Local partners continue to work on the project or broader issue**: Following completion of their engagement with innovation processes, local partners use the new skills and capacities they have gained to continue developing and scaling the project, if it is successful, or, if the tested innovation is not successful, to continue working to develop solutions to the emergent issues and problems.

Approaches to gender equity for resilience and innovation

Humanitarian and development organizations mandate policies, and fund programmes, designed to advance protections and rights for traditionally repressed and/or marginalized groups. This is increasingly seen as an integral part of programming and is usually described using the term gender equity and social inclusion (GESI), where gender equity predominantly refers to women's rights. Although important and pressing issues of social inclusion extend to a vast array of discriminations, intolerances, and injustices against all lesser-power (or *other*) groups, in general, institutions tend to prioritise gender groups, specifically women, to drive GESI because of the scope and magnitude of women's issues globally. It has long been considered as proven in development theory that GESI programmes and their successes are extremely valuable because development dollars spent on and for women not only directly support the women themselves but also offer overwhelming benefits to the larger community, especially in relation to programmes that direct and provide access to the same capital for men. However, in many places, women and other marginalized groups are primarily perceived as end-of-line beneficiaries or recipients of special consideration or services, rather than as community members qualified to be involved in the planning or implementation of women-oriented programmes.

When prompted, local partners articulate that the lower capacity of women or other groups – a perception that is itself a result of traditional marginalization – means that efforts to fully incorporate them into the planning, management, or execution of initiatives would result in unacceptable exceptions being made (i.e., standards would be lowered), undermining programmes and thus serving no one. The socio-cultural challenges implicated in targeting expanded capacity building for girls and women, in both rural and urban contexts, are, therefore, doubly significant and complex. Essentialist gender roles are embedded within familial and matrimonial expectations, reinforced constantly by family and community social standards, and have broad impacts across educational and professional development.

Simultaneously, changes in lifestyles and livelihoods of able-bodied men, such as migration to urban centres in-country or abroad, is fundamentally driving the emergence of a household structure that is dually globalized and divided. The structural nature of oppression means it is hard to isolate an identified women's issue because there are always implications for functional programme areas such as education, healthcare, and citizenship across the humanitarian and development agenda. Thus, while the aim may be to advance women's rights, in order to do so, any intervention must understand and target the various underlying issues that contribute to the marginal status of women. Such a framing erodes the tendency to classify specific issues as 'women's issues' and makes clear that, in fact, women's issues expand and should be a consideration in every humanitarian and development programme.

To this end, and by the nature of their extensive social fixedness, nearly all GESI issues demand innovation in order to make substantive progress and deliver significant gains. It is very unlikely that a first-round intervention will succeed in laying bare the nuances and complexity of structurally ingrained social issues; instead, programmes require dedication and commitment to progress through adaptive iterations where the policy, process, or project may reflexively challenge its own assumptions and thus move incrementally and deliberately towards the desired outcome. The deliberate but incremental change that comes from working with local partners within the innovation process previously outlined lends itself to disruption of social hierarchies in non-disruptive ways, with incremental gains validated and accepted at each stage by both the women themselves and their immediate families and communities – the people who have a direct influence and control over their standing and privileges. Within GESI mandates, community acceptance is understood as a proxy for the acceptance of the higher-power party. Since this may be achieved through local partnership, such local partnerships become even more essential.

Lastly, it is important to realize that, despite being a useful overarching grouping, women cannot be presumed to be or understood as a monolithic social group. Indivisibility from their gender does not dismiss the intersection of many other demographic identifiers and background characteristics such as race and ethnicity, class, locale, and so on. At the individual, household, and community levels, strategies for resilience and innovation must be adapted to the varying demographics of group members in order to tailor projects to the most relevant and appropriate cultural context. In no way is such a framing advocating for separate but equal treatment, rather it is an acknowledgement that any programme should carefully consider and develop the capacity-building and innovation strategy based on the varying baselines of a community's members. When a programme is developed considering such a spectrum, individuals are liberated to insert themselves into it in ways which best suit their needs and desired outcomes, as well as to flexibly shift within the programme as those needs evolve. Such shifts could constitute accelerations, lateral shifts, reviews or sharing of foundational stages, and pauses which may be deep-dives or even sabbaticals. Programmes that are genuinely designed to empower the individual should be conceived in a way that acknowledges and affords individuals the autonomy and flexibility to make the decisions they deem to be in their best interest for themselves. Of course, it requires a well-attuned and reflexive programme to deliver such freedom while simultaneously insulating members from potential external coercion.

Opportunities for empowerment

Understanding these challenges, it is clear that a more deliberate framework to integrate and advocate for *and with* women (or any marginalized group) is required in order to foster women's active participation, engagement, and leadership in humanitarian aid and development – thus mainstreaming and advancing women's rights across sectors. Substantive partnerships for and with women should *proactively* consider and pursue the following measures.

Recruitment and retention of women as partners throughout the project: This includes every phase of the project from conception to execution and every project role from the leadership team to women in the community. Incorporating women is frequently challenged and met with claims that women are not present, not available, not qualified, not interested, or even some combination of all of these. Any such claim should be vigorously investigated and, when this is done, it is likely to be determined that it is either unfounded or, at the most, surmountable. Where metrics of qualification are embedded within the structural development of women relative to men, setting a threshold that woman must demonstrate or achieve in order to be considered qualified is a fundamentally discriminatory screening practice. To overcome such structural bias, a system must be developed based on possibility – that a woman is as capable as she is enabled to be. Such a process leads to self-actualization that may then release the woman from dependence – even on the group or body that initiated her transformation.

Dedication to decision-making and leadership development for all women: In order to target the institutionalized context of women's position relative to men, priority should be dedicated to initiatives and projects that incorporate women as equal partners in the development and implementation – *regardless* of the designation of the project, all projects are an opportunity. Women should no longer be viewed as the key benefactors because this is a reflexive labelling of woman as victim that is subsumed into the psyche of the women, communities, and the aid sector itself. Rather, women should be incorporated into vision planning and the complete cycle of project implementation and development. In order to overcome overwhelming essentialist bias, women must be built up as leaders and this will, in turn, elicit or embolden critical qualities. It is clear that women themselves are often equally, if not more, convinced that their role and purpose is that defined by their society. The stronger the social structure that dictates such roles, the more critical it is that any development programme works with the community to create space for and acceptance of alternatives. A woman needs her family and her community – her support structure – in the same way that any human being does. Therefore, programmes must also be in place to demonstrate the value of her development to, on behalf of, and at the scale of her family and her community. Thus, one needs partners to deconstruct and redefine the potential of women partners.

Research, identify, and work to counteract – if not eliminate – intersectional systems that subvert or undermine opportunities for women: Recognizing the structural nature of women's oppression remains essential to understanding, and thus navigating, the ecosystem of women's development, partnership, and leadership within the humanitarian and development sectors. Countless laws, policies, and standards delineating a citizen's right and access to education, healthcare, and economic opportunities have a massive impact on women – and these are only a few examples. Even the legal regime itself may be complicit. No matter whether an effect is intentional or unintentional, any purported second-order effect should be reframed as a direct effect. The seemingly indirect nature of some mandates is easily deployed to obfuscate the disadvantaged outcomes for women. Such institutions are thus essential components of the status quo that must be first revealed, then challenged. This type of ecosystem awareness also effectively maps the field of laws or policies that (independently or, even more hidden, in synthesis) may coalesce into primary obstacles or blocks that have extensive consequences for women and should be targeted as priorities. As it is such a complex and structurally integrated issue, any conceptual or operating model for women's rights that lacks such wide-field view is essentially blind.

Conclusion

The importance of partnerships, specifically with local organizations, is regularly raised as a key way to contextualize and improve processes and projects. The specific benefits of partnerships to a given process or project are many: local partnerships provide the venue through which to develop and refine an innovation, test it, scale up, and communicate its potential benefits. Throughout the innovation process, there are many roles for partners to play and there are different types of partners that could be engaged. It is important to look beyond the generic term and identify the specific roles and responsibilities of different actors and organizations.

However, beyond the specific benefits that partnerships bring, there are corollary benefits to engagement with the process that contribute to resilience, equity, and inclusion. Taking on the roles and responsibilities of partnership, developing networks, practising new analysis and decision-making skills, and increasing understanding of issues all contribute to an enhanced capacity to learn and reorganize, a core tenet of resilience for actors and institutions. The increased resilience partnership offers to people from traditionally marginalized groups also contributes to their ability to be more active members of communities responding to change and disturbance, and thus helps overcome the traditional structures of marginalization.

Inherent in the process of innovation is an understanding that failure is part of the process. Each failure helps you understand what does not work, and better refine ideas of what might work in the future. This, however, is at odds with the traditional culture in humanitarian and development sectors, where success is measured and judged against a pre-identified set of indicators.

A key element that is needed to ensure innovation continues to move forward is communication of both successes and failures. While successes are easily communicated, failures are harder to share and, especially in development and humanitarian sectors, often quietly hidden. However, innovators can contribute to a growing body of knowledge across the sector, and help future innovators avoid previously encountered pitfalls. Recognizing that failure contributes to both this growing body of knowledge and the capacity of different partners can make it easier for people to be comfortable talking about failures.

Understanding that partnerships contribute to a greater capacity for resilience can help bridge the gap between the importance of failure in innovation and the need for demonstrable successes in development. By using partnership to build resilience, donors and international organizations can start to see potential benefits in supporting humanitarian innovation.

About the authors

Justin Henceroth is a co-Founder of FieldSight, a resident of the Nepal Innovation Lab, and an innovation advisor to UN Office for Project Services (UNOPS). He is a Luce Scholar and a Boettcher Scholar with a bachelors degree in Biology from Colorado College and a Masters in Risk and Resilience from the Harvard Graduate School of Design.

Ashley Thompson is a design researcher working in humanitarian aid and disaster assistance with a focus on gender equity and social inclusion. She is an Air Force veteran with a professional Bachelors of Architecture from Rice University and a Masters in Risk and Resilience from Harvard Graduate School of Design.

CHAPTER 13

Influencing innovation adoption using the matrix of influence

Duncan McNicholl

This chapter begins with the provocative contention that good ideas are often challenged and fail to engage others. Thus, innovating becomes a dual challenge of perseverance and framing. A matrix which provides a practical framework for understanding perceived importance and control for use in prioritizing decisions around innovation is presented. The chapter ends by considering different stakeholders, weighing factors that affect the perceived importance of, and control over, a problem in an innovation process.

Keywords: innovation process, stakeholders, collaboration, influencing

No one cares about your good ideas

From the process of developing your innovation, you probably have a good view of what is not working and what should be done differently. You might be right. To make a bigger difference, you probably need to convince others to adopt your ideas. The bad news is that others might not care what you think. Even if you have a well-founded criticism or a potentially useful idea, many will not listen.

Being rejected hurts. Rejection can come in various forms including flat-out refusal or simply an unwillingness to follow up. It could be that you developed an idea years ago and still cannot figure out why so few have picked it up. It can be discouraging. The challenge is how to handle the frustration when things do not work: how to pick up the pieces, learn from the experience, and to find a way to persevere.

Innovating therefore becomes a dual challenge of perseverance and framing. Organizations face many issues such as budgetary constraints, institutional inertia, and other barriers – perceived or real – that keep them running as usual instead of adopting new innovations. This is a frustrating reality. Successful innovators must therefore be able to frame the value of their ideas in ways that appeal to the broader interests of other stakeholders.

Influencing others to adopt an idea means considering its value for them. Simply having an innovative solution might not sufficiently motivate others to adopt it. If that is the case, an idea might need to appeal to more values in order to encourage widespread uptake.

http://dx.doi.org/10.3362/9781780449531.013

The matrix of influence

Influencing other organizations to change is often an important part of successful innovation, and stakeholders may not care about a specific problem to the extent that you do. This chapter offers a framework to help pitch your ideas to others. The framework can help you to find alignment between what you want others to do, what they want to do, and what they can do.

Stakeholder-mapping tools examine stakeholder influence and power to identify key stakeholders, potential advocates, potential saboteurs, and potential time-wasters. The influence matrix presented in this chapter builds on stakeholder-mapping techniques by examining how a single stakeholder perceives an issue that you are trying to convince them to address. It is designed to help you influence people to adopt your innovation.

The framework (Figure 13.1) considers two aspects of the guiding rationale of the stakeholder you are trying to influence. The first aspect is their perception of the importance of the issue that your innovation seeks to address. The second is the level of control they have over implementing your proposed solution. This creates four quadrants describing their potential willingness to adopt your idea. Each quadrant of Figure 13.1 contains a description of how the stakeholder might react to your innovation.

Stakeholders do not care about problems that are not relevant to them. If your innovation addresses a problem that the other perceives as unimportant, they will be unlikely to adopt it. These are, perhaps, stakeholders you not should focus your efforts on. This is especially true if they also have little ability to implement your idea. Issues that fall into the low-importance and low-control quadrant are probably things they will not be motivated to address. The exception is if they have the opportunity to solve an unimportant problem with relative ease. This is the low-importance and high-control quadrant. If your innovation is seen as effective and easy to implement, a stakeholder may consider adopting it.

Issues that are perceived as important are likely to get more attention. What makes issues exciting instead of frustrating is the degree of control the stakeholder perceives they have over the issue. If they believe they cannot adopt your innovation for whatever reason, real or perceived, they might feel helpless. They might wish the problem could be solved, but feel powerless to work on it.

Winning ideas are likely to be ones that address important issues with approaches the stakeholder thinks they can implement. Being in this high-degree-of-importance and high-degree-of-control quadrant could inspire a commitment to action. This is the territory of shared value. Instead of pressuring others to adopt an idea, such stakeholders might be willing and able to take it directly on board themselves.

Depending on the relationship, this framework can even be applied collaboratively in open conversation with the target organization. A team I worked with once sat down with a major lending institution to map where

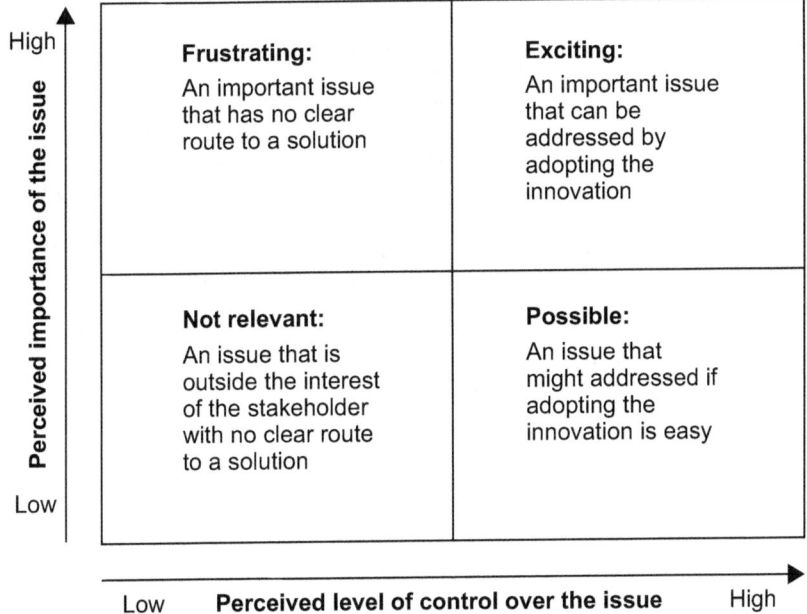

Figure 13.1 Perceived importance and control in prioritizing

our numerous recommendations fitted with respect to the importance of the issues and the institution's ability to adopt the recommendations. The end result highlighted which recommendations addressed the biggest issues and which of these were also within their power to implement.

Stakeholders

In going through this process, it is important to consider the types of stakeholders you might need to influence, and factors that affect both their control over the problem and their perceptions of its importance. Different stakeholders have different values and costs they are willing to tolerate. Potential factors affecting perceptions of importance and level of control over a problem are presented in Table 13.1, which illustrates how these values can differ for different stakeholder groups. It is not a definitive list. The more accurately you can understand those you aim to influence, the more likely you are to succeed.

A key challenge is that both the importance of an issue and the ability to implement a solution are perceptions of those you are trying to influence. You might have different perceptions of the importance of a problem, possibly because you have different values or organizational priorities. You might also have different perceptions of the ease of implementation. Large bureaucracies might struggle to implement seemingly straightforward ideas. Understanding

Table 13.1 Stakeholder groups: Problem importance and level of control

Stakeholder group	Possible factors affecting perceived problem importance	Possible factors affecting perceived level of control
NGOs	Mission; ability to demonstrate impact; likelihood of success; value for money	Time and resource constraints; project rigidity; organizational structure; organizational competencies
Government – civil servants	Mandate; accountability structures; incentive structures	Time and resource constraints; institutional structure; capacity; constraints within hierarchy
Government – elected and appointed officials	Visibility of the problem; ability to attribute solutions for political gain	Duration of political terms; trade-offs between different issues; political clout
Donors	Mission; understanding of local contexts; value for money	Bureaucracy; head-office priorities; rigidity of project design
Private sector	Costs and revenues; competitive benefit; opportunity cost	Core competencies; assets and resources; stability of business model
Individuals/affected people	Relationship to overall wellbeing; opportunity cost; personal values	Size of the problem; understanding of the solution; available resources

issues from their perspective is an important part of framing your innovation attractively, and your pitch can influence perceptions of what is important and what is possible.

The framework will not eliminate all challenges of pitching ideas to others. Hopefully, however, it can help you to consider how appealing your ideas are, and how to strengthen your position so that more of your good ideas can spread.

About the author

Duncan McNicholl is a PhD researcher at Cambridge University where he studies stakeholder networks in service delivery systems in Africa, Asia, and South America. He previously worked with Engineers Without Borders, Canada in Malawi, where he was programme manager of the Water and Sanitation Programme.

PART IV
Lessons from the frontline

With an emphasis on the practical and what can be learned from the experience of others, this part presents case studies, applied models, and illustrative examples. Because this book focuses on hardware solutions, the various topics presented include cutting-edge manufacturing, labs, and other recent advances. Specifically, this part focuses on:

- advanced manufacturing
- humanitarian innovation labs
- collaboration and the importance of process
- design identification
- organizational approaches to innovation in the field

CHAPTER 14
Additive manufacturing and humanitarian aid

Brenna Sniderman, Parker Baum and Vikram Rajan

As the need for post-crisis humanitarian aid increases, 3D printing can have a profound impact on aid efforts. While it can start by addressing the single largest challenge in relief work – getting the aid on-site – 3D printing also has the potential to drive a new, sustainable approach to aid. The technology can be used in the field to augment humanitarian efforts in several ways, along a continuum of complexity depending upon the need on the ground: redefining the supply chain, producing customized goods that address situation-specific needs, creating a blueprint for future on-site 3D printing efforts, and potentially promoting an engine for economic development.

Keywords: 3D printing, additive manufacturing, supply chain, customization, rapid prototyping

Crises of significant magnitude require massive amounts of humanitarian aid. Humanitarian aid totalled $24.5 billion globally in 2014, up from $20.5 billion in 2013 – an increase of 19 per cent year-on-year (Swithern et al., 2015). In 2016, it was estimated that 89.3 million people would receive aid that year alone – but, sadly, that many more in need would not (James and Gilman, 2016). In the days immediately after a disaster, humanitarian groups rush in to help those affected, but the magnitude of the devastation can limit aid workers' ability to reach those who are most in need.

The demand for aid shows no signs of slowing. Indeed, in 2015, 346 natural disasters occurred, impacting 98.6 million people, (EM-DAT, 2016) and António Guterres (UN Secretary General and former UN High Commissioner for Refugees) noted that, with 'the exponential increase in needs we have seen just in the last three years, the humanitarian financing system is nearly bankrupt' (James and Gilman, 2015). Delivering aid is an expensive endeavour. Aid is delivered via 'channels of delivery': mobilized groups that set up supply chains and deliver assistance, with associated costs in both time and money (Swithern et al., 2015).

While the use of advanced technologies in the service of humanitarian aid is relatively nascent, they are still proving valuable (Deloitte and the World Humanitarian Summit, 2015). Digital and smartcard-based technologies have revolutionized the delivery of financial aid for Syrian refugees

(Overseas Development Institute, 2015), while drones can speed delivery of goods to remote areas (Shingles et al., 2016). Advanced technologies can not only drive more effective aid efforts but may also have a ripple effect, transforming local economies and organizations alike, and addressing many of the challenges current aid efforts face (Shingles et al., 2016).

Less explored in the technology space – but no less significant – are the impacts that additive manufacturing (AM) can have on humanitarian endeavours. The ways in which AM technologies – most specifically, 3D printing – can provide solutions to humanitarian challenges are many, and they are profound (Deloitte and the World Humanitarian Summit, 2015). Indeed, the attributes that make 3D printing so attractive to manufacturers also make it well suited to improving the lives of the world's most vulnerable populations: the ability to print physical objects anytime, anywhere, has tremendous potential impacts on the speed of aid; and its lack of reliance on traditional manufacturing constraints enables design optimization for the situation at hand. In addition, the set of technologies that comprise AM – including 3D printing – can break performance trade-offs, freeing aid providers from challenges related to economies of scale or scope (Cotteleer and Joyce, 2014). Three-dimensional printing is also versatile enough that it can be used in tandem with traditional approaches to aid where required.

This chapter explores how organizations are using 3D printing in the field to augment their humanitarian efforts: redefining the supply chain, producing customized goods that address situation-specific needs, creating a blueprint for future 3D printing-related on-site efforts, and potentially promoting an engine for economic development that even goes beyond disaster relief to ongoing sustainable solutions. We will also consider some significant takeaways from these efforts that can enable organizations to develop capabilities offering a competitive advantage more broadly.

The additive manufacturing framework

The origins of AM go back nearly three decades. Its importance is derived from its ability to break existing performance trade-offs in two fundamental ways. First, AM reduces the capital required to achieve economies of scale. Capital versus scale is an important consideration when minimum efficient scale can shape supply chains. AM has the potential to reduce the capital required to reach minimum efficient scale for production, thus lowering the manufacturing barriers to entry for a given location.

Second, it increases flexibility and reduces the capital required to achieve scope. Capital versus scope is an important consideration where economies of scope influence how and what products can be made. The flexibility of AM facilitates an increase in the variety of products a unit of capital can produce, reducing the costs associated with production changeovers and customization and, thus, the overall amount of required capital.

Changing the capital versus scale relationship has the potential to impact how supply chains are configured, and changing the capital versus scope relationship

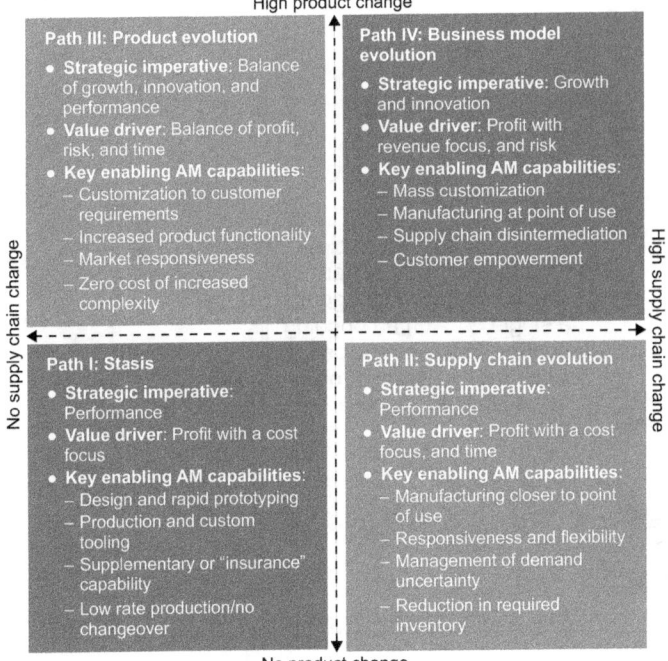

Figure 14.1 Additive manufacturing paths and value framework
Source: Mark Cotteleer and Jim Joyce, "3D opportunity: Additive manufacturing paths to performance, innovation, and growth," *Deloitte Review*, January 17, 2014

has the potential to impact product designs. These impacts present organizations with choices on how to deploy AM across their businesses. Organizations pursuing AM capabilities choose between divergent paths (Figure 14.1):

Path I: Organizations do not seek radical alterations in either supply chains or products, but they may explore AM technologies to improve value delivery for current products within existing supply chains.

Path II: Organizations take advantage of scale economies offered by AM as a potential enabler of supply-chain transformation for the products they offer.

Path III: Organizations take advantage of the scope economies offered by AM technologies to achieve new levels of performance or innovation in the products they offer.

Path IV: Organizations alter both supply chains and products in pursuit of new business models.

3D printing's progression in humanitarian relief: a potential transformation

Three-dimensional printing can impact the way organizations provide aid by addressing the single largest challenge in humanitarian relief: getting the aid on-site. Viewed through the lens of the AM framework, use of 3D printing in

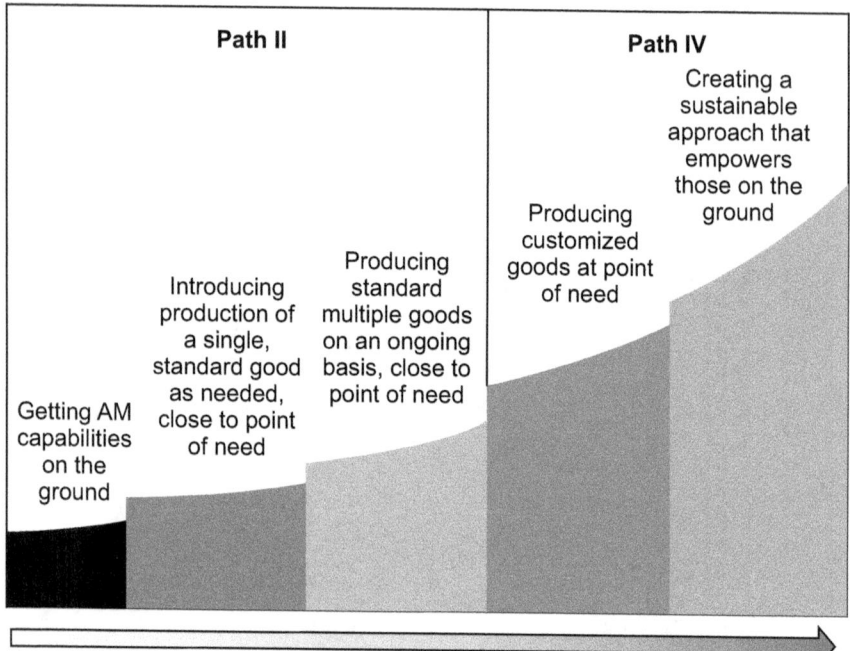

Figure 14.2 Aid across the additive manufacturing framework

humanitarian aid progresses along a continuum (see Figure 14.2), depending on the need on the ground. This progression begins with initial applications that are crucial to subsequent use of the technology: establishing or redefining a supply chain through the downstream relocation of the point of manufacturing (path II). It evolves into a more complex approach to providing aid: producing customized parts and products at or close to the point of need (path IV), and using lessons from aid experiences to inform future aid endeavours and promote sustainable approaches that can empower locals. While there are applications for 3D printing along path I, in rapid prototyping of aid supplies, the technology's most dramatic potential lies in its ability to deliver economies of scope at point of use; therefore, we focus our discussion along paths II and IV.

Progression along additive manufacturing framework

Once a functioning 3D printer is in place, it can be used to produce small-batch goods that address a specific requirement at, or close to, the point of need. The next stage of path II can be to use 3D printing machines as an ongoing production point: creating standardized goods – such as medical tools – on an as-needed basis, obviating the need to wait for shipments. This longer-term use can exploit some of the manufacturing capabilities of 3D printing machines, such as the ability to produce multiple products without machine changeover or retooling time (Cotteleer et al., 2014). Progressing beyond path II to path IV can produce goods tailored to specific local needs at or near the point of use. Finally, it can lead to a sustainable, ongoing and maintainable system; in essence, 3D printing technology can empower those on the ground and drive a new, sustainable approach to aid.

As with commercial manufacturing, AM can coexist with conventional methods, augmenting and replacing them in areas in which it is uniquely suited to do so. Organizations can deploy 3D printing strategically for situation-specific needs while using traditional aid approaches such as food-drops and monetary relief to fulfil more universal relief needs.

Getting additive manufacturing capabilities to the ground

Humanitarian aid, at its core, is centred on protecting and ensuring the wellbeing of disaster-affected populations. In many cases, this translates into delivering goods and services necessary to daily life, often as quickly and completely as possible. Thus, the successful delivery of aid begins with the establishment of a functional supply chain. Establishing such a supply chain is costly: 60–80 per cent of humanitarian aid is spent on logistics and shipping, adding up to $15 billion annually to aid costs (Tatham and Pettit, 2010). The process is complicated, as locations may be remote; typical shipping routes may be impassable or non-existent due to aftershocks, flooding, or conflict; and infrastructure may be limited. Due to these challenges, the last-mile problem – that is, the supply-chain challenge of getting goods from a port, station, or shipping hub to the final point of need – can prove challenging.

Organizations using a traditional aid model may struggle to deliver supplies and often cannot accommodate unexpected, yet sometimes inevitable, surges in demand without a significant lag in response time, spelling potential failure (Zeimpekis et al., 2013). Even in situations where the supply of aid has been accurately matched to demand, challenging environments mean that equipment can break down at any time, leading to a need for spare parts on demand – or parts may arrive broken due to unfavourable shipping conditions (Tatham et al., 2014).

Three-dimensional printing can provide significant benefits here. Creating a deployable 3D printing solution can move the point of production further down the supply chain, addressing many of the challenges organizations face as they seek to transport humanitarian aid – particularly cost and lag time (Marchese et al., 2015). In other words, AM can enable aid organizations to address the last-mile challenge by creating some goods on-site.

Thus, the first step in using 3D printing to address humanitarian needs is the most straightforward: getting the printer and printing materials to, or close to, the point of need. Using 3D printing to bring the point of production further down the supply chain in this way can simplify many of the logistical and distribution challenges that humanitarian aid providers face. Production equipment would only need to be transported once, and raw materials such as printing filament can be used to produce a variety of products on the ground.

This translates to fewer goods to track during the logistics process – cutting down on costs – and potentially the ability to ship other, previously deprioritized, goods to the site due to newly available space on shipping pallets. Further, raw materials in the form of powders and filaments are denser and therefore can be shipped more efficiently, and they can often be transported with less protective packaging, since there are no parts to break.

A recent study demonstrated two printers outfitted with solar panels, capable of printing in any location – even one lacking access to an electrical grid (King et al., 2014). One of the printers, a mobile machine meant for use in schools or local makerspaces, uses RepRap technology, allowing it to print continuously while also providing power to several computers for design purposes. The second printer can be 'completely packed into a standard suitcase, allow[ing] for specialist travel from community to community to provide the ability to custom manufacture … as needed, anywhere' (King et al., 2014: 25).

Both of these approaches demonstrate ways to potentially sidestep supply-chain challenges. They not only move production directly on-site at the point of need, but also adapt to local infrastructure challenges, making their functions more self-sufficient. They can also teach organizations how to use new local materials and understand how differing production technologies and techniques may be better suited to certain environments.

Introducing production of a single, standard good as needed, close to point of need

AM-enabled supply chains in humanitarian zones can take a variety of forms, including hub-and-spoke and more distributed models, as described below. Organizations should consider the needs on the ground as they prioritize when, where, and how to use 3D printing to provide aid. Often, the first application on the ground can be addressing an unexpected, urgent need – one in which waiting for aid to arrive via traditional means can lead to greater casualties or risk.

Field Ready's work in Nepal is an example at the far left of the continuum (Figure 14.2), where the organization was able to take 3D printing capability directly to the source of need, assess the need, and address it. During the 2015 earthquake, aftershocks destroyed water pipes, hindering the community's access to potable water. Water-pipe fittings provided via traditional relief efforts arrived missing parts, leading to leaks. Using the battery of an automobile as a power source, Field Ready was able to print a replacement part and fit it within two hours, restoring functionality and avoiding a wait of several weeks for new parts (Scott, 2015).

Producing standard multiple goods on an ongoing basis, close to point of need

Beyond producing single parts, established 3D printers already at the point of need can produce a range of goods and services – profoundly impacting the way in which aid is distributed. Put simply, it is extremely difficult for organizations to get the *right* aid to those in need. Crises come without warning, leaving little ability to plan not only for on-the-ground conditions but also for location-specific needs.

Disconnects make planning a challenge. In the view of humanitarian aid professionals, 'it is almost inevitable that, to a greater or lesser extent, there will be a mismatch between the demand and supply situation' (Tatham et al., 2014: 4). This often translates to a one-size-fits-all approach to aid, in which NGOs stockpile inventories of goods they think will be most broadly useful. The International Federation of Red Cross and Red Crescent Societies (IFRC), for example, maintains a catalogue of about 10,000 items – mostly medical equipment – that it uses for any humanitarian condition it encounters (Tatham et al., 2014). Three-dimensional printing offers hope for a solution to this challenge.

Having a production point capable of producing a diverse range of products, however, will create new challenges for organizations such as prioritizing which of a wide range products to print, and anticipating and responding to unexpected surges in demand or the sudden need for wholly new objects that must be designed or iterated on the spot. Addressing these challenges can provide organizations with important lessons about manufacturing flexibility, leading to new insights into demand planning and inventory management, both in the field and on a commercial factory floor.

Furthermore, unforeseen events that impact and potentially disrupt production will be the norm rather than the exception in aid situations. Power may be intermittent, printers may break down, and there may be a 3D printing learning curve for those on the ground. As they resolve these situations, organizations can again use these as opportunities to learn, to create more self-sufficient production facilities, and to develop response mechanisms to production crashes.

Producing customized goods at the point of need

Beyond supply-chain considerations, 3D printing has the potential to alter what is actually produced to support humanitarian and developmental aid efforts, in particular at the point of consumption. In this way, organizations can exploit 3D printing's strengths to address specific local needs. This approach can have the added benefit of teaching an organization how to manage large-scale local development – maintaining a network of production points, with each producing goods uniquely suited to its immediate population.

A case study from the University of Auckland examined the ways in which 3D printing can be used to address water and sanitation issues post-natural disaster, as clean drinking water and proper disposal of wastewater pose significant health concerns following a crisis. Reviewing Oxfam's field catalogue of aid supplies, researchers demonstrated how they could print an elbow joint on a desktop fused deposition modelling (FDM) printer in 45 minutes with no post-finishing required. The project also explored other options using different materials and printer types.

They further noted the ability to use 3D printing to make ad-hoc customizations to original designs as needed – changing a 90-degree bend to 120 degrees in order to address vagaries in local water pipes, for example. Researchers also noted the technology's potential to alter the internal geometries of the design to add water filtration capabilities to 3D printed fittings. The researchers estimated that a customized in-field print would take two to three hours – a notable improvement over traditional shipping methods (Tatham et al., 2014).

The Auckland study also demonstrated how 3D printing can join disparate parts from two different equipment suppliers. The lack of standardization and communication across aid suppliers can present a major challenge in the field: when replacement parts do arrive, they may not fit the system for which they were intended, making repairs difficult or impossible. Mechanical couplings are one approach that aid organizations currently use to solve this problem in the context of remote water supply systems (World Health Organisation, 1989). Three-dimensional printing can make the process faster not only by sidestepping shipping lag, but also by potentially offering an open-source design file that users on the ground can customize as needed – enabling greater communication between organizations.

Creating a sustainable approach that empowers those on the ground

After addressing supply-chain and product customization, organizations using 3D printing for social impact and aid can use lessons learned from each field experience to transform aid beyond the initial post-disaster push, making it more sustainable over the longer term. They can do so by teaching technical 3D printing skills to locals, and by supplying open-source software and part designs to enable them to continue to produce parts and products on-demand once organizations have left. This type of education and training can develop a local, sustainable talent pool that can design and produce goods on-site for new markets – which, in turn, encourages economic development, potentially helping to break the cycle of unemployment and poverty (Vazquez et al., 2014).

This strategy can transform aid by providing not just a customizable set of disaster-preparedness skills to transform responses to future crises, but also training in 3D printing-related skills to locals to promote economic sustainability (Perretty, 2015). Organizations can even learn from such efforts in the developing world and apply the capabilities learned to build sustainable skills in developed regions (in the reverse or trickle-up innovation described by Altay in Chapter 2 of this book). In the United States, open-source software and AM-related initiatives aimed at building technological skills have helped individuals develop a sense of entrepreneurialism, build new engineering skills, and pave the way for new jobs (Viswanathan, 2014). The University of Illinois, for example, has introduced an extension programme course focused on AM that is aimed at addressing poverty through providing underprivileged youth with marketable skills. The four-phase programme is based on similar programmes in Tanzania and India (Schiller, 2014).

Beyond the disaster: ongoing economic and social transformation through sustainable aid

Maimonides' aphorism 'buy a man a fish, and you feed him for a day. Teach a man to fish, and you feed him for a lifetime' speaks to the importance of passing on skills. For its part, post-disaster humanitarian aid focused on emergency food-drops, medical supplies, and temporary shelters is necessary in the short term, but humanitarian crises continue to persist long after the initial news coverage. And, indeed, these forms of aid are not meant to stimulate growth, but rather to ensure survival (Radelet et al., 2014).

In fact, the line between crisis-driven humanitarian aid and developmental aid are often blurred; immediate efforts to aid survival and prop up infrastructure inevitably give way to rebuilding and developing countries that have lost what precious little infrastructure they had and may struggle to regain it. Witness Haiti, which experienced a devastating earthquake in 2010 and still experiences extreme challenges establishing effective supply chains for medical supplies nearly six years later. Likewise, immediate war-related disaster relief often involves the creation of refugee camps, where refugees may live for years, necessitating developmental aid such as education and healthcare (James and Gilman, 2015).

Stable, complex production to solve ongoing, complex problems

AM changes the way organizations can respond to each of these situations, even enabling a source of stable production for complex objects (Cotteleer et al., 2014). For example, the US Army Rapid Equipping Force deployed fabrication labs ('fab labs'), to Afghanistan in 2013. The Expeditionary Lab Mobile is a 20-foot container manned by two engineers. Its equipment includes 3D printers; computer numeric control (CNC) machines; laser, plasma, and water cutters; and welding tools, as well as generators and satellite communications for power and connectivity (Kuneinen, 2013). The fab lab enables faster solutions to problems and repairs for broken equipment through on-site prototyping and rapid testing. These labs allow engineers to combine AM with other types of production, increasing fabrication options and offering a potentially viable model for humanitarian efforts.

Tapping into locally-driven innovation

By giving locals access to a new manufacturing technology, they have the opportunity to address ongoing needs with new ideas, and create solutions to problems outsiders may not see. This can enable organizations to meet hyperlocal, heretofore-unrecognized demands. This sort of outcome would not be unprecedented; rapid smartphone adoption in Africa made it the world's second-most mobile-connected region – and also enabled the financial services industry to use mobile banking to tap into the continent's millions of unbanked. As the sector grew, so did local mobile banking organizations such as Paga in Nigeria and M-PESA in Kenya (both cash transfer companies that rely on users' cell phones), a development that in turn led to growth in the retail sector, enabling retailers to establish regional fulfilment centres in areas where they might never have sold goods before at that scale (Jidenma, 2014).

In one example, researchers in Kenya explored the potential to 3D print recyclable, individually customized shoes from reused plastic to help address the local problem of foot parasites called jiggers. Developed in a fab lab at the University of Nairobi, this innovation can potentially help to stem cases of severe inflammation, auto-amputations, and tetanus (Ibrahim et al., 2015 Mathai, 2012).

Enabling education and economic development
In India, two million of the country's poorest people sift through landfills for plastic refuse they can sell for scrap, netting about $1 per day. Enterprises such as Protoprint have set up filament labs adjacent to landfill sites in several regions to purchase the plastic and turn it into ethical filament for 3D printers (Pai, 2014). These organizations can pay waste-pickers as much as 15 times their previous wage, adhering to fair-trade standards (Feeley et al., 2014). In some cases, these labs also teach the waste-pickers new skills and technologies, encouraging entrepreneurialism. The ethical filament is, in turn, provided to academic institutions at a low cost, so they can develop affordable 3D printing facilities and add the technology to academic programmes, enabling students and professionals to learn about AM (Zareva, 2014). Small 3D printing shops and facilities now dot India, including those run by 3DPD and Divide by Zero, among others.

Making mass customization of prosthetics, medicine, and glasses more affordable
Three-dimensional printing is being used to customize prosthetics for individuals in the developing world (Phan, 2015). By 3D printing parts, prosthetics can be created to fit personal measurements, making them more functional for their users. Replacement parts can also be 3D printed, making them easier to repair then their conventional counterparts (Dally et al., 2015). One group from the University of Victoria has begun training local populations in the use of 3D printing to build and maintain prostheses, making the process sustainable (in what is known as the Victoria Hand Project). PCEA Kikuyu orthopaedic hospital in Africa worked with 3D LifePrints to use open-source software to produce customized prosthetic limbs. Using a design available via e-NABLE, 3D LifePrints produced prosthetic hands and legs that accommodated individuals' unique measurements. The prostheses have been shown to perform better than those from the Red Cross, and have a total cost of less than $50 (Sher, 2015).

With the first 3D printed drug approved for use in the US, experts have speculated that the technology could have applications for disaster relief – printing dosages of medicine, or vaccination beads (Molitch-Hou, 2013) to serve as visual medical charts, on-site as needed (Ibrahim et al., 2015). As the technology – and access to it – evolves and is further tested in real-life scenarios, it may have the potential to improve ongoing healthcare in the developing world, as well as the administration and dissemination of medications during times of disaster.

Three-dimensional printing also has the potential to make strides in treating visual impairment, an issue that afflicts over 282 million individuals who live in low-income areas (Phan, 2015). A recent case study showed how it could be used to make adjustable, customized eyeglass frames for individuals in impoverished or isolated regions of the developing world, leveraging distributed production methods to provide low-cost treatment (Gwamuri et al., 2014).

Preparing for technology-driven humanitarian aid

As organizations consider adding 3D printing to their aid capabilities, they will need to ensure they are well positioned to scale technology to their needs. Depending on the organization's priorities and objectives along the AM-driven aid continuum (shown in Figure 14.2), a number of considerations should be taken into account. These might also be helpful when considering other technologies and innovations which are only now at the conceptual stage.

Consider where and how 3D printing fits into the wider aid mission. Not all aid situations will need the same level of AM. By assessing the level of AM actually needed in any given situation, organizations can ensure that they match capabilities and investments in resources, technology, and talent to the specific needs on the ground. Likewise, organizations should recognize that needs are different in each and every aid situation – and can even change during a single mission. Even within a single crisis event, organizations may find that multiple approaches along the continuum may be needed, while in others, one will suffice. Thus, organizations should regularly assess and adjust their capabilities to meet current realities.

Train a sustainable workforce based on the level of need. Simply put, organizations cannot implement 3D printing in humanitarian aid without trained workers who can use the technology on the ground – but the skillset required depends on how it will be used. For initial uses, such as printing replacement parts, workers may get by with a relatively basic skillset. As applications progress further along the aid continuum, individuals are likely to need deeper skills, such as manipulating designs to create customized parts, and designing new parts and goods (Vazquez et al., 2016). In order to create a sustainable approach that empowers locals, organizations should consider developing a team that is not only capable of implementing the technologies, but also of training locals to use it long term.

Address and ensure quality at the appropriate levels. Quality assurance remains a crucial aspect of 3D printing; parts need to work, and they need to work well enough (Wing et al., 2015). Organizations should consider what level of quality will be appropriate for each part, based on its intended use, in contexts starting with production of a single, standard good as needed, all the way to a long-term, sustainable approach to 3D printing and aid (Wing et al., 2015). In some cases, basic functionality in the short term may be enough for a 3D printer-produced object; for others, long-term use may be the goal.

Consider the technology requirements needed to operationalize AM aid delivery. As organizations spool up their use of 3D printing in the field, they can consider the technologies they will need to meet their objectives. At their most fundamental, these requirements can include a printer, power source, materials, and design files. As use evolves along the continuum, technology needs might grow to include a design repository, additional material types and printers, complementary technologies including CNC machines and other manufacturing tools, and a data management system to enable organizations to continue improving upon and adjusting designs for future use – in short, a fully functioning digital thread (Cotteleer et al., 2016).

Three-dimensional printing technologies can have a profound impact on humanitarian challenges. The uses can stretch far beyond simply serving immediate relief needs. The ripple effects of a customized, immediate response to aid can inform future humanitarian response, enable more efficient and faster response, evolve the supply chain; and create ongoing benefits, building skills that extend well beyond the immediacy of disaster toward sustainable growth and development.

References

Cotteleer, M. and Joyce, J. (2014) '3D Opportunity: Additive manufacturing paths to performance, innovation, and growth', *Deloitte Review*, 14.

Cotteleer, M., Holdowsky, J. and Mahto, M. (2014) 'The 3D Opportunity Primer: The basics of additive manufacturing', *Deloitte University Press*, 15.

Cotteleer, M., Trouton, S. and Dobner, E. (2016) '3D Opportunity and the Digital Thread: additive manufacturing ties it all together'. *Deloitte University Press*.

Dally, C., Johnson, D., Canon, M., Ritter, S. & Mehta, K. (2015) 'Characteristics of a 3D Printed Prosthetic Hand for Use in Developing Countries', *IEEE 2015 Global Humanitarian Technology Conference*, pp. 66–70 <http://ieeexplore.ieee.org/stamp/stamp.jsp?tp=&arnumber=7343956> [accessed 28 September 2017].

Deloitte and the World Humanitarian Summit (2015) *The Humanitarian R&D Imperative: How Other Sectors Overcame Impediments to Innovation* <http://www2.deloitte.com/content/dam/Deloitte/global/Documents/About-Deloitte/dttl_cr_humanitarian_r&d_imperative.pdf> [accessed 28 September 2017].

EM-DAT (2016) *2015 Disasters in Numbers*, Centre for Research on the Epidemiology of Diseases and IRSS, Université Catholique de Louvain <http://reliefweb.int/sites/reliefweb.int/files/resources/47791_infograph-2015disastertrendsfinal.pdf> [accessed 28 September 2017].

Feeley, S.R., Wijnen, B. and Pearce, J. M. (2014) 'Evaluation of Potential Fair Trade Standards for an Ethical 3D Printing Filament', *Journal of Sustainable Development*, 7(5), pp. 1–12.

Gwamuri, J., Wittbrodt, B. T., Anzalone, N.C. and Pearce, J. M. (2014) 'Reversing the Trend of Large Scale and Centralization in Manufacturing: The Case of Distributed Manufacturing of Customizable 3D Printable Self-Adjustable Glasses', *Challenges in Sustainability*, 2(1), pp. 30–40.

Ibrahim, A.M.S., Jose, R.R., Rabie, A.N., Gerstle, T.L., Lee, B.T. & Lin, S.J. (2015) 'Three-Dimensional Printing in Developing Countries', *Plastic and Reconstructive Surgery Global Open*, 3(7), <http://doi.org/10.1097/GOX.0000000000000298> [accessed 28 September 2017].

James, E. and Gilman, D. (2015) *Shrinking the Supply Chain: Hyperlocal Manufacturing and 3D printing in Humanitarian Response*, United Nations Office of Coordination of Humanitarian Affairs <https://docs.unocha.org/sites/dms/Documents/OCHA_OP14_3D%20printing_online.pdf> [accessed 28 September 2017].

Jidenma, N. (2014) 'How Africa's Mobile Revolution is Disrupting the Continent,' *CNN.com*, <http://www.cnn.com/2014/01/24/business/davos-africa-mobile-explosion/> [accessed 28 September 2017].

King, D., Babasola, A., Rozario, J. & Pearce, J. M. (2014) 'Mobile Open-Source Solar-Powered 3-D Printers for Distributed Manufacturing in Off-Grid Communities', *Challenges in Sustainability*, 2(1), pp. 18–27.

Kuneinen, E. (2013) 'U.S. Army Deploying Mobile FabLabs', *3D Printing Industry*, <http://3dprintingindustry.com/2013/03/06/u-s-army-deploying-mobile-fablabs/>.

Marchese, K., Crane, J. and Haley, C. (2015) '3D Opportunity for the Supply Chain: Additive Manufacturing Delivers', *Deloitte University Press*.

Mathai, J. (2012) 'Imaginarium: Tapping into 3D Printing', *SpaceBlogs*, <http://textually.org/3DPrinting/2012/12/031454.html>.

Molitch-Hou, M. (2013) '3D Printers for Peace Contest - the Results Are In', *3D Printing Industry*, <http://3dprintingindustry.com/2013/09/06/3d-printers-for-peace-contest-the-results-are-in/> [accessed 28 September 2017].

Overseas Development Institute and Centre for Global Development (2015) *Doing Cash Differently: How Cash Transfers Can Transform Humanitarian Aid*, Report of the High Level Panel on Humanitarian Cash Transfers <http://www.odi.org/sites/odi.org.uk/files/odi-assets/publications-opinion-files/9828.pdf> [accessed 28 September 2017].

Pai, S. (2014) 'Protoprint: Converting Waste Plastic into 3D Printer Filament', *Massachusetts Institute of Technology* <https://d-lab.mit.edu/scale-ups/protoprint> [accessed 28 September 2017].

Perretty, D. (2015) '3D Printing Medical Tools in Haiti and Beyond', *Core77* <http://www.core77.com/posts/28179/3d-printing-medical-tools-in-haiti-and-beyond-28179> [accessed 28 September 2017].

Phan, S. (2015) '3D Printers: Significance in Alleviating Poverty', *Borgen Magazine*, <http://www.borgenmagazine.com/3d-printers-significance-alleviating-poverty/> [accessed 28 September 2017].

Radelet, S., Clemens, M. and Bhavnani, R. (2014) *Aid and Growth: The Current Debate and Some New Evidence*, Center for Global Development, Pennsylvania State University, <http://citeseerx.ist.psu.edu/viewdoc/download?doi=10.1.1.422.8164&rep=rep1&type=pdf> [accessed 28 September 2017].

Schiller, B. (2014) 'Can 3-D Printing Help Teach The Business Skills To Lift People Out Of Poverty?', *Co.Exist* <http://www.fastcoexist.com/3039477/can-3d-printing-help-teach-the-business-skills-to-lift-people-out-of-poverty> [accessed 28 September 2017].

Scott, C. (2015) 'A Simple, 3D Printed Pipe Fitting Has Huge Implications for Disaster Relief', *3DPrint.com*, <http://3dprint.com/113155/field-ready-nepal-earthquake/> [accessed 28 September 2017].

Sher, D. (2015) '3D LifePrints Achieves Many Firsts in Africa with 3D Printed Prosthetics', *3D Printing Industry*, <http://3dprintingindustry.com/2015/06/09/3d-lifeprints-reaches-africas-first-3d-printed-prosthetic-hands-leg-covers/>.

Shingles, M., Briggs, B. and O'Dwyer, J. (2016) 'Social Impact of Exponential Technologies: Corporate Social Responsibility 2.0', *Deloitte University Press*.

Swithern, S. (2015) *Global Humanitarian Assistance Report 2015*, Global Humanitarian Assistance, <http://devinit.org/post/gha-report-2015/#> [accessed 28 September 2017].

Tatham, P. and Pettit, S.J. (2010) 'Transforming Humanitarian Logistics: The Journey to Supply Network Management', *International Journal of Physical Distribution and Logistics Management*, 40(8/9), pp. 609–622.

Tatham, P., Loy, J. and Peretti, U. (2014) '3D Printing (3DP): A Humanitarian Logistic Game Changer?', *12th ANZAM Operations, Supply Chain and Services Management Symposium*, <http://docs.business.auckland.ac.nz/Doc/Tatham-anzamsymposium2014_submission_104-final.pdf> [accessed 28 September 2017].

Vazquez, E., Passaretti, M. and Valenzuela, P. (2016) '3D Opportunity for Workforce Development: Additive Manufacturing Minds the Talent Gap', *Deloitte University Press*.

Viswanathan, M., Rindfleisch, A. and Sachdev, V. (2014) 'Teaching Marketplace Literacy with the Help of 3D Printing', *Stanford Social Innovation Review* <http://ssir.org/articles/entry/teaching_marketplace_literacy_with_the_help_of_3d_printing> [accessed 28 September 2017].

Wing, I., Gorham, R. and Sniderman, B. (2015) '3D Opportunity for Quality Assurance: Additive Manufacturing Clears the Bar', *Deloitte University Press*.

World Health Organisation (1989) *Maintenance and Operation of Rural Water Supply and Sanitation Systems*, Water, Engineering and Development Centre, World Health Organisation Eastern Mediterranean Regional Office Centre for Environmental Health Activities <http://www.ircwash.org/sites/default/files/202.6-89MA-12188.pdf> [accessed 28 September 2017].

Zareva, T. (2014) 'Wealth From Waste: How 'The First Ethical' 3D Printer Filament Empowers The Lowest Class In India', *Big Think* <http://bigthink.com/design-for-good/wealth-from-waste-how-the-first-ethical-3d-printer-filament-empowers-the-lowest-class-in-india> [accessed 28 September 2017].

Zeimpekis, V., Ichoua, S. and Minis, I. (eds.) (2013) *Humanitarian and Relief Logistics: Research Issues, Case Studies and Future Trends*, Springer-Verlag, New York, NY.

About the authors

Brenna Sniderman is a researcher and subject-matter specialist at Deloitte Consulting LLP who focuses on the strategic and organizational impacts of advanced digital and physical technologies on manufacturing, production, and the supply network. She works with other thought leaders to deliver insights into the strategic, organizational, and human implications of these technological changes.

Parker Baum is a senior consultant with Deloitte's Supply-Chain Strategy practice. He focuses on advising clients across the commercial and public sector on end-to-end supply-chain strategy, disruptive technologies, and mergers and acquisitions.

Vikram Rajan supports the Technology and Strategy & Operations practices of Deloitte Consulting LLP by defining and implementing technology strategies, with a focus on manufacturing, defence, and healthcare. He has developed and presented market-defining business strategies for additive manufacturing, and pulls from his experiences as a graduate of Johns Hopkins University's Biomedical Engineering MSE programme and as a registered patent agent.

CHAPTER 15

Humanitarian innovation labs: Bridging innovators and humanitarian challenges

Kate Wharton, Adam Arabian, Dave Levin, Jamil Wyne, with William Altman and Natalie Chang

This chapter examines humanitarian innovation labs, their purpose and characteristics. It suggests that the fabrication laboratory provides a foundational model that has been replicated by others and includes good practices such as co-creation, using available infrastructure, host-community involvement, gender considerations, and tailoring to technology. It then presents a case study of Refugee Open Ware (ROW), a social enterprise that harnesses advanced technology, co-creation, and open innovation to reduce suffering, fulfil basic needs, and accelerate inclusive development in fragile and conflict-affected areas. The chapter concludes with a set of recommendations for different stakeholders including policymakers, donors, and those involved in following through the innovative process.

Keywords: humanitarian innovation, labs, 3D printing, training, Research and Development

The technologies and knowledge of the next industrial revolution can help to mitigate the costs and inefficiencies facing the global humanitarian sector. These improvements could span the entire supply chain and ecosystem of humanitarian services. First, delivery of services and logistics, which have traditionally relied heavily on manual implementation, can be expedited and costs reduced by increasing integration of information and communication technologies (Kopczak and Thomas, 2005). Second, with access to advanced technologies and educational opportunities, entrepreneurs and innovators in displaced communities can more quickly obtain resources and skills needed to deliver their own products and services, potentially to a global audience.

With growing integration of these tools and methods, these technologies can facilitate self-reliance, creative expression, and the pursuit of purpose and identity within migrant communities. This empowerment can also carry over to host communities, helping them to access skills, services, and even new business ventures that arise from a thorough and thoughtful implementation of advanced technologies.

http://dx.doi.org/10.3362/9781780449531.015

Humanitarian innovation labs: purpose and characteristics

Given the need for new models for humanitarian assistance, and the simultaneous surge of new technologies, innovation labs can be an effective mechanism for connecting challenge with opportunity. They offer a powerful means by which to bridge communities affected by humanitarian crises – both displaced and host communities – with the technologies of the next industrial revolution in a way that promotes local ownership and solutions. These facilities can take a variety of forms depending on local context and needs: makerspaces, fabrication laboratories (fab labs), micro-factories, hardware incubators, humanitarian labs, social innovation hubs, innovation centres, and even entire innovation districts, particularly in special economic zones (SEZs).

Beyond helping to address some of the immediate humanitarian needs of the community, innovation labs support longer-term economic development by building skills and capabilities in the technologies of the next industrial revolution, skills which will be increasingly in demand in both developed and developing countries.

Humanitarian innovation labs are defined by several distinguishing characteristics:

- **Shared purpose**: Targeting the world's toughest humanitarian challenges via crowd-sourcing, co-creation, and field-testing of solutions.
- **Primary-user engagement**: Affected communities (both displaced and host communities), supported by local and/or international experts.
- **Innovative technologies**: Advanced manufacturing equipment, traditional manufacturing tools, and physical computing. This includes the most promising, yet accessible, technologies of the coming decade, such as 3D printing, the Internet of Things, robotics, artificial intelligence, and virtual/augmented reality. In more advanced settings, and with the support of research institutes, universities, and corporate partners, these facilities could also support research into applications of advanced materials and synthetic biology to humanitarian relief.
- **Locally and globally targeted services**: Depending on the needs identified with the community, services built upon these platforms may include R&D; rapid prototyping; skills development; job creation; entrepreneurship training; science, technology, engineering, art, and mathematics (STEAM) education; co-working and informal knowledge exchange; programmes promoting social cohesion and gender equality; and psychosocial support through interactive creative expression.

The fab lab as a foundational model

Globally, the maker movement is on the rise. Between 2006 and 2016, the number of makerspaces (facilities providing the general public with access to modern creation and prototyping equipment) increased 14 times to around 1,400 (Lou and Peek, 2016). The largest network of makerspaces is based on the fab lab model, a digital fabrication lab concept which was a product of the Center for Bits & Atoms at the Massachusetts Institute of Technology (MIT).

A fab lab facility enables technical prototyping for innovation and invention, sharing common tools and processes with a global network of over 1,000 labs across the world. Fab labs provide a platform from which a community's technical challenges can be shared with this international network, which can help solve problems and design solutions with and for the community. Building innovation spaces as fab labs immediately connects communities affected by fragility and conflict with a global network of open-source innovation.

The core capabilities of the fab lab include a range of tools and equipment such as milling machines, sign-cutters, and programming tools for low-cost high-speed embedded processors. There is also a computer-controlled laser cutter, for press-fit assembly of 3D structures from 2D parts, and a precision (micron resolution) milling machine to make three-dimensional moulds and surface-mount circuit boards.

While the fab lab serves as the foundational model, it is easily tailored to meet the needs of local societies and cultures: the concept is highly amenable to localization. Fab labs can be considered a foundation upon which additional equipment, services, and specializations are added according to the needs of the community. There are at least four areas in which an innovation lab may specialize:

- **Education, training and capacity building**: Skill building in the use of 3D printing, algorithm development, and other competencies needed to build and use the advanced technologies discussed in this chapter is a core service of any innovation lab. These capacities can be leveraged competitively across various organizations, by both entrepreneurs and employees. Ultimately, labs can provide training to empower their target communities, enabling them to obtain gainful employment and remain relevant contributors to their local economy.
- **Enterprise creation and entrepreneurship**: The entrepreneurial mindsets and energies within refugee populations are forces that can be harnessed to foster job creation and, if properly integrated into local communities, create large-scale economic value.
- **Community development and engagement**: Labs can build communities within their facilities – a cohort of learners, educators, technologists, researchers, makers, and innovators. Humanitarian innovation labs can provide a platform from which a community's technical challenges can be shared among local constituents, as well as with partner labs in other geographies. These long-distance connections between communities, including those affected by fragility and conflict, can be a catalyst for large-scale community development around the theme of open-source innovation. Additionally, labs can help to enhance

a sense of community ownership, building local consortia and long-term engagement.
- **Psychosocial support**: Psychological trauma is one of the most pervasive and profound challenges facing forcibly displaced persons, particularly those who are victims of conflict. Access to art, creative tools, and collaborative projects can all aid in psychosocial support, especially for children and young people. Victims of conflict can benefit from therapeutic activities within labs. With access to self-expression, mentorship, and general creative activities, constituents' psychosocial wellbeing can improve. Impact can also be measured in terms of increased economic integration, as well as improved social cohesion with host communities.

Elements of good practice

The following elements of good practice are based on experience supporting the ecosystem for humanitarian innovation in Syria, Jordan, Turkey, Greece, and Germany. These five elements are co-creation, alignment with available infrastructure, involving host communities, gender considerations, and tailoring to thematic areas.

Co-creation

The central guiding principle for the community-embedded humanitarian innovation lab is co-creation. The lab should enable self-reliance by providing affected communities with advanced manufacturing tools, training, raw materials, and access to international experts, such as open-source communities. Not only does this reduce the cost of humanitarian relief in the near term, but it also trains affected populations on the skills of the future – the skills they will need to rebuild their countries. Best practices for promoting co-creation include:

- Engaging affected communities from start to finish, including during the lab design
- Prioritizing the training of affected communities, particularly refugees
- Providing affected communities with both training and access to resources to put this training to practice
- Where appropriate, leveraging international experts from the region who share a common language and understanding

Alignment with available infrastructure

Where they exist, SEZs can serve as spaces for experimentation with new models of humanitarian relief. The notion of self-reliance for refugees becomes significantly more practical if they have the right to work, sell products, and start companies. SEZs can play a role in attracting foreign direct investment by companies seeking to contribute to relief efforts. Additionally, they provide a space to implement policies that may not be possible elsewhere in the country: for example, allowing refugees the right to work in Jordan's King Hussein Bin Talal Development Area, located in the north of the country. This makes SEZs a prime location for humanitarian innovation labs, particularly those that will serve as business incubators. Best practices for SEZs include:

- Where possible, locating labs in SEZs or other locations where refugees have or can be given the right to work
- Aligning skill-building efforts with the needs of local or foreign companies so that there is alignment of supply and demand for trained workers
- Where appropriate, supporting business incubation for entrepreneurs and inventors in affected communities

Host-community involvement

There are often tensions between refugees and host communities, particularly where host communities are already marginalized or are facing challenging economic circumstances. This tension can lead to government restrictions on the provision of services such as training and employment for the displaced. Offering programmes to both refugees and host communities can help ease tensions, while also promoting wellbeing and equity. Good practice for involving host communities includes aligning the vision and strategy for humanitarian innovation labs with the economic and social development objectives of the host community. It can also be helpful to collaborate with local players to conduct targeted outreach to the most vulnerable populations of the host community.

Gender considerations

As a principle, women and men should have equal access to labs. However, gender *equity* requires addressing specific barriers that women may face in accessing services. It also requires creating a welcoming environment in facilities designed with and for women's use. Suggested actions to promote gender equity include:

- Consult local communities to identify an appropriate approach to gender equity
- Consult women to understand how they intended to use the space and their equipment needs, and ensure that these needs are incorporated into the design and bill of materials
- Consider dedicating certain hours of operation to women only
- Ensure equal quality of services, particularly if there are separate spaces and equipment for women and men

- Offer services such as on-site childcare or transportation to incentivize and facilitate women's participation
- Recruit female trainers and international experts, who can serve as role models to women using the facility

Tailoring to thematic areas

Labs should be tailored to needs. Each facility can enable innovation across several thematic areas, but the lab generally has a primary motivation. Four thematic specializations are common:

Technology R&D such as provision of basic services such as health; water, sanitation, and hygiene; and shelter.

- Empower affected communities to lead or meaningfully contribute to R&D
- Use and/or create do-it-yourself (DIY) open-source designs
- Offer free services for the community
- Use recycled materials for production where possible

Training and education such as experiences that help foster vocational training and STEAM subjects.

- Fab labs can provide robust curricula but may require localization
- Children and young people who have been out of the formal education system for years may lack foundational knowledge, such as mathematics
- Match supply with demand for vocational training by working with potential employers to design training programmes

Entrepreneurship and job creation including business incubation and youth employment generation.

- Provide both training and resources for entrepreneurs, particularly financing
- If applicable, help connect entrepreneurs with international markets
- Support entrepreneurs to hire from within affected communities, and ensure that potential hires have the necessary training

Community wellbeing including activities that promote social cohesion and psychosocial support.

- Training, access to technology, and the means for creative expression that enhances agency, dignity, and purpose
- Engage experts on psychosocial support, art, and facilitation to help design and execute activities
- For integration, promote meaningful interaction with host communities
- Accelerated economic and social integration of refugees through education, training, and psychosocial support

Case study: 3D printing prosthetics

Three-dimensional printing technology is central to fab labs and makerspaces, and its impact in humanitarian crises is increasingly visible. The following case study highlights the means through which Refugee Open Ware (ROW) used the platform of a makerspace to address local medical needs – specifically, for prototyping prosthetic limbs. The experience highlights the importance of engaging the recipient in the design process, while also demonstrating that 3D printing is a teachable skillset that can create opportunities to further economic and social wellbeing.

Additive manufacturing is a transformative tool that can positively impact refugee scenarios and disasters. Medical services and devices are critically important in these contexts. Providing prosthetic limbs typically requires highly trained practitioners and incurs significant logistical demands, making it an attractive opportunity for automation and on-demand production capacity.

In 2014, ROW and 3Dmena used a makerspace in Amman, Jordan to create a set of personalized prosthetic limbs for amputees. ROW used open-source designs to create replacement prosthetic limbs, with the goal of producing more cost-effective solutions of comparable quality to commercially produced prosthetics. These devices were specifically designed for those suffering from partial hand amputation, who typically had several fingers amputated but some portion of the hand remaining.

ROW partnered with the Jordanian Royal Medical Services, Médecins Sans Frontiers (MSF), and local charities to provide devices to victims of war who fled to Jordan. There were four patients – two young women in their mid-twenties and two boys aged six and eleven. Each of these patients had a partial hand amputation – three as the result of war injuries, and one as the result of a household injury. After establishing a makerspace in Amman, ROW and 3Dmena recruited and trained local personnel to operate the 3D printers and other equipment. The project was executed by a team of Jordanians, Europeans, and Americans, with support from a Syrian refugee and amputee who was recruited and trained on 3D printing, model creation and customization, and maintenance of the printers. The team used open-source designs disseminated by eNABLE.

The field trials offer several lessons:

- **Co-creation**: It is exceptionally difficult to make culturally appropriate aesthetic decisions without designing with and for the specific end-user. Co-creation, the process of designing alongside the user and community, allows the designer to create products that are more likely to be accepted by the individual and his or her community.
- **Expanded portfolio**: For future operations, it will be critical to expand the design portfolio of available devices and solutions to accommodate a broader range of patients, particularly those suffering from transradial and transhumeral amputations.

- **Educational hubs**: In addition to demonstrating the usefulness of the technology in the context of prosthetics, the trials showed the potential for training and education. For example, the Syrian operator was able to use 3D printing to create a replacement component for his prosthetic foot for a fraction of the cost of ordering it from a prosthetist. The printers also formed the basis of a regional hub for education that served as outreach to both the local host and refugee communities.
- **Not a panacea**: Despite the notable impact that 3D printing had in supporting refugees, this technology is not a panacea. Incorporating 3D printing into a workflow takes time and effort, and is dependent upon skilled designers who generate the computer models to be printed. However, these tools improve daily as manufacturers produce more robust machines, stronger materials, and more reliable processes. Its limitations notwithstanding, digital manufacturing can contribute substantially to technical-skills development and real-time problem solving on the ground.

Recommendations

Beyond the innovation lab's management team, various stakeholders influence its trajectory and impact. Policymakers, investors, entrepreneurs, and leaders in the global makerspace communities, among others, can all play a vital role in bolstering humanitarian innovation labs. Each can make specific contributions to ensuring that humanitarian innovation labs evolve into dynamic, high-impact efforts.

Policymakers: The policy space is instrumental to creating the regulatory environment needed to support the innovation, entrepreneurship, resource acquisition, and general processes that characterize the fab lab.

- Promote a favourable regulatory environment that eases import of advanced technologies and machinery, including the tools for their upkeep
- Streamline the business start-up process so that entrepreneurs are able to launch new enterprises quickly and with minimal administrative costs
- Provide displaced persons with the right to work and mobility within the host country
- Provide a favourable investment climate for venture capital, angel investors, and commercial banks
- Promote solutions that support both refugees and host communities

Investors: Provide capital and expertise to guide entrepreneurs in fab labs and help them to scale their companies.

- Recognize and plan for a longer-term horizon for returns
- Value the social returns of humanitarian ventures
- Recruit new investors to support humanitarian technology start-ups

Entrepreneurs: Entrepreneurs will be some of the main users and beneficiaries of the fab lab and entrepreneurial methods are key.

- Bring new technologies, innovations, and skill sets to fab lab
- Help create deal flow for investors
- Promote a collaborative environment and shape the fab lab's culture
- Serve as mentors and future investors in humanitarian technology start-ups
- Integrate new trained practitioners into the global economy, particularly through roles and projects that can be performed remotely

Global practitioners: Experts in digital fabrication and advanced technology can provide access to best practices, resources and general know-how.

- Integrate fab labs into a global network to facilitate collaborations and knowledge exchange
- Enable idea and resource sharing, capacity building, and the creation of joint ventures, as well as peer education throughout global fab lab networks
- Promote open-source principles to establish a common culture of sharing and collaboration between fab labs globally

References

Kopczak, L. and Thomas, A. (2005) *From Logistics to Supply Chain Management: The Path Forward in The Humanitarian Sector*, Fritz Institute.

Lou, N. and Peek, K. (2016) 'By the Numbers: The Rise of the Makerspace', *Popular Science*.

About the authors

Kate Wharton is an advisor to Refugee Open Ware and Hala Systems and previously served as chief operating officer of both organizations. While at Deloitte's U.S. Federal Consulting practice, she co-founded a global social impact programme and supported energy and infrastructure projects in emerging markets for USAID and the World Bank.

Adam Arabian Ph.D. P.E., is the chief technology officer of Refugee Open Ware. He is an associate professor of engineering at Seattle Pacific University and senior technical advisor for Hala Systems. He has researched, published, and engaged extensively in the field of appropriate applications of technology to humanitarian crises.

Dave Levin is the founder and executive director of Refugee Open Ware, as well as co-founder and head of strategy at Hala Systems. Previously,

Dave worked at LeapFrog Investments, McKinsey and Co. and the UN Global Compact. He was also a Fulbright Scholar in India, pioneering mobile banking products for the poor.

Jamil Wyne is an advisor to Refugee Open Ware. He founded the Wamda Research Lab, served as a Fulbright Fellow and has consulted with the World Bank and International Finance Corporation. His work has appeared or been cited in the *Wall Street Journal* and Stanford, Wharton, and WEF publications, among others.

William Altman works at CB Insights where he is a Senior Intelligence Analyst for Cybersecurity.

Natalie Chang is a Coordinator at the Office of International Affairs at Stanford University.

CHAPTER 16

Lessons learned from the Nepal innovation lab

Sebastien Maupas, David Kaldor, and Jennifer MacCann

The Nepal Innovation Lab (NLab) was set up in late 2015 by World Vision International's earthquake response office. It has since become the site of various innovations and a potential model for other humanitarian situations. This chapter presents the lessons learned in setting up and operating this lab. After describing the lab and the context in which it was formed and operates, the chapter concludes by outlining a number of guiding conditions and principles such as the importance of leadership, setting up loose operational boundaries, and remaining nimble and responsive to the shifting context.

Keywords: innovation labs, humanitarianism, lessons learned, principles

The Nepal Innovation Lab (NLab) was set up to foster innovative and inclusive solutions to humanitarian challenges. It was established in December 2015 by World Vision International's earthquake response office as a platform to improve the humanitarian recovery efforts in Nepal through the nurturing of new thinking and more effective, efficient, and appropriate solutions.

Key projects supported during the first year included: the 3D printing of humanitarian supplies, a remote-monitoring system for construction sites, a community-driven landscape mapping toolkit, a peer-to-peer disaster recovery digital platform, and an early warning system.

The NLab's initial offering centred on a residency programme that supported project teams to test and refine innovations in the field. Within six months, the NLab had expanded this to include a set of programmes aimed at fostering a local community of innovation practice, and the rapid testing of early stage ideas.

The NLab programmes offered *physical resources*, such as office space for project teams and uninterrupted access to power and internet; *strategic resources*, such as access to sector specialists and a community of peers working on innovation projects; and *financial resources* through a grants mechanism.

This chapter presents lessons learned during the first year of the NLab's operation. The analysis first considers the design and set-up of the NLab's team, culture, and programmes. It then goes on to explore challenges associated with the process of integrating the NLab into local, international, and humanitarian ecosystems. Finally, it draws on the NLab's experience to present a set of conditions and principles that we see as being integral to the establishment of a successful lab.

Lab design: creating a space for innovation

Given the experimental nature of the lab, a large emphasis was placed on attracting people and partners who could bring a diversity of skills, knowledge, and experience so as to forge the NLab's culture and direction through practice. Early participants at the lab were seen as partners, and were involved in the process of determining the NLab's strategic direction.

The NLab aimed to maintain a very lean structure, in order to build a culture of collaboration with external partners and to focus resources on testing projects. Expertise was brought in through a mixture of strategic, academic, and technical partnerships, with the NLab playing a connecting role. The NLab team initially comprised a lab manager and a range of consultants from the humanitarian sector, the private sector, and academia. Back-office (finance, human resources, procurement, IT, etc.) and sectoral support (shelter, health, livelihoods, WASH, education, etc.) was provided through World Vision.

It was tempting to rely on experienced international consultants and advisors, but this approach was found to delay early set-up processes because the outputs from remote support did not always match realities on the ground. Remote support should, therefore, either be limited, or framed with highly specific objectives. The experience of the NLab was that, without this specificity, remote consultancy could consume, rather than increase, the already limited capacity of a lean team on the ground. The NLab learned that having a strong, collaborative team with complementary skills on the ground from the start was key to kick-starting the formation of the lab.

The NLab found that it was necessary to move beyond the traditional humanitarian recruitment channels to find the skills required for lab management. It took longer than anticipated to identify both international and local candidates for these roles. This delay in recruitment slowed initial impact, with later growth of the team accelerating the NLab's capacity to support more projects, deliver more events, and further leverage capacities. While it is important to stay lean during set-up, human resources and hiring should be prioritized.

During the lab's set-up, a balance was needed between established and experimental methods of design and management. While the NLab sought to build its strategy with reference to lessons from existing initiatives and research into local needs and capacities, it also found that practical experimentation using untested thinking could fast-track successful design.

The NLab team therefore found it useful to separate the roles of day-to-day management and hosting from longer-term strategic design and business development. This allowed an approach in which the team could remain responsive during early stages by experimenting with methods while keeping within the broader constraints of a longer-term vision.

It is critical that the core processes of an innovation lab create a flexible environment that allows the lab itself to lead by example, to inspire lab residents and projects to experiment and push the boundaries. Flexible conditions here included the lab's opening hours, the frequency and format of lab residents' interactions, the entry points through which the wider community could engage with the lab, and the methods the lab used to communicate its activities and learnings to a wider audience.

In designing the NLab's culture, it was important to find out what 'just enough structure' looked like for the various lab users and projects. This was achieved by:

- Working closely with project teams to articulate a tailored innovation roadmap
- Developing terms of agreement that referenced the roadmap of activity, while acknowledging the inherent uncertainty in innovation processes and maintaining room for flexibility in the delivery of specific outputs
- Establishing a schedule of regular progress updates from project teams with the clear aim of supporting them to achieve their intended outcomes
- Encouraging autonomy for teams and individuals but offering regular support
- Building a structured operating rhythm for the lab community while offering a diversity of tools and experiences for users to interact with, so allowing a range of projects and people to get what they need to succeed.

To ensure reflection on and iteration of the lab model, the NLab instituted a process of review and redefinition of core principles after six months. The process enabled the formal integration of ways of working that had evolved organically, allowed for flexibility, and provided a mechanism to address principles that were not serving the aims of the lab. Strategy design and roll-out for such a lab should be a continuous iterative process that gradually steers the organization in the intended direction, rather than a periodic process that has heavily prescriptive long-term activities and milestones.

Developing the criteria to monitor and evaluate the NLab's projects proved difficult. This was primarily due to the very nature of innovation, as well as the wide variation in focus area (infrastructure, health, supply chains, education, etc.) and innovation type (product, service, programme, delivery model, etc.) of the projects being pursued. After selection, it was not possible to apply standardized tracking metrics to the projects. It was therefore necessary to define these metrics on a project-by-project basis.

While the NLab sought to pursue certain areas of focus based on obvious demand (shelter, connectivity, energy), these themes were not made a formal requirement for entry to the lab. This open approach enabled the lab to seize different – and, at times, unexpected – opportunities. However, it also created difficulty in building specific expertise and a knowledge base to use to process and collate data, and to drive momentum to specific areas of need.

After launching the lab with a core six-month residency programme, it quickly became clear that potential lab users were looking for a wider range of entry points. A diverse set of programmes was built, offering shorter residencies (to scope-out early stage concepts) and even-lighter-touch connection points, such as events and workshops (to help build a community of practice around the lab, and to initiate conversations with new partners). While this approach of defining programmes did not preclude ad hoc forms of engagement, it greatly simplified the messaging about how to engage with the lab and streamlined the subsequent application process – ultimately strengthening the pipeline of lab projects.

In setting up the NLab, it was necessary to build or adapt a suite of tools and platforms to support the lab's management. Developing platforms to manage operational processes – such as stakeholder-relationship management, opportunity pipelines, project tracking, team collaboration, document storage, and knowledge management – proved to be a time-consuming process. Establishing strong connections to learn from similar initiatives (such as accelerators, incubators and co-working spaces) can enable the initial set-up of this type of 'soft architecture' to be more efficient and effective.

A critical component of the NLab's set-up was the establishment of a dedicated working space – a dynamic, multi-use environment that offered full-time access to power and internet, quiet (as quiet as is possible in bustling Kathmandu) desk spaces, meeting and presentation zones, video-conferencing facilities, and a small workshop for manual experimentation. The lab is primarily intended for use by project teams; however, it has been set up to welcome a wider community during key events such as workshops and presentations. The space is continually evolving, but resources were invested early to ensure it is an inspiring place to work from – and this has had a positive effect on lab residents and visitors.

The NLab was hosted by World Vision, and this greatly accelerated the initial set-up. The lab was able to leverage the existing processes (finance, human resources, IT, legal, etc.) of an established organization, allowing it to fast-track into operation. This essentially meant that critical set-up processes only needed to be adapted and built upon to meet the needs of the lab, rather than designed from the ground up.

A significant challenge arose in the need to create a legal framework for the NLab to engage with its users. Representing a new modality for initiating humanitarian projects, the lab needed to go beyond existing organization frameworks to create new contracts that reflected the new kinds of partnerships that were being brokered between World Vision, as the host of the NLab, and its collaborators.

Lab context: integrating the NLab into local, international and humanitarian ecosystems

The local innovation ecosystem of Nepal is in its infancy, and, therefore, initially proved difficult to navigate. This slowed down the process of identifying local partners and recruiting a core team, and the NLab relied initially on international innovations to bridge the apparent gap in the ecosystem. While local pockets of innovation were gradually being identified, this proved a successful strategy. Much activity occurred at an informal level, and, over time, came together to form the beginnings of a community of practice. The lessons are clear: mapping the local innovation ecosystem to understand its depth and key participants should be amongst the first activities undertaken in establishing a lab such as this; and the sooner local humanitarian innovators can be identified, the quicker traction can be gained in the national context.

In order to build these local networks and integrate with the existing ecosystem, the NLab relied heavily on networking with private-sector innovators, communities, and social-service providers. The best way to build these networks was to use a diverse range of channels: online (Facebook, in particular, is very popular in Nepal); conferences and workshops; and existing staff and partner networks.

The humanitarian sector is increasingly recognizing the importance of integrating local capacities for long-term solutions, and investing in nurturing local capacity where gaps exist. Labs need to decide what role they aim to play in local capacity building for innovation and, similarly, in connecting international partners with the capacities of local innovators.

Central to the initial NLab concept was the formation of international partnerships leading to collaboration between international and local expertise. In practice, it proved difficult to engage international organizations that did not already have a commitment to operating in Nepal. However, those that were prepared to commit to being on the ground brought significant value during early stages – both in the design and management of the lab and in collaboration on lab projects. Attempts to engage international partners remotely did not achieve a comparable level of interaction, often resulting in conversations moving slowly or stalling due to a lack of insight into the rapidly shifting needs at ground level.

In order to better frame the possible entry points and opportunities for potential partners, the NLab made attempts to provide context for local challenges – for example, collaborating with graduates from the Harvard School of Design to produce a situation report on energy challenges during a nationwide fuel shortage. Research of this kind was used to initiate conversations with potential collaborators, both locally and internationally.

It was also important for the lab to play a role in framing the risks and barriers associated with working in Nepal. It was necessary to strike a balance between generating momentum and excitement around collaboration, while supporting partners to get established on the ground amid uncertain and continuously shifting conditions.

In trying to respond to the most systemic humanitarian needs in Nepal, the NLab found that humanitarian actors typically find it hard to articulate the challenges they face. The same broad challenges frequently emerge (resources, budget, communication). However, it can be difficult to identify specific areas and tipping points that will catalyse significant change. The complex, multifaceted challenges risk becoming over-simplified, resulting in solutions that are ineffective. An innovation lab should dedicate significant resources to helping innovators to frame the problems they seek to address.

While open and collaborative approaches are increasingly being explored by humanitarian agencies, the NLab initially found it difficult to leverage its relationships with other NGOs on the ground. This was due to barriers in the humanitarian sector, such as potential partners having 'no time', 'no organizational support', 'little incentive to innovate' and being wary of risk and failure. The NLab sought to overcome this through a series of activities (such as networking events, expert review of projects, and workshops) designed to build confidence and strengthen these relationships. This approach proved somewhat successful, but needed to be creatively renewed on a regular basis to maintain a high level of engagement.

The NLab's experience reinforces the importance of fostering an understanding of the lab's purpose, and entry points for collaboration, amongst its stakeholders and intended users from an early stage. Lab residents were often dealing with an idea in its early stages, one that would not result in tangible benefit to communities until much later; it was therefore important to capture and convey progress stories and lessons learned to the wider community. Significant resources should be invested to document the innovation journeys of lab projects. Rich narrative content such as photo- and video-journalism proved most effective in building interest and momentum around innovations during testing phases as innovations moved towards reaching the potential for widespread adoption.

Guiding conditions and principles

In reflecting on the NLab's set-up and first year of operation, the following conditions and principles have been put forward as having been critical to the lab's ongoing success:

- Leadership support from World Vision's Response Manager to enable the NLab to be flexible, to move outside of compliance-based response systems, to secure sufficient funding, to ensure prioritization of innovation with the internal organizational response team (which facilitated connections between the lab and World Vision), and provide links to external networks at a high level.

- Initial funding to support projects, including a small-grants mechanism to launch ideas that may otherwise not be funded (due to risk, time and prioritization).
- Connections to both global and local innovators to ensure the 'right kind of people' are in the lab. The lab was built through partnerships as an enabling space for positive deviants to grow. This succeeded best when the right people from organizations were brought together and given time, space, and support with the right purpose and vision.
- A mix of global and local organizations and people led to the strongest projects and ideas. The diversity of sectors (academic, NGO, private) and perspectives from different countries and cultures enabled creative friction and unexpected thinking.
- Support from large humanitarian organizations to provide a strong grounding in humanitarian methods and values, and from a range of other local and international organizations to inject outside expertise and perspective into existing approaches.
- Set loose operational boundaries and trust the process. The following principles have been used by the lab management team as a mantra to move through uncertainty: trust the creation process, be patient, listen carefully, then build, learn, and adjust the approach as the organization grows.
- Remain nimble and responsive to the shifting context to ensure the lab can respond to unexpected opportunities, re-organize around unforeseen changes, and evolve alongside the disaster response phases – from relief to recovery to rehabilitation and integration into development. A lab must be able to measure its success within the timeframes and context of a disaster.
- Roadmaps for scaling innovation should be considered with every investment. Each project should begin with a clear sense of the opportunities for future scale, including potential partners, users, or funding streams that could support it. Certainty is not necessary but a good consideration of scale from the beginning increases overall impact and effectiveness of the lab in the long term.

The NLab is a live project that continues to evolve as it enters its second year of operation – testing and refining its own operating model and set of programme offerings – in support of inclusive and innovative humanitarian solutions in Nepal and beyond.

About the authors

Sebastien Maupas leads teams and organizations of all size (start-up, not for profit, corporate and government) to drive creative thinking and innovation through human-centred design and design thinking to solve large complex problems. He has developed specific expertise in sustainability, social enterprises, social, and humanitarian innovation. In 2016, he was manager of the Nepal Innovation Lab.

David Kaldor is a designer and strategist who works closely with organizations and communities to shape solutions that foster resilience and sustainability. David has learned the value of inclusive and innovative design first-hand through his practice – from designing better ways to respond to natural disaster with earthquake-affected communities in Nepal, to the co-design of programmes to improve education outcomes for young Indigenous people in Australia.

Jennifer MacCann is the director of the Response Innovation Lab. She has extensive experience in humanitarian programming having led World Vision's Nepal earthquake response and held leadership roles in the responses to Typhoon Haiyan in the Philippines and the Haiti earthquake. She has also worked in West, East and Southern Africa and Palestine.

CHAPTER 17

Turning a conversation into an opportunity

Abi Bush

Many established organizations in the humanitarian sector are seeking to innovate through engaging and partnering with other organizations that already employ innovative approaches. However, many organizations employing innovative approaches are young, small, and can have non-conventional organizational structures, cultures, and processes. This can make the journey from a chance conversation to a contracted opportunity incredibly frustrating for both the small and large partner, as procedural differences, assumptions, and misunderstandings throw up barrier after barrier, eventually leading to abandonment of the project. This chapter looks at how many of the skills usually associated with building a contextually sensitive response, such as clear problem identification, communication, and empathy, can be applied to develop a successful conversation between potential partners.

Keywords: partnerships, innovation, collaboration, scaling

Introduction

There is increasing recognition of the highly complex and long-term nature of humanitarian crises. Humanitarian organizations are looking to innovate and build new capabilities to solve complex problems. Discussion of what it takes to build a more effective response points to greater focus on clear problem identification, collaboration, process over product, and building as many opportunities for communication and empathy into response programmes as possible. This advice usually focuses on how NGOs interact with affected communities; however, it works equally well when directed at discussions between established NGOs and young innovative organizations looking to work together.

The journey from a positive conversation to a contracted opportunity can be a frustrating experience for the parties involved. This frustration arises as differences in organizational procedures and assumptions and misunderstandings accumulate. This eventually leads to the cost of forming a partnership outweighing the positive potential impact of the opportunity itself. For example, the costs that must be met before a contract is agreed include worker hours (e.g., for meetings, discussions, and assessment trips), transport, documentation, and due diligence. A lengthy and costly process

http://dx.doi.org/10.3362/9781780449531.017

often ends before it begins for small innovative organizations, who may see the value of a small amount of funding to complete a project with a larger organization entirely absorbed by the time and effort input to win the project in the first place.

Avoiding this trap can be done in a number of ways:

- Keeping the conversation succinct and managing the risks that are inherent in any project
- Taking time to build an empathetic relationship that has the potential to grow into a long-term partnership
- Developing a carefully defined project while recognizing that it will need resources to cover the cost of the time and effort expended in forming it.

Ultimately, any relationship will be smoother and less costly if there is a high level of trust. A number of steps can help instil this trust, including demonstrating respect, clarifying expectations, keeping commitments, and extending trust in the first place. To help develop partnerships based on high trust, the remainder of this chapter looks at a few of the obstacles and how to overcome them. By working this way, it is possible to transform a chance conversation into an opportunity. Four key areas are looked at from the perspective of the first attempts to collaborate (when an initial 'short productive conversation' occurs) to the longer-term work to develop a partnership.

Formal processes and procedures

There are often bureaucratic requirements that form obstacles to partnership. Long formal documentation procedures, audits, and checks can make it impossible for a small organization to pursue a small-budget project or pilot with a large organization, because of the costs incurred from time absorbed in first understanding and then completing the tasks. Additionally, small, young organizations may simply not have the documentation required (e.g., new organizations will not have extensive financial audit data and may lack other information often required in a due diligence process).

For short productive conversations

- Large organizations:
  - Do you have a streamlined process for pilot/innovation projects; i.e. under a certain project budget, are you able to offer a simplified, lightweight process?
  - If not, can you sort your usual collaboration requirements into 'nice-to-haves' and 'deal-breakers', and address the deal-breakers early on in the conversation?

- Small organizations:
  - Do you have someone who can advise on the documentation typically required as you grow and take on larger projects? Do you have as much of it ready to go as possible?
  - How many people are involved in writing and signing off a project proposal – can this be reduced?

For building a long-term partnership

- Map out the procedures and processes required on both sides together. Highlight areas that may cause challenges.
- Large organizations:
  - Seek to eliminate or reduce requirements that pose a challenge.
  - For 'deal-breakers', be prepared to be patient while small organizations find the capacity to address the requirement.

Organizational structure and decision-making processes

Different organizations, big and small, can have very different structures. It is useful early on to map out the key people on both sides who will be involved in making decisions.

For short productive conversations

Minimize the amount of time spent communicating by identifying the key people needed for sign-off, and engaging only with them.

- Large organizations:
  - Is the person you are talking to the person who can sign off the project? Is the person you are talking to going to be the lead on the project, or might they hand you over to someone else?
  - Who else is involved? Particularly with technically novel projects, the person you meet at a conference may not have the technical knowledge to sense-check the project. Get the person with the technical know-how to reality-check the discussions early on.
- Small organizations:
  - Who holds the budget?
  - Who has to approve the project?
  - Who would you actually be working with – are you involving them in the discussion?
  - Is there an 'Innovation' group or department you can engage with at local level? Approach with care, particularly at an international level; when 'innovation' is someone's job there can be powerful but quite

fixed ideas about what innovation is and isn't. Innovations that do not fit the definition may quickly be shut down.

For building a long-term partnership

For longer, higher-budget projects changes to the scope later on will significantly increase costs. It will be worth investing the time to fully engage all stakeholders, whereas for a smaller project, the rewards would not justify the costs.

- Small organizations:
  - Will the person you are talking to champion you inside their organization? Do you have a video, leaflet, or one-pager you can give to them to share with others?
  - Be prepared to make exactly the same pitch and answer the same questions in front of different people, often in front of the same people. Take the time to get everyone on board.

What risks does this conversation expose people to?

For short productive conversations

- Small organizations:
  - What type of funding is the project from? Low-risk funding sources include budget surplus or designated innovation funds. Project funds, not intended for innovation, are more risky for a manager to allocate to innovation. For a short conversation, actively seek low-risk funds where decisions should not cause too much personal liability.
  - Is the person you are talking to willing to accept the risks of being the decision-maker? How big are the personal risks to their career if the project fails?

For building a long-term partnership

- Small organizations
  - If your funding source or situation place your champion at high personal risk, be prepared to commit more time to building trust and relationships. A higher-risk decision will need the buy-in of more people, as no single person will want to accept full responsibility.
  - Empathize with the costs of change your innovation may incur, and the risk this places on your collaborator. Your innovation may be

cheaper and faster, but does this outweigh the cost of dismantling existing systems?

- Large organizations:
  - Empathize with cash flow difficulties and the fact that most jobs are being done by a small number of people. The person you are talking to may be doing sales, but they might also be managing two projects, writing grants, and managing the company accounts.

Problem identification

The usual vocabulary surrounding solving problems in the field often consists of identifying needs through interacting with people experiencing the problem and trying to collaborate or co-create a solution (the instruction not to push 'a solution in need of a problem' is often added). This is good general advice, but fails to capture the full perspective of what it is like to solve humanitarian problems. In particular, it fails to acknowledge that capabilities and resources on hand also need to be taken into account. It also invites the supposition that problems can be neatly isolated and solved with community input. Often problems are complex, systemic, and not obvious or interesting to those affected by them.

For short productive conversations

Problems and solutions can be difficult and it can be time consuming to pin down all the correct measures of progress and success. Rather than identifying highly specific outputs, focus on generating a hypothesis to test that everyone can agree to work on, but be flexible in the face of new data.

- Small organizations:
  - Are you solving a problem faced by the partner, or by the end beneficiary? Be clear on this, and where you should therefore direct your time and effort. Needs assessments and other forms of data are powerful tools for a quick win.
  - Listen closely and try to understand what is being said around you; do not be afraid to evolve your offering or to change focus based on interests that emerge through subsequent conversations.
- Large organizations:
  - Take care to understand the capabilities on offer – they may be being offered in a very different way than usual. Are your partners offering a service, a consultancy, to be a supplier, etc.? Why are you excited about leveraging this capability? What impact could it have on your organization's future success?

For building a long-term partnership

Clearer project outputs will be required in longer-term contexts. However, since innovative projects can bring to light radically new information that can completely change the nature of a project, sometimes setting clear outputs can be uncomfortable. However, defining a physical output which leaves the impact of the project undefined can be a good resolution to this issue. This could take the form of a report, evaluation, or video. Removing uncertainty by conducting initial assessments can also be a good way of managing this issue.

Small organizations:

- Do not assume the potential partner is truly familiar with either their own or the end beneficiaries' problems. For example, a budget holder is unlikely to be spending much time in the field. An aid worker in the field is unlikely to want to admit they have problems. The culture at field level may be geared towards delivery, not problem identification.
- Be prepared to do the legwork to determine the on-the-ground relevance of your innovation – ask to go out to the field to do assessments with the organization.
- Take your time – a new concept can take a while to sink in. Describe the problem being solved using examples and broad conceptual ideas. Your potential partner may see the relevance of your work after one week, two months, or a year.

About the author

Abi Bush is a technical advisor for Field Ready and led the organization's efforts in Nepal in 2016. She previously worked for SimPrints and The EcoHouse Initiative. Abi holds a MEng in Manufacturing Engineering from the University of Cambridge.

CHAPTER 18

Collaboration and the importance of process

Robin Borrud and Stephanie Gliege

Focusing on process over product empowers disaster-hit communities, leads to cross-sector communication, collaboration and innovation, and fills gaps in the humanitarian response. This chapter presents the work of Communitere International, an INGO that draws disaster-affected communities together by providing the space to work together, exchange ideas, share resources, and collaborate through developing cooperative resource centres in post-disaster areas.

Keywords: humanitarian innovation, makerspace, local engagement, locally driven process, local empowerment, process over product

In the chaos and devastation following a major catastrophe, disaster-response organizations compete for scarce local resources like tools, materials, technical equipment, meeting spaces, reliable internet access, and lodging. In addition, response efforts are often driven by the priorities of foreign donors and policy-makers, disempowering the disaster-hit communities and leaving residents without the resources they need to rebuild their own lives.

The phrase 'process over product' refers to an emphasis on the practice and methods of innovation rather than simply the tangible outputs. It is a concept often used to describe the importance of creating, doing, and sharing in fields such as visual and performance art. In the context of humanitarian innovation, it can be seen as an approach to engaging affected people and communities in a way that is as important – if not more important – than the final product delivered. A project that creates something without community engagement may be less valuable than a project with a lot of community engagement, regardless of outcome.

Communitere International is an INGO that draws disaster-affected communities together by providing the space to work together, exchange ideas, share resources, and collaborate through developing cooperative resource centres in post-disaster areas. It has developed and supported resource centres in Haiti (March 2010), the Philippines (late 2013), Nepal (June 2015), and Greece (2017).

http://dx.doi.org/10.3362/9781780449531.018

What is a resource centre?

Resource centre is the term used by Communitere International to refer to a fab lab, innovation lab, makerspace, innovation hub, or other similar unrestricted area that facilitates communication, collaboration, and innovation through empowering the space-users with the tools, materials, and space to create. Designed to operate indefinitely, the resource centres become permanent structures giving communities the capacity to develop and rebuild their lives long after the initial flood of international aid recedes. Communitere International supports local resource centres to help individuals, relief agencies, private companies, NGOs, and local groups to reduce overheads by providing the space, support, and tools needed to rebuild in the wake of humanitarian disasters.

Communitere International believes that empowering local residents to design and run the resource centres enables affected communities to create spaces that best serve their humanitarian and development needs. The spaces created naturally facilitate cross-sector communication, collaboration, and innovation, and, as a result, unforeseen gaps in the humanitarian response, early recovery, and long-term development planning are filled based upon needs identified by the local population. Resource centres are used by a wide range of actors:

- Local groups and individuals use the resource centres to collaborate, share resources, and rebuild their lives on their own terms.
- Start-ups that design products and services specifically for their region but lack the resources to build their own trial centres have used resource centres for field testing.
- NGOs borrow tools and rent space to keep their own infrastructure lithe and nimble.

Process-over-product philosophy

Our organization's experiences in Haiti and the Philippines taught us that the key to successful community participation and empowerment is the process of setting up the resource centre itself (not necessarily the ultimate products of the centre). The process-over-product approach to setting up a community-centred project means that it is intended to become a permanent part of a community after a humanitarian disaster.

Focusing on thoroughly engaging the community at the design phase of the project and maintaining this engagement can have a significant impact on the effectiveness and long-term sustainability of the project by:

- Ensuring the project truly serves the needs of the community, empowering the community to rebuild on its own terms
- Investing in local leadership for the project from the very beginning – it is more difficult to bring in local leaders at a later stage in the project
- Creating a culture of innovation before the project commences
- Enabling the project team to be flexible, and remain flexible, to meet the changing needs of the affected community

Therefore, it is not the product of the resource centre or space that the organization focuses its energy on, it is the process of designing and creating that space and, thereby, building a resource centre to be used for learning, sharing, borrowing resources, co-working, and networking.

Traditionally, little focus has been placed on the value of the process taken to get to the end product. While it makes sense that putting, for example, food in the hand of a person who is starving will give them the chance to eat, that solution does not address the deeper emotional and spiritual recovery that needs to take place for them to truly begin to rebuild their lives. Such a person's needs would be met more holistically through involving them in the process that put food into their hand. More importantly, they would be seen as participants rather than beneficiaries; they are put on equal footing with the first responders and donor community and so can begin walking the path to restore their humanity.

Setting up a resource centre in post-earthquake Nepal

In each successive disaster, Communitere International uses lessons learned from the previous disaster response to inform development of the next resource centre. In April 2015, after Nepal was struck by a 7.8-magnitude earthquake, a long-time volunteer flew to Nepal to support the disaster-mapping efforts. Our volunteer's drone footage gave information on the situation in distant and hard-to-reach areas and showed how badly the affected areas were hit. The devastation was widespread. Over 8,000 people had already died, nearly 18,000 people were now known to have been injured, and over 10 per cent of the country's homes were destroyed or damaged. Another massive earthquake that struck in May of that year increased those numbers and intensified the needs in Nepal.

Communitere International's process-over-product philosophy means that the processes of designing, constructing, supplying, and operating cooperative resource centres must be locally led. Therefore, we developed Nepal Communitere through a six-week-long consultative process, our longest and most comprehensive planning phase thus far. The initial priority was to identify local and international partners on the ground in Kathmandu who would be an integral part of our deployment.

Engaging the local community: creating a network

Once on the ground, the Communitere International team focused on engaging the local community to build up a local team and network. This was a long process, ultimately taking more than four months. Key learnings can be used by organizations seeking to build a local network.

- The initial deployment should, ideally, include team members with existing contacts in the affected community, in national NGOs, or in INGOs with a presence in the country.
- Use these pre-existing connections to develop a wider network. NGO and INGO staff have a good understanding of the local context and the

organizations operating there – beyond their own official partners – and can be an excellent place to start.
- Take time with the process. In Nepal, we spent four weeks building relationships before convening the first design workshop.
- INGOs in the field frequently do not have mechanisms to directly partner with or fund other organizations, especially international organizations. However, the support of individuals working within those organizations can be invaluable, particularly in terms of making connections with local actors.
- Manage expectations. Setting up community-centred projects takes time, so it is important to bring potential partners in with the understanding that it will be a long journey.

Design workshop

Over the first month, our small team built up a strong local network and convened a comprehensive design workshop with 40 participants from 25 organizations; while some of these organizations were INGOs, most were local NGOs. Participants were primarily young leaders playing a significant role in post-disaster relief and community development initiatives.

The purpose of the design workshop was to collaborate with the participants to identify what Nepal Communitere could do as a local organization that aims to serve the people of Nepal. It was the first of a series of workshops facilitated with local organizations to engage the community and ensure local priorities were identified and addressed in designing and building Nepal Communitere. Some of the general guidelines followed included:

- Do not start with a product in mind.
- Roadmaps are better than strict guidelines and prescribed steps.
- Capture creative ideas by whatever means works.
- Figure out what is known and not known.
- Nothing is set in stone.

During the workshop, participants divided into small groups of four or five to come up with innovative and creative ideas of what the resource centre in Nepal could offer. These included:

- A mobile resource centre that goes out to various communities affected by the earthquake.
- Office space shared with other local organizations.
- Space to host different events to raise funds that could be a centre for yoga, meditation, and other activities.

During the third session, the facilitator invited all participants to work in groups on a variety of key topics including: location, centre-design wish list, tools and equipment wish list, self-funding, and inclusivity. Each group presented their ideas, most of which addressed the cultural, social, political and emotional needs. The workshop ended with participants sitting in a circle and discussing key issues in an open forum, including money-handling and ensuring Nepal Communitere became sufficiently known. The richness of the conversations between participants served as the foundation of Nepal Communitere's design and helped bridge the gap between individuals who were able and willing to help and organizations that could effect change. Central to that commitment was the notion that communication, information, and strategic partnerships are vital to an effective, relevant emergency response and recovery and renewal of the affected communities.

Conclusion

Focusing a substantial amount of energy on the design phase of a humanitarian response presents a number of challenges, the most substantial being the age-old issues of time and money. Time is of the essence in the early stages of disaster recovery and, quite often, long-term solutions are exchanged for short-term gains. Although painstaking, Communitere has learned that putting time into the design phase and thoroughly engaging the local community at the start of the project ensures that a community-based resource centre truly serves the needs of the community in the short- and longer-term. This process creates the space for innovation before the resource centre is even built. A local board and strong local relationships ensure the consultative process continues throughout the creation and operation of the centre. While the process can present challenges with donors who are used to seeing immediate, tangible results, Communitere has learned that this local engagement is the key to rebuilding – and continuing to effectively serve – disaster-affected communities. Focusing on a collaborative process creates a resource centre that is used for learning, sharing, borrowing resources, co-working, networking, and rebuilding.

About the authors

Robin Borrud is an international social entrepreneur, philanthropist, and previous board member of Communitere International. Robin's professional background is in media sales and marketing: she spent seven years in local and national television sales in the United States.

Stephanie Gliege is director of operations and legal advisor for Communitere International. A US-qualified lawyer, she previously worked for other non-profits and was a coordinator in Darfur, Sudan, for the International Organization of Migration.

CHAPTER 19
Three-stage design process

Desiree Matel-Anderson

Traditional assessment methodologies can be time-consuming, and even the 'lite' versions that are geared for rapid response can lead to a lack of alignment between data and activities, and missed opportunities for creative solutions. The Field Innovation Team (FIT), a US non-profit, developed a three-step design process to adapt these different approaches to disaster response. This chapter describes this rapid process and presents a case study of a situation where this proved successful.

Keywords: assessment, design process, disaster relief, partnership

The merging of relief, design thinking, and rapid prototyping can be a genuine challenge in disaster response, particularly when under pressure to deliver results in the initial stages. A process that enables innovative thinking can lead to novel approaches. Some examples include flying drones and 3D printing topography maps in the US state of Washington in 2014, public-health gaming and off-the-grid power in the Nepal earthquakes of 2015, and artificial intelligence with partners using the WhatsApp platform and X2ai in the Syrian refugee crisis in Lebanon in 2016. The Field Innovation Team (FIT), a US non-profit, uses a three-step design process to develop different approaches to disaster response, such as these.

Traditional assessment methodologies can be time-consuming, and even the 'lite' versions, which are geared for rapid response, can lead to a lack of alignment between data and activities, and missed opportunities for creative solutions. FIT has used theories of change, log-frame analysis, and other models in past grant opportunities. Although these take time to create, they are useful in certain cases. In a humanitarian setting, where survival can be a matter of timing and quick thinking, a framework that is quickly and easily understood is a definite asset. The FIT team needed an approach that could be built quickly and easily adjusted until it is right. Three steps are easy to remember.

Step 1: What? Assess the situation to determine the problem(s).
Step 2: Who and why? Complete the following sentence: _____ needs a way to _____ because/in order to _____.
Step 3: How? Develop different solutions that will address the problem(s).

The first step in the design process is to gain a good awareness of the situation to ensure that everyone can focus on the essential elements. It is important

http://dx.doi.org/10.3362/9781780449531.019

to observe the event, obtain as much information as you can, and pinpoint where you will focus. For instance, are you looking to contain an area, triage survivors, or facilitate an evacuation process? In addition to directly observing what is going on in the emergency, collect data through social media. When they are available, photos, identifying words, and overall sentiment analysis of posts on social media such as Twitter, Instagram and Facebook can provide the perspective of other individuals who are experiencing the emergency.

After gathering as much external data as possible through your own personal account and the accounts of the community impacted by the emergency, we encourage people to graphically illustrate what the team is focusing on rather than simply writing it down. Graphic facilitation is an effective communication method when interacting with populations that do not all speak the same language and/or have limited time to discuss with responders. We used illustrations to record information and project results to Syrians who only spoke Arabic to get permission for our plastic upcycling initiative to create cold-weather insulation in the Syrian refugee camps in Lebanon.

FIT's second stage is to develop a 'challenge statement'. This statement establishes who will benefit from the project the most and why. It is imperative that this is as targeted as possible – too broad, or with too many grey areas, and it is likely that you will end up generating a range of solutions none of which focuses on those who need the solution or why you are solving it.

Third, FIT defines the specific activities needed to address the challenge identified in step two.

- During this phase, you will come up with as many different ideas as you can, providing rough sketches or notes of each of the ideas. There are several design techniques to extract variations on ideas to build additional options for solving the challenge statement in step two.
- It is also important not to rule out ideas. FIT uses an improvisational activity called 'Yes, and …' where, before the next idea is given, you must state and complete the phrase 'Yes, and …' to make sure not to disqualify any ideas.

Once there has been an opportunity to come up with a variety of solutions to satisfy the 'how', then narrow it down to select one that best fits the requirements of the challenge. Flowing selection, an emergency prototyping process that involves building the solution (and, at times, building upon an already existing prototype), can be used to make day-to-day non-emergency decisions as well. This process can be completed within 24 to 48 hours (sometimes even more quickly). This timeframe should be sufficient to roll out potential solutions for testing in the ongoing situation.

Three-step model case study

In March 2014, a landslide struck the US state of Washington, leaving scores dead and causing at least $50 million in damages. Eyewitness survivors in the decimated area described a wall of mud, perhaps eight metres high, racing across the valley toward them with the sound of freight trains. Landslide debris was as much as 18 metres deep, covered roughly 50 homes, and closed a highway for nearly two months.

Step 1: To gain situational awareness, FIT deployed a team to the area where they were able to view the slide, take photos, and understand the magnitude of the disaster. They listened to the local authorities who had formed an 'Incident Command' (a mechanism that brings police, fire, and rescue services under a single management structure), survivors, and the community to get an understanding of the situation. There were a myriad of problems connected with the mudslide that could have been selected, but listening to the Incident Command led FIT to focus on the mudslide in its entirety, and this is what was shown in the first-stage drawing.

Step 2: FIT developed the challenge statement. Search and rescue teams needed a way to map out where the teams would go to continue recovery efforts each day that would ensure they were safe and could carry out their mission efficiently. Our challenge statement filled in the 'who' and 'why' blanks by writing; 'Responders need a way to observe the entire disaster zone in order to strategically place search and rescue teams in stable areas for recovery efforts.'

Step 3: The organization thought of many solutions using the 'Yes, and …' approach. One proposal was to use of trampolines to disperse the weight of responders and allow them to navigate across the slide using a 'leapfrog' approach. Although this solution seemed unrealistic to a risk manager concerned about liability, it led the team to the eventual solution of flying drones to collect data and imagery that could be used to 3D print a topographical map of the mudslide for the emergency management. FIT provided first responders with the tools to create an interactive 3D model of the mudslide.

About the author

Desiree (Desi) Matel-Anderson, JD, is FIT's chief wrangler. She deploys teams into disasters to empower humans to create cutting-edge solutions. She is a former chief innovation advisor of FEMA and a graduate of Harvard's National Preparedness Leadership Institute.

CHAPTER 20
Design identification: Planting the seeds of empathy

Rich Lehrer and Annie Johnson

Authentic and purposeful design can have a significant impact on producing innovative results. To scale and create even larger impact, passing this knowledge on to others – through training and education – is essential. This chapter describes recent efforts by the authors to pass design skills on to students in order to not only build knowledge of process and technology, but also to foster empathy toward others. This approach can have a range of applications in international aid. The chapter includes a number of lessons learned about the importance of interviewing, prototyping and rapid iteration.

Keywords: design, learning, empathy, technology

How can we use authentic and purposeful design projects to help people become more empathic individuals? This is a worthwhile question in a number of humanitarian settings and, in particular, in the education sector.

There has been a recent acknowledgement of the importance of teaching so-called success skills – skills that will allow students to be successful in a rapidly changing future. As our world becomes more and more connected, and young people have greater opportunities to interact with others, the skill of being able to consider another's perspective is becoming increasingly important. So, in the same way that educators would never expect students to become better collaborators, users of technology, communicators, or problem solvers without the explicit teaching of these skills, educators are coming to realize that the key to students becoming more empathic individuals is building opportunities to practice, reflect on, and improve these skills into the school day.

Projects steeped in design thinking and, in particular, those centring on students working to contribute solutions to others' problems, provide powerful opportunities for students to be put in a position of *having* to consider perspectives other than their own. Of these, experiences involving 3D modelling and printing appear to be particularly well suited to this type of empathy education. These powerful tools allow students, working with others, to co-identify design problems in their lives, communities, and world; and to use any of a suite of free and effective design programmes to rapidly prototype, iterate, and implement high quality authentic solutions. Although students can begin to feel like actual engineers through this work, they quickly learn that the keys to an effective solution are surprisingly human in nature. Conversing, listening, understanding, empathizing, receiving feedback, and reflecting – combined with frequent and increasingly specific 'check ins' – end up being far more important to the production of successful and functional solutions than engineering or design skills.

At Brookwood School in Manchester, Massachusetts, we have been exploring some interesting territory in terms of the use of 3D design and authentic STEM (science, technology, engineering, and mathematics) work to help our students become more empathic. In 2013, we became one of the first schools in the world to create a 3D printed prosthetic for a child, a project which effectively launched us into the world of authentic 3D design. With this initial powerful example of the potential of this technology, and a burgeoning partnership with the Enable Community Foundation, came the realization that there were incredibly valuable educational experiences and empathy-training opportunities to be explored. Soon, we were expanding our work by having students move beyond the simple printing and assembly of devices for this boy to the creation of small, activity-specific clips to fit an e-NABLE adaptor created by a team at Seattle Pacific University.

Looking for expanded opportunities for our students to have the opportunity to engage with members of our school community in the generation of solutions to their problems, in 2014 our school created a tool called the Brookwood 3D-Design Problem Bank. This online platform allows anyone from our community to post a problem in need of a solution. Students select a problem from the collection to work on and then enter into an ongoing relationship with the problem's poster centred around the creation of ever-improving iterations of solutions until a refined and functional solution is created.

Success with this model led us to search for design relationships in the community outside of our school. In May 2016 we connected with the Harborlight House, an affordable housing residence for seniors in the US town of Beverly, Massachusetts. They had indicated a willingness to work with our sixth-grade students in problem finding and solving efforts. Following a presentation about the nature of 3D printing, pairs of students began by developing connections with individual residents and moved to conversations about areas of the residents' lives that might be made easier with the creation of personalized assistive devices. Multiple visits to the residence, repeated sharing of different iterations, and considerable opportunities to implement resident feedback in the improvement of designs led to surprisingly deep connections between students and residents and the development of sophisticated student inventions such as cardholders, key sleeves, cup spill catchers, and improved bingo chips that proved surprisingly functional and helpful to the residents.

Along our journey toward having students create real solutions to authentic design challenges, we have learned some important lessons:

- Interviewing for empathy is a key to effective designing for others.
- Prototyping with conventional materials is important in helping students 'get their heads around' design solutions.
- Rapid iteration and going through the design cycle many times (redesigning, printing, testing, and evaluating), is the engine that churns out excellent student solutions.
- Efforts to decrease the time needed to print ever-improving iterations (focusing on slices of a device, or outlines of parts in order to confirm specifications) paid huge dividends.

New technologies are allowing young people to conceive and create hyper-effective solutions to problems and are creating unparalleled opportunities to engage in community and global problem finding and solving. These deep relationships between students and community members in search of solutions provide fertile ground for seeds of empathy to grow into deep understanding, empowered digital humanitarianism, and a sense of agency rarely seen in schools.

About the authors

Rich Lehrer is innovation coordinator at the Brookwood School in Manchester, Massachusetts and was the education coordinator for the Enable Community Foundation. He has been exploring the use of authentic STEM and design work to engage students and help them develop empathy since 2010.

Annie Johnson is a science teacher who has been using authentic STEM projects to engage students and inspire teachers in the US and Zimbabwe since 2001. She has worked at Brookwood School since 2007 as the sixth-grade science teacher and science department coordinator. Currently serving as the interim upper-school division head, Annie believes deeply in the importance of global competency education and the use of authentic STEM and design projects to help students find their place in the world.

CHAPTER 21
Open-source 3D printing

Joshua M. Pearce

3D printing can have a definitive role in fostering innovation by enabling local production of materials from recycled waste, and off-grid solar photovoltaic-powered distributed manufacturing of high-value products. The technological improvements and innovations resulting from open-source 3D printing being used as a distributed manufacturing technology can benefit resource-constrained areas, including those undergoing crisis. This includes the ability to locally fabricate 3D printers, useful products, and the printing filament to make them using local materials. Work in these areas shows enormous potential for radically improving the lives of people and communities affected by disaster.

Keywords: 3D printing, appropriate technology, distributed manufacturing, open source, recycling

The development of the open-source RepRap (self-replicating rapid prototyper) project (Sells et al., 2010; Jones et al., 2011; Bowyer, 2014) created enough competition in the 3D printing market to aggressively reduce the costs (Rundle, 2014). The costs of these libre and open-source 3D printers have now dropped to a few hundred dollars, making them viable candidates for a new model of humanitarian distributed manufacturing in both the developed and the developing worlds (Pearce et al., 2010; Rifkin, 2012 and 2014; Birtchnell and Hoyle, 2014).

As 3D printers can manufacture bespoke components or products from an exponentially increasing list of free designs (Wittbrodt et al., 2013) they can be used for both disaster relief (e.g., by Field Ready) and providing access to fabrication (e.g., iLab Haiti) while reducing the costs of products for the world's poorest people. This chapter reviews the current status of humanitarian applications of open-source 3D printing and its role in fostering innovation; discusses tools and mechanisms to enable local production of 3D printing materials; and analyses the current state and technical viability of off-grid solar-powered 3D printing.

Open-source 3D printing fostering innovation in humanitarian applications

The RepRap project uses fused filament fabrication (FFF) that can make most of its own parts as well as millions of products and product components. FFF creates an object by depositing material in layers, applying a heated new layer

http://dx.doi.org/10.3362/9781780449531.021

to those already in place. When Bowyer originally released RepRap designs and software they were both free and open source (reprap.org). Since then, hundreds of individuals, groups, and companies from all over the world have improved the technology by increasing speed, improving resolution and reliability, expanding the variety of materials used, and increasing the build volume, all while decreasing the number of parts, assembly time, and costs. Thus, following the free and open-source technical development model, the RepRap itself is an example of how the innovation cycle is accelerated when many people work together on technology free of intellectual property impediments (Raymond, 2001; Rundle, 2014).

Although open-source 3D printing itself can be thought of as a humanitarian technology, it is also a tool for producing a wide range of products or components that have humanitarian applications. First, and foremost, it can be used for inexpensive rapid prototyping to try new ideas without investing significant capital or time in conventional prototyping. However, 3D printing also enables low-cost distributed production that can be used to produce less-expensive and custom end products.

For example, 3D printing could radically improve access to eye care by enabling consumers to fabricate self-refractive glasses for a tiny fraction of the cost of either conventional glasses or commercial self-adjustable systems (Gwamuri et al., 2014). Thus, open-source 3D printing provides the capacity to locally fabricate and optimize products. For example, organic farmers on small plots of land may appreciate being able to print hand tools like a fruit picker, food-processing tools like cassava presses, animal management tools such as a chicken feeder, and water-related components like spigots and pumps (Pearce, 2015a). Similarly, high quality bicycle replacement parts can be fabricated with a 3D printer (Tanikella, et al., 2017). These and many other open-source appropriate technologies (OSAT) (Pearce, 2012) housed on Appropedia (appropedia.org) and other websites can be 3D printed in the community that can decide exactly what it needs. This can provide substantial economic value to rural communities.

Open-source 3D printing can also be readily used for humanitarian medical applications. For example, Enabling the Future (enablingthefuture.org) is a global community of over 7,000 volunteers who own or operate 3D printers and use them to print low-cost prosthetics for children around the world (Schull, 2015). The open-source 3D printable prosthetic hands have the potential to help many people who do not have the ability to pay for expensive proprietary prosthetics sold commercially. They can give people the opportunity to do work and make money in a way that they were not previously able to because of physical constraints. There are clearly many such opportunities to help one another in the global community.

Local recycling for local 3D printing materials

Commercial 3D printing filament is often unavailable in developing communities and the cost is, potentially, prohibitive for the poorest communities. 3D printing filament generally costs $20/kg or more.

However, these costs can be reduced to well under $1/kg by obtaining filament using recyclebot technology and waste plastic (Baechler et al., 2013, Zhong & Pearce, 2018) for single or even multiple cycles (Cruz et al., 2015; Sanchez, et al. 2017).

The Ethical Filament Foundation (ef.techfortrade.org) is a non-profit organization whose goal is to grow the waste-plastic recycling industry through the underdeveloped world using 3D printing-filament fabrication with recyclebots and their variants. They assist waste pickers to increase their income, which is normally limited to pennies per day. This is done by waste pickers taking plastics from landfills and using recyclebots to make low-cost filament while being paid fairly for their work. This will benefit both people and the planet as these plastics articles will be used again immediately instead of decaying over centuries in landfills. To obtain the Ethical Filament stamp of approval, which shows that the filament was ethically produced and is of high quality, the filament produced is tested for quality (Feeley et al., 2014).

Solar-powered 3D printing for off-grid households

For open-source 3D printing to be viable in most communities in developing countries there must be a source of electric power. However, roughly 79 per cent of the people in the world's 50 poorest nations have no access to electricity (Gronewold, 2009). Generally, people in the most need live in remotely located and isolated communities without access to a reliable road network or the electrical grid.

Fortunately, off-grid solar-powered 3D printers have been developed for semi-mobile (e.g., located at a school) and mobile systems (King et al., 2014, Wong, 2015, Gwamuri et al., 2016). The mobile systems can be used by relief or development workers to make, for example, replacement parts for any rural development centre (Pearce et al., 2010), school science programme (Pearce, 2013), medical clinic (Pearce, 2015b), or for items for disaster relief (Dotz, 2015). Thus, this technology has the potential to help alleviate the problems of science-equipment shortages in developing-world schools, which has a direct effect on innovation in those areas. Finally, open-source 3D printing also makes it possible to deliver just-in-time equipment to medical centres by making much-needed hardware available at a fraction of the cost of the equivalent items from conventional sources.

Conclusions

It is clear from the work being done on open-source 3D printers, free designs, recycling waste plastic into 3D filament, and solar-powered 3D printers that the open-source paradigm applied to distributed additive manufacturing has enormous potential for radically improving the lives of people and communities affected by disasters.

References

Baechler, C., DeVuono, M. and Pearce, J.M. (2013) 'Distributed Recycling of Waste Polymer into RepRap Feedstock', *Rapid Prototyping Journal*, 19(2), pp. 118–125.

Birtchnell, T. and Hoyle, W. (2014) *3D Printing for Development in the Global South: The 3D4D Challenge*, Springer.

Bowyer, A. (2014) 3D Printing and Humanity's First Imperfect Replicator, *3D Printing and Additive Manufacturing*, 1(1), pp. 4–5.

Cruz, F., Lanza, S., Boudaoud, H., Hoppe, S. and Camargo, M. (2015) 'Polymer Recycling and Additive Manufacturing in an Open Source Context: Optimization of Processes and Methods', Solid Freeform Fabrication Symposium, Austin, TX, pp. 10–12.

Dotz, A.D. (2015) 'A Pilot of 3D Printing of Medical Devices in Haiti', in S. Hostettler, E. Hazboun and J.-C. Bolay, (eds.) *Technologies for Development: What is Essential?*, pp. 33–44, Springer International Publishing, Switzerland.

Feeley, S.R., Wijnen, B. and Pearce, J.M. (2014) 'Evaluation of Potential Fair Trade Standards for an Ethical 3D Printing Filament', *Journal of Sustainable Development*, 7(5), pp. 1–12.

Gronewold, N. (2009) 'One-Quarter of World's Population Lacks Electricity', *Scientific American*, 24.

Gwamuri, J., Franco, D., Khan, K.Y., Gauchia, L. and Pearce, J.M. (2016) 'High-Efficiency Solar-Powered 3D Printers for Sustainable Development', *Machines*, 4(1), p. 3.

Gwamuri, J., Wittbrodt, B.T., Anzalone, N.C. and Pearce, J.M. (2014) 'Reversing the Trend of Large Scale and in Manufacturing: The Case of Distributed Manufacturing of Customizable 3D Printable Self-Adjustable Glasses', *Challenges in Sustainability*, 2(1), pp. 30–40.

Jones, R., Haufe, P., Sells, E., Iravani, P., Olliver, V., Palmer, C. and Bowyer, A. (2011) 'RepRap–the Replicating Rapid Prototyper', *Robotica*, 29(1), pp. 177-191.

King, D., Babasola, A., Rozario, J. & Pearce, J.M. (2014) 'Mobile Open-Source Solar-Powered 3D Printers for Distributed Manufacturing in Off-Grid Communities', *Challenges in Sustainability*, 2(1), pp. 18–27.

Pearce, J.M. (2012) The Case for Open Source Appropriate Technology, *Environment, Development and Sustainability*, 14(3), pp. 425–431.

Pearce, J.M. (2013) *Open-Source Lab: How to Build Your Own Hardware and Reduce Research Costs*, Elsevier, Waltham MA.

Pearce, J.M. (2015a) 'Applications of Open Source 3D Printing on Small Farms', *Organic Farming*, 1(1), pp. 19–35.

Pearce, J.M. (2015b) 'Maximizing Return on Investment for Public Health with Open-Source Medical Hardware', *Gaceta Sanitaria*, 29(4), p. 319.

Pearce, J.M., Blair, C.M., Laciak, K.J., Andrews, R., Nosrat, A. and Zelenika-Zovko, I. (2010) 3D Printing of Open Source Appropriate Technologies for Self-Directed Sustainable Development, *Journal of Sustainable Development*, 3(4), pp. 17–29.

Raymond, E.S. (2001) *The Cathedral & the Bazaar: Musings on Linux and Open Source by an Accidental Revolutionary*. O'Reilly Media, Inc.: Sebastopol, CA.

Rifkin, J. (2012) 'The Third Industrial Revolution: How the Internet, Green Electricity, and 3D Printing are Ushering in a Sustainable Era of Distributed Capitalism', *World Financial Review*, pp. 4052–4057.

Rifkin, J. (2014) *The Zero Marginal Cost Society: The Internet of Things, The Collaborative Commons, and the Eclipse of Capitalism*, Palgrave Macmillan, New York, NY.

Rundle, G. (2014) *A Revolution in the Making: 3D Printing, Robots and the Future*, Affirm Press, Melbourne.

Sanchez, F. A. C., Boudaoud, H., Hoppe, S. and Camargo, M. (2017), 'Polymer recycling in an open-source additive manufacturing context: Mechanical issues', *Additive Manufacturing*, *17*, pp. 87–105.

Schull, J. (2015) 'Enabling the Future: Crowdsourced 3D printed Prosthetics as a Model for Open Source Assistive Technology Innovation and Mutual Aid', *Proceedings of the 17th International ACM SIGACCESS Conference on Computers & Accessibility*, ACM.

Sells, E., Smith, Z., Bailard, S., Bowyer, A. and Olliver, V. (2010) 'RepRap: The Replicating Rapid Prototyper: Maximizing Customizability by Breeding the Means of Production', *Handbook of Research in Mass Customization and Personalization*, pp. 568–580.

Tanikella, N.G., Savonen, B., Gershenson, J. and Pearce, J.M. (2017), 'Viability of distributed manufacturing of bicycle components with 3-D printing: CEN standardized polylactic acid pedal testing', *Journal of Humanitarian Engineering*, 5(1), pp. 8–17.

Wittbrodt, B.T., Glover, A.G., Laureto, J., Anzalone, G.C., Oppliger, D., Irwin, J.L. and Pearce, J.M. (2013) 'Life-Cycle Economic Analysis of Distributed Manufacturing with Open-Source 3D printers' *Mechatronics*, 23(6), pp. 713–726.

Wong, J.Y. (2015) 'Ultra-Portable Solar-Powered 3D Printers for Onsite Manufacturing of Medical Resources', *Aerospace medicine and human performance*, 86(9), pp. 830–834.

Zhong, S. and Pearce, J.M. (2018), 'Tightening the loop on the circular economy: Coupled distributed recycling and manufacturing with recyclebot and RepRap 3-D printing', *Resources, Conservation and Recycling*, *128*, pp. 48–58.

About the author

Joshua M. Pearce, PhD, runs the Open Sustainability Technology Research Group in the Department of Materials Science & Engineering and Department of Electrical and Computer Engineering, Michigan Technological University. His research concentrates on the use of open-source appropriate technology in sustainability and poverty reduction.

CHAPTER 22

Piloting 3D printing technology to increase access to prosthetic devices

Matt Ratto

This chapter considers the case study of Nia Technology Inc. (Nia), a Canadian non-profit social enterprise that develops and deploys 3D printed prosthetics, and the challenges they faced navigating the pilot phase of a technical innovation. This chapter describes the principles used to design and implement the innovation; the long process of 'proving' and iterating the innovation; some of the obstacles (which, in large part, stemmed from the 'newness' of the technology); and early thinking on a future business model.

Keywords: 3D printing, prosthetic devices, design, technology

Throughout the pilot stage of an innovation, humanitarian-innovation managers must navigate challenges of programme design, implementation and iteration. This case study looks at the pilot phase of a technical innovation through the lens of the experiences of Nia Technology Inc. Nia, a Canadian non-profit social enterprise, was created by charitable organization cbm Canada to develop and deploy innovations in the orthopaedic space. In the following four sections, the chapter will examine the principles used to design and implement the innovation; the long process of 'proving' and iterating the innovation; some of the obstacles faced by Nia (which, in large part, stemmed from the 'newness' of the technology); and early thinking on a future business model.

Nia is developing a system that merges traditional orthopaedic expertise and skills in manual production with 3D design and printing technologies to create a digital toolchain (3D PrintAbility) that will enable orthopaedic clinicians to produce more mobility devices in low- and middle-income countries.

Nia's initial aim is to use 3D PrintAbility to produce devices for children and young people (5–25 years old) with lower-limb disabilities. Preliminary research shows that 3D PrintAbility enables orthopaedic workshops to produce high-quality devices more quickly than with the conventional manual methods used in developing countries.

Design and implementation: aspiring to long-term transformation

With the aim of creating a long-term improvement, Nia uses the following methods and principles (which apply to both the technology itself and

http://dx.doi.org/10.3362/9781780449531.022

the approach to implementing the technology) to develop and iterate the innovation:

- Design with local needs in mind (in response to what is perceived locally as an issue or problem)
- Develop collaboratively and field-test/evaluate in target clinical settings
- Design to enable orthopaedic clinicians in low-income countries to adopt the product and adapt it to their local environment and workflow
- Manage and maintain locally (with ongoing technical support from Nia)
- Focus on long-term benefits to local people (people with disabilities, clinicians, and hospital administrators etc.).

Nia manages the innovation by beginning with a change process that is designed to make it very easy for existing systems to adapt to and adopt the innovation, then moves towards approaches that align with the longer-term purposes of aid efforts, i.e. to build local capacity. In short, we focus on long-term transformation by using the following short-term tactics:

Fitting in with existing aid efforts and established systems: The aim of the innovation is to speed up the process of producing and fitting a prosthetic or orthotic device for a child by using commodity 3D technologies. Commodity technology refers to widely available, affordable, standard-issue products, including commercially available 3D scanners, design software, and printers, as opposed to highly specialized high-performance products. To simplify adoption, the innovation is designed to mirror the polypropylene process (first developed by the ICRC in 1979) for producing custom prosthetics and orthotics. The innovation reflects each step in the traditional manual process (plaster casting and thermoforming with polypropylene) with digital tools that speed up the slowest parts of the existing process and keep a digital record of the design.

In field trials carried out by Nia, manual manipulation of the plaster cast and thermo-plaster process is replaced by 3D scanning, design, and printing. With traditional manual methods, the production of a prosthetic lower limb takes about five days. When digital tools are combined with an experienced clinician's knowledge and skill, the design and production process is cut to about a day and a half.

Enhancing, rather than replacing, local capacities: The innovation was developed with a focus on enhancing the capacity of local clinicians (as opposed to developing a parallel process that might bypass existing professionals). The main barrier to procurement and use of prosthetics and orthotic devices in the developing world is a lack of access to trained and skilled orthopaedic clinicians. The issue is one of capacity and cannot be solved simply by adding funding. Training on, and access to, 3D printing technology increases existing clinical capacity by providing the means for orthopaedic clinicians to make prosthetics and orthotic devices more quickly. It does not reduce or remove the need for orthopaedic clinicians in a clinical or rehabilitation setting.

By building on clinical skills and expertise, the 3D PrintAbility innovation enables clinicians to minimize time spent on manual production and maximize time spent making decisions about device design, fit, and patient care. The 3D technology becomes another tool in the orthopaedic workshop: the clinician takes a scan of the patient's residual limb, and uses software developed by Nia to create a biomechanically accurate design. The component is then printed and integrated with the mass-produced components from ICRC. Our system only replaces the custom parts: the mass-produced parts – such as connectors, pylons, and feet – are cheaper if sourced through ICRC rather than 3D printed.

The motivation to find a viable solution to the real problem is demonstrated here by the focus on working within the pre-existing social, professional, and technical context by building on existing efforts, systems, and local capacities. It seems that too many innovation projects are motivated by the application, or scaling, of a purely technological solution without the due consideration of the context that would make it viable. The former motivation offers a greater chance of implementing a long-term solution to a problem; the latter motivation can result in interventions that are not possible to sustain without the physical presence of outside short-term technical experts (who may prevent the building of more permanent capacity).

Proving and iterating the innovation

For all new innovations, it is important to build up an evidence base to prove the efficacy of the innovation, especially when the innovation integrates technology that is new or unfamiliar to the sector (in this case, to both the humanitarian and medial sectors).

At the time of writing, Nia is undertaking a large-scale clinical evaluation of its 3D PrintAbility innovation (by the end of the field-testing phase, over 200 patients at four clinical sites in three low-income countries will have been tested over the course of two years). The goal of the trial is to be able to make statistically significant claims about the durability, fit, accuracy, and overall use of the 3D printed device when directly compared to traditional devices. Nia set this goal for two key reasons:

- To prove that the technology is sufficient for both the developing and developed world
- To show ministries, governments, and larger organizations that usually provide medical assistance in the relevant contexts that the process is effective.

A third, unexpected, benefit to the trials quickly emerged:

- The trials demonstrated Nia's commitment to improving the clinical process to clinicians and other stakeholders, thereby strengthening key relationships.

Nia has used the pilot phase (field-testing) to iterate the innovation. Getting the technology right for the context is, clearly, of vital importance to maximizing the impact of the innovation. The clinical evaluation phase provided time for Nia to test its assumptions about what the appropriate trade-offs were. As an example, the team decided to use a 3D printer that is relatively easy to maintain and repair in situ, as opposed to the easiest-to-use printer available. This decision required the team to trust the technical capacity of the orthopaedic clinicians (as professionals already working with a range of tools and equipment), but significantly enhanced the durability of the innovation.

Obstacles

There are at least three key obstacles worth considering if launching a similar set of activities.

Managing expectations: There are several considerations about the realities of 3D printing that need to be taken into account. People across the board perceive 3D printing as a magical technology, and 3D printing of prosthetics as a solved problem. Media rhetoric around 3D printing has required Nia to educate people (particularly funders) on how to interpret claims made by other projects or researchers.

Scepticism of professionals: In part due to the rhetoric around 3D printing, it has taken Nia some time to convince orthopaedic clinicians in the developed world of the merits and potential of 3D technologies. Key to overcoming this challenge was helping the profession understand that 3D printing technologies would not replace clinicians with computer-aided design (CAD) designers in Canada (or elsewhere), nor would their craft and expertise be transformed into manual labour. Integrating 3D technologies into the profession by retaining the clinician at the centre of the design and production process remains a major aspect of Nia's work.

Knowledge and approach of funders: Not all funders are set up to fund projects that are not designed to produce large-scale, quantifiable results in the short term. Investment in professional development, quality, and patient care takes time and significant resources. Technology funders, in particular, have grown accustomed to a specific notion of scale: one that says technology innovations can be scaled quickly, leading to quick and large-scale results, providing opportunities for funders that require a relatively short-term commitment.

Business model: opportunities and challenges

Over the course of the pilot, a number of thoughts emerged about the future business model. Questions have emerged around going beyond philanthropy, a dual-market approach, and Nia's attitude to openness.

The next step for Nia is to establish a business model for the innovation – a step that many innovative organizations, large and small, are grappling with.

Generally speaking, small organizations focused on fostering a product or process innovation face the demand to wean themselves off grant funding; larger organizations which foster innovation within a much broader operation commonly face a consideration of whether a given innovation can thrive within the organization or whether it must 'spin out' in order to reach scale. Generating a revenue stream that is not dependent only on philanthropic grants or on resource extraction from the developing world is a requirement of one of Nia's major funders, and has been encouraged by other funders. Nia and its funders believe that moving away from reliance on philanthropic funding partnerships will contribute to long-term stability and sustainability for the organization. It would enhance Nia's ability to proactively adapt to and shape procurement, technological change, monitoring, and evaluation.

Nia's current focus is, therefore, on developing a dual-market strategy: a business model that creates a balance between developing- and developed-world revenue streams while selling similar products in both markets. The key to this approach is finding a niche for the innovation in the developed world which resembles the developing-world context.

One way to increase impact, possibly at the cost of sustainability for the organization, would be to open source all of the research and testing undertaken by Nia over the course of the project. This would go beyond the existing academic publications to producing how-to guides and releasing the software that enables clinicians to operate the process. However, this raises two key concerns: sustaining funding for the core organization could become more difficult; and safeguarding the process would become impossible for Nia.

As an organization introducing a new technical innovation to a clinical environment, Nia has an ethical responsibility to ensure that applications are safe and appropriate. Nia currently vets and validates the clinical settings into which the innovation is introduced. It ensures that the setting has adequate infrastructure, experienced orthopaedic clinicians, and a sufficient level of training in the profession. This provides assurance that the people using the system are using their professional knowledge to create good patient outcomes. If the innovation was open sourced, there would be nothing to prevent a design student or a biomedical student from taking the technology to, for example, a refugee camp and becoming the prosthetist, making prostheses and leaving. The result would be poor long-term patient outcomes (e.g., poorly made or fitted prosthetics) and long-term damage to the profession by replacing existing capacity with capacity from the developed world.

About the author

Matt Ratto, PhD, is an associate professor in the Faculty of Information at the University of Toronto and directs the Semaphore Research cluster on inclusive design, mobile and pervasive computing and, as part of Semaphore, the Critical Making lab. He is also chief science officer at Nia Technologies.

CHAPTER 23

Opportunities and challenges in the HELIOS project

Martijn Blansjaar

The software package known as HELIOS was developed to help meet the demands of humanitarian supply-chain management and integrate logistics into programme design and planning. Initiated by the Fritz Institute and a number of NGOs following the 2004 Asian tsunami, it was envisaged as a sector-wide generic supply-chain information system. This chapter explains the development of HELIOS and reflects on the challenges faced by Oxfam in trying to implement this innovation. Finally, it describes barriers to developing a sector-wide solution through multi-agency collaboration.

Keywords: ICT, supply-chain management, innovation process, collaboration

Innovations related to information communications technology (ICT) have been making their way into the humanitarian sector increasingly over the last decade. The purpose of many of these innovations is to improve processes that are key to the back-office operation of humanitarian organizations; these are process innovations. Examples that have been piloted and implemented on a large scale include systems supporting beneficiary registrations, distribution management, and market analysis.

To help meet the demands of humanitarian supply-chain management (SCM) and integrate logistics into programme design and planning, a software package known as HELIOS was developed. This was initiated by the Fritz Institute, in partnership with a number of NGOs, in the aftermath of the 2004 Asian tsunami. It was envisaged as a sector-wide generic supply-chain information system.

The remainder of this chapter will explain the background to the development of HELIOS, before reflecting on the challenges faced by Oxfam while developing and implementing the innovation. Finally, it will consider barriers to developing a sector-wide solution through multi-agency collaboration. The intention is to draw out lessons from the process of developing and implementing HELIOS that are useful for those who are engaged in developing and implementing a process innovation within an organization, or in developing a cross-sector innovation to address a common challenge.

http://dx.doi.org/10.3362/9781780449531.023

Rolling out the system

In 2008, Oxfam took the strategic decision to implement HELIOS across the majority of its programmes. After a year of further development and testing, the large-scale implementation of HELIOS was undertaken rapidly; the aim was to implement the system in 18 programme countries, covering 70 per cent of Oxfam's portfolio in financial terms, over a five-year period. HELIOS was intended to fundamentally update two aspects of the process of SCM within Oxfam.

First, HELIOS established a new way of managing logistics. Rather than simply automating existing processes, the new system introduced the requirement for periodic collaborative supply planning in every project. Changing circumstances, such as fluctuating beneficiary numbers, can change supply needs on the ground. HELIOS therefore improved the previous system by providing logisticians with up-to-date information.

Second, HELIOS instituted an automated request-to-delivery process with the associated advantage of tighter controls and better visibility. While there was a diligent and detailed administration of expenditure across Oxfam's programmes prior to the implementation of HELIOS, this did not provide a real-time and accessible view of supply-chain transactions and inventory rules. There was, therefore, no way to examine supply-chain performance and to identify possible improvements. HELIOS introduced detailed real-time information within and, to some extent, across programmes, enabling quantitative analysis, evaluation, and target setting.

At least two key challenges were identified in the HELIOS project. These resulted in part from a disconnect between the development of the HELIOS software and the realities of implementation in the field.

Technology infrastructure: The deployment of online SCM software required solid infrastructure and connectivity, training, considerable time to organize and load data, and dedicated change management. It is of vital importance that software developers fully understand the reality of field operations and that decision makers and budget holders at headquarters sufficiently recognize the investment necessary to prepare field offices to adopt the new system.

Complex reality: Relief and development programmes are complex. Programmes are anything but fixed, repeatable processes. The extent to which operational variety and complexity would challenge implementation of the HELIOS system was not fully realized in advance. For example, in Oxfam programmes there were six ways to buy fuel with different delivery and payment methods. Several ways may have been in use in one country, yet not all were possible everywhere. Introducing a single way of doing things risked paralyzing operations or alienating staff who would then resort to their old ways of doing business. Either of these eventualities would undermine the implementation of the new system.

While Oxfam was prepared for some of the challenges encountered during the development and implementation of HELIOS, it had not anticipated them all prior to the roll-out. Rapidly implementing HELIOS across the majority of Oxfam programmes was not a good way of dealing with challenges as they arose.

An incremental roll-out may have allowed Oxfam to get things right before moving to the next country programme. It would have given a greater degree of flexibility in local implementation, and it would have allowed for more time to achieve a high level of local-user skill. However, it would also have taken much longer to achieve the same volume of benefits and, given the more marginal trajectory, the question is whether such an approach would have been able to maintain the necessary level of management support.

One significant lesson from the implementation of HELIOS in Oxfam was that measuring the quantifiable impact of the innovation on the SCM system was more difficult and took longer than expected. The main anticipated advantages put forward in the internal case for support were: reductions in supply-chain wastage, supply-chain fraud, transport cost, and logistician time; improved planning (leading to better achievement of an on-schedule delivery) and tracking of materials through the supply chain; and better and more timely information supporting better management practices.

Despite the anticipated advantages, the HELIOS Foundation came up against numerous barriers in efforts to engage with other agencies. Examining these barriers begins to explain some of the underlying obstacles to using innovation to improve back-office operations of humanitarian organizations, as well as obstacles to collaborating on such efforts.

'Not invented here'

The development of a single SCM information system was hampered by each NGO's belief that their requirements were unique and, therefore, that they required a bespoke solution. However, from working with individual agencies through the five-agency trial, the HELIOS Foundation found that the requirements were actually quite close. The biggest hurdle to understanding the closeness of the match between different systems turned out to be in the language of the requirements. Some requirements were easy to describe and agree upon, but the majority were harder to describe in a manner that did not leave room for interpretation.

In the analysis of the START Network (then known as the Consortium of British Humanitarian Agencies, CBHA) multi-agency pilot project, the narrative of each requirement that was not a strong fit was examined. Each requirement was put into one of the following three categories:

a. Processes that would be rendered obsolete by the implementation of an information system.
b. Processes beyond the intended scope of the HELIOS system (i.e., improving the management of supply-chain information and streamlining SCM processes), such as financial or fleet management.
c. Valid features that future versions of the system should consider.

State of the product

Some organizations were tempted to wait for the system to be developed to a point where it could be deemed a perfect solution. Software projects continuously evolve, with improvements to functionality and the discovery and fixing of bugs. Many organizations will hold off on selecting software until that software system is 'finished' – a point that, in practice, may never actually be reached.

Willingness to invest

The budgets of logistics teams usually consist of funds that are restricted to individual programmes or responses. However, investment in improvements to logistics practices or, in this case, the development and deployment of a new organization-wide IS/IT system for SCM must come from unrestricted sources. Individuals spearheading process innovations must therefore make a strong internal case to compete for scarce unrestricted funds.

Limits to organizational competence

Developing and deploying a process innovation requires significant capacity in terms of time, financial resource and skill. If the organization is either unwilling or unable to supply an internal team with the appropriate skills and capacity, then the roll-out of the innovation is likely to falter or fail. For example, the logistical capacity within organizations may not be sufficient to engage with a collaborative (or similarly complex) project.

Furthermore, it was clear from the beginning of the project that the selection of a new information system is not typically within the range of expertise of most people working in a humanitarian relief organization. Further, ICT departments in many NGOs operate at full capacity. Consequently, the normal process is to contract an external consultant to guide them in the selection process. Based on our experience, many of these contracted solutions are not as sustainable as we would like because contractors are often predisposed to offer the following types of solutions:

- **Safe solution**: Being part of the herd and choosing a mainstream product protects the consultant from backlash from any software problems that arise further down the line.
- **Bespoke solution**: Where a bespoke system needs to be built, NGOs should take into account that the external consultant will have moved on to new projects before promises fail to materialize or problems with the software arise.
- **Preferred solution**: Some consultants have a preferred solution which is often provided by a company with which they have contacts who can refer business back in the future. Human factors are likely to be present, even when the selection looks unbiased on paper.

The perception of a requirements gap (i.e. the difference between what is needed and what is available) also affected the process of selection of the software system. Any system that exists and can be tested before selection is liable to find itself at a disadvantage when compared to proposed systems that are yet to be developed. This is because it is easy at the pre-sale stage to promise to meet ambitious or vague requirements.

A further selection bias can cause problems for ICT project management: suppliers who estimate low (and are, therefore, cheaper) are more likely to win a contract than suppliers who estimate more realistically and, as a result, appear to be more expensive (Jørgensen, 2013). If the contract is well written, the supplier should absorb the financial cost of any overruns, although, in practice, there would still be time implications.

In addition, NGO ICT departments may have pre-selected a strategy that excludes certain technologies or types of supplier. This is certainly the case in the government sector where only suppliers on an approved list may be used, but the practice of pre-selecting vendors can occur in the aid sector as well.

Summary

While the experience of the HELIOS project might not be reflected in the sector as a whole, vital lessons can be drawn that are applicable to multiple types of initiatives: process innovations, collaborative innovations and software innovations.

The experience of Oxfam demonstrates that implementing a large-scale ICT innovation to update a significant back-office function is a long, challenging, and resource-intensive task. High-level internal support for and commitment to the project was vital to the successful implementation of HELIOS in Oxfam.

The potential benefits of developing a collaborative solution to common challenges are significant: cost savings, greater expertise and knowledge sharing, and inter-operability. Here too, however, serious barriers exist that can hinder the initiation of a project, let alone the garnering of long-term commitment to it.

There is, clearly, still some way to go to achieve the establishment of a broad, common supply-chain information platform in the sector. Nonetheless, the approach taken to management and ownership of this software and the knowledge sharing (through the HELIOS Foundation) ensured that the project has helped to bring resource barriers down by offering a relatively simple way to take up ICT in SCM.

Reference

Jørgensen, M. (2013) 'The Influence of Selection Bias on Effort Overruns in Software Development Projects', *Information and Software Technology*, 55(9), pp. 1640–1650.

Further reading

Blansjaar, M. and Van der Merwe, C. (2011), 'The Importance of Information Technology in Humanitarian Supply Chains: Opportunities and Challenges in the HELIOS Project', in Christopher, Martin and Tatham, Peter (eds.), *Humanitarian Logistics: Meeting the Challenge of Preparing for and Responding to Disasters*, 1st edition, Kogan Page, London, pp. 47–63.

Blansjaar, M. and Stephens, F. (2014) 'Information Technology in Humanitarian Supply Chains' in Christopher, M. and Tatham, P. (eds.), *Humanitarian Logistics: Meeting the Challenge of Preparing for and Responding to Disasters*, 2nd edition, Kogan Page, London, pp. 57–76.

About the author

Martijn Blansjaar is head of supply and logistics for Oxfam GB. He has 30 years of experience in international aid and collaboration, of which 25 have been in senior positions managing programmes, technical support, and global supply chains.

CHAPTER 24
The Tao of extreme making

Brad Halsey

This chapter presents an actionable way of carrying out making (manufacturing) in a challenging relief context. It outlines three practical steps to successfully effect change on the ground. The first step is to get deeply involved with those in the field (to 'roll in it') in order to gain their perspective and have a full understanding of the problems faced. The second step is to build something useful, even if it is a rough prototype, and test it out (in other words, to 'make it/break it'). The final step is to quickly provide the end-user with what has been made (i.e., 'deliver, fast'). This simple process can make the difference between those who talk about doing something and those who actually make an impact.

Keywords: making, local manufacturing, disaster relief, assessment, partnership

The big secret? Making stuff is easy. What to make? Now that's the hard part. And that's no different whether you're in Baghdad, the Caribbean or your basement. Understanding the problem and implementing the solution are considerably more difficult than making the tech, regardless of complexity. But the making is arguably more fun – and less dangerous.

Following the devastating hurricanes that swept through the Caribbean in 2017, I volunteered for Field Ready, the NGO transforming aid by localizing manufacturing. The first thing we saw in St. Thomas, US Virgin Islands, was the utter destruction left behind by the storms. The problem was almost too big to comprehend. How do we even *begin* to dig in and make a difference? To me, it's sort of like peeling an orange: you just jam your thumb in and get on with it. If done right, it starts to have the trim tab effect described in Chapter 9.

I first learned to do this in an extreme place – flying into Baghdad in early 2008. I was hired as a civilian 'embedded geek' to help the Coalition forces improve equipment and solve on-the-ground problems with making and technology. As I travelled around Iraq trying to help, it became very apparent that to solve problems successfully I needed to immerse myself in the end-user's world. I went into the field to witness issues first-hand. I saw the tech and infrastructure people had to work with, and used what existed as a starting point for innovative solutions that actually worked.

http://dx.doi.org/10.3362/9781780449531.024

From that time in Iraq to my recent disaster relief work in the Caribbean, I have been formulating and refining the process for humanitarian problem-solving and making. It is an approach I am comfortable with, and one that is being pioneered by Field Ready worldwide. I have used them to develop a rough and totally non-comprehensive set of loose guidelines that might help others peel the orange.

The similarities between man-made and so-called natural disasters are striking. Turns out, there are really only three things you need to do to successfully effect change in these situations: (1) roll in it; (2) make it/break it; and (3) deliver, fast.

Although I have listed these things in sequence, reality dictates they happen rather more concurrently. At the very least, this process is iterative, moves fast, and becomes intertwined quickly.

Roll in it

Any effective approach to disaster response needs to be practical, no-nonsense, and centred on the user. The problems can be more blurry. The immense destruction is overwhelming and finding a starting point seems impossible. But, at some point, you just have to jam your thumb in the orange: find a place/group/organization that is doing something related to building or making solutions, and jump in. Think again about peeling an orange: the juice soon starts dripping and you're immersed in the experience as your mouth waters.

In the Caribbean, we found, among other things, a project run by a local NGO (My Brother's Workshop in St. Thomas) that was trying to repair roofs on a few houses. On the first day, we jumped in to assist, interacting with the community and their problems. We dove in deep, we immersed ourselves, we got dirty ... we rolled in it. And that led us to identify other problems we could work on – and then projects we could make and deliver. This all happened in the first twenty-four hours on the island and generated momentum to create several tech solutions during my week there.

Immersion must be with eyes and ears open, brain firing, and also with mouth moving. Communicating ideas and understandings of the problem to others – whether they are disaster-affected people, colleagues, or other stakeholders – concisely and frequently helps the rapid prototyping process – even if a particular prototype is designed, developed, tested, and, if necessary, passed over just in your head.

Make it/break it

Don't roll in it for too long. The environment is always changing and the situation evolves. Start making! Many makers have a tendency to learn as much as possible about the problem before getting to work. More information reduces stress and makes the development process more comfortable, right? Well, prepare to be uncomfortable. Recall the Cynefin Framework described in Chapter 7: it is never possible to obtain enough information to make a complex situation or problem into an obvious one. Optimization can only take you so far.

I have *never* had the entire picture or all the parameters when I have been in the thick of it. At some point I just made something. It likely didn't work, and probably frustrated a few people. I threw it out and tried again. I would break all sorts of tools and tech in the process. I have burned up whole laboratories, power supplies, furniture, computers, expensive motors, and most types of power tool. I have destroyed nearly every piece of tech I have used at least once. But that's how I do it. Experimentation makes way for iteration.

But really it's about fear. Not necessarily the fear of breaking something or screwing it up, but the fear of looking like a failure to people who need me to solve problems. The fear of feeling I just can't learn the tech. The pressure we learned as school children emerges and put brakes on our openness and creativity. I am supposed to be the professional problem-solver, right? And yet sometimes I produce failures. This *can't* be how extreme making is done, can it?

Unfortunately, yes, this is exactly how making in extreme environments is done. This how you quickly get to the solution. This is probably not a great method for learning to land a plane: iteration past the first time is a waste (or far worse). But when you need to make tech solutions, iteration may be your best friend. Besides, in relief situations, there should be a higher tolerance for risk. You really don't have the time to be afraid of digging in or learning a new tool – just do it. It's actually kind of a luxury to not have time to think whether you should or shouldn't try something. It is, perhaps, a mindset we should all adopt more often.

Deliver, fast

Over the last several years, I have had the privilege of training nearly two hundred well-qualified scientists, engineers, teachers, and professionals in extreme making. I tell them that the single most important thing you can do when making a solution for someone is to deliver it. A potential solution buried in a computer or sitting on a shelf doesn't help anyone. Show up and deliver – the single most important thing you can do. It sounds obvious, but doing it is hard. And sometimes it's very hard.

One evening in Baghdad, I received an email from a unit that was under constant attack. Insurgents would hide in alleyways and shoot at vehicles as they passed. The unit needed a camera that would allow them to view what was front of their vehicle. The cameras could help identify threats such as bombs hidden alongside the road. That was all the info I had to work with but it was enough to get started.

To help solve this problem, I worked all through the night on a pan/tilt and zoom camera system that could be mounted on an existing pole. I scheduled a trip to deliver it the next afternoon. I showed up that evening with a scrappy but workable prototype. They were astounded that I had received the email just twenty-four hours ago and was at their doorstep with something passable as a tech solution. I installed the system at first light and went out on a mission with them that day to ensure it worked. By doing this, I proved to them that I could be counted on to deliver at short notice. That trust sprouted several iterations of the camera system, as well as leading to other projects that helped a unit in a dire situation.

Delivering quickly might prove to be even more important in disaster recovery scenarios where the population is already suffering, exhausted, and feeling abandoned. Talking and working with survivors only becomes fruitful when you return the next day with a solution, however jury-rigged. Doing so makes the community feel that they are part of the rebuilding process, even if it is through what someone else has made.

In the Caribbean, this is exactly what Field Ready did. Quickly finding workable problems to solve, we made useful things and delivered them, fast. We were able to roll in and, working with a great partner, we found on the first day that many systemic issues could be traced back to lack of power. Families couldn't find loved ones because they couldn't charge their cell phones; diabetes medicine was going bad because of a lack of refrigeration; and people couldn't even register for aid because this had to be done on an online portal. We found that most of the damaged solar panels on the islands still worked. We collected a couple, spent the night rigging a system to make them functional, and tested them in the early morning sunshine. By 8:30 that morning, we had presented a new solution that could be replicated and scaled.

Conclusion

The important lesson is this: all of that rolling in it and iterative making is for naught if you don't show up quickly with something in your hand. Not in a month – tomorrow. Extreme making (now a trending term on Twitter) demands this kind of turnaround. Because if you can't deliver quickly, the people in need will lose faith in your ability to help them. You'll quickly become a marginalized battlefield or disaster-zone tinkerer. And that's not cool.

Not all solutions can be made this way, nor this quickly. But I think elements of this rapid problem-solving process should be interwoven into all making and creating. The world needs to see and experience your ideas. Life is short. So dig into whatever orange you find. Make something important.

About the author

Brad Halsey is the chief executive officer of Building Momentum, a company that brings a conflict-zone, humanitarian making and prototyping experience to the classroom through scenario-driven problem-solving workshops. He has trained hundreds of scientists, engineers, educators, military personnel, and industry professionals to solve problems using today's technology.

CHAPTER 25
Field Ready: Transforming aid worldwide

Tessa Fixsen-Lavdiotis

Field Ready, a humanitarian organization dedicated to transforming logistics through technology, innovative design, and engaging people in new ways, has developed a practical approach to innovation. This incorporates a systematic means to reach scalability.

Keywords: innovation process, scaling, design, livelihoods, health, search and rescue

An organizational approach to innovation

Field Ready is pioneering an approach that addresses the burden of slow, expensive, and cumbersome humanitarian supply chains. Field Ready has developed an organizational approach that bypasses supply-chain issues by innovating ways to make supplies and train others to do so. The result is the development of unique products and services that are faster, less expensive and, ultimately, better than existing logistical supply chains.

Our focus is on people and their problems where they experience them. For Field Ready, technology is simply a means to an end; tools that help achieve clear goals. We use exponential technology as well as appropriate technology to carry out local manufacturing in ways that have never been done before in the field. A focus on human-centred problem solving is more important than simple application of technology. By working closely with others – through meaningful partnerships, operating within existing systems and frameworks, and sharing our knowledge widely – Field Ready is a 'trim tab' in areas that will transform the way aid is delivered worldwide.

Field Ready has developed a five-step, non-linear process that enables us to work across sectors (whether DRR, search and rescue, health, WASH, livelihoods, education or food security). In following this process, we engage in a number of practices which help us arrive at novel solutions to very difficult problems. These include having a bias toward action, not differentiating between 'creative' and 'non-creative' team members, and iterating by making lots of prototypes (which means allowing for failure but also for small successes that lead to bigger results). This process also helps us understand and work within the four Cs (see chapter 4). The steps are described below.

1. Assess

To understand the context and those we work with, an assessment is undertaken. This uses mixed methods such as rapid participatory interaction, human-centred design (HCD) and lean methods. In the process, Field Ready develops a deep understanding and empathy that allows us to work toward practical and sustainable solutions with other aid workers and affected people.

2. Design

Using an iterative process, Field Ready takes into consideration smart design, technology, and how people can benefit from its proper use. The organization works closely with end users where they live and work to ensure viable impact.

3. Make

Field Ready uses experienced people and the right technology when working with local makers and manufacturers so that genuine needs can be met, regardless of the sector or challenge faced. We possess the capacity to meet unique needs and then take solutions to scale.

4. Share

Timely distribution is the essential element of an effective supply chain and this represents one of the key advantages of local manufacturing. We share not only the items we repair, make unique parts for and mass-produce them, but also the knowledge that has been developed through hard-earned experience. We do this through training and other capacity-building measures at all steps of this process.

5. Lead

By pioneering our approach, we have been able to set an example for others to follow. Contributing to improving our sector is a key indicator of our success. This is done with humility and with partnership in mind. We also use digital platforms to bring groups together.

This approach is enabling us to take different products, described below, to scale as well as services such as training and technical advice. The following three case studies show a range of ways in which we manage innovation. Each has an explicit goal, a clearly formed problem statement, employs a tangible technology, and has a definitive result.

Case Study #1: Radio antennas in Nepal

Goal: To make better, more reliable antennas and increase radio coverage. A group of amateur radio enthusiasts played an important role in the aftermath of the 2015 Nepal earthquake, using their home radio stations to

Figure 25.1 Engineering measuring hardware

relay messages to the army and police. However, the earthquake destroyed many ground stations in their network and, unfortunately, there were still some earthquake-affected areas they could not communicate with.

In preparation for future disasters, this group was seeking to increase radio coverage in Nepal by installing antennas that do not rely on station-to-station communication, but instead communicate via satellite. However, they were having trouble getting their radio antennas to work.

Problem framing: There were many small problems that accumulated to inhibit the performance of the antenna, such as the type of antenna, impedance matching, the quality of soldering, and assembly accuracy. We compared importance with difficulty for each of these, searching for the one that would yield the most impact on performance for the least time and effort. We chose to focus on assembly accuracy. For radio transmissions, the higher the frequency of the radio waves being transmitted the smaller the antenna must be. The frequency for communicating via satellite is much higher than that used for ground station-to-station communication, hence the antennas that the team were working with were much smaller than those they were used to. It is possible to easily build a large antenna by hand because errors in dimensions and inexact placement of parts do not matter much. However, small inaccuracies can lead to large differences in performance for smaller antennas.

Antenna accuracy was a good problem to focus on because it was likely to have a positive impact on antenna performance, and a prototype could be developed and tested within a couple of days. Focusing on type of antenna, impedance matching, and soldering may have had just as much impact on performance, but the issues were not as straightforward to test or solve.

Technology: Field Ready worked with the team to design some simple 3D printed parts to help quickly and accurately assemble the antenna, by allowing the components to be snapped into pre-defined locations. The 3D printed plastic chassis holds the metal rods of the antenna precisely at the correct locations, ensuring accurate assembly from unit to unit.

Results: The work resulted in a significantly improved antenna, and a design that could easily and accurately be replicated. The antenna design was used in other contexts with similar results.

Case Study #2: Umbilical-cord clamps in Haiti

Goal: To design and 3D print sterile umbilical-cord clamps and other medical items for babies, mothers, and medical personnel.

Problem framing: Small clinics in rural Haiti often have no access to sterile medical supplies. Many of these supplies are unavailable, while others are too expensive for many clinics to afford. One example is the clamp used to close the umbilical cord during delivery. The lack of sterile clamps poses a health risk to mothers and babies. Neonatal sepsis, a type of infection that can originate at the umbilical cord, is one of the leading causes of death among infants in the region.

The Field Ready team interviewed personnel at a number of clinics, which led to the identification of various immediate needs. One clinic, for example, needed birthing kits to give out to pregnant mothers because, often, women who go into labour may be five or ten miles from the clinic with no means of transportation. After assessing multiple clinics and learning more about the delivery process and the needs of rural clinics in Haiti, it became clear that expanding access to sterile items like clamps would significantly improve the health of mothers, babies, and medical personnel. The Field Ready team set out to design an umbilical-cord clamp that would fulfil particular requirements. The clamp had to be sanitary and should not be reusable: therefore, it was designed to break after the first use. It needed to be intuitive to use and easy to grip. It needed to be easy and cheap to produce: this meant coming up with a design that minimized the amount of material used. It had to remain on the baby for three to five days so it would preferably be made from a non-porous, medical-grade material to minimize the risk of bacteria and infection.

Technology: Field Ready made clamps of different designs using 3D printing.

Results: Working with a local partner, batches of umbilical-cord clamps were manufactured and distributed at several sites in Haiti. This product has since been added to an array of useful items that can be made locally using a production kit.

Case Study #3: Rescue airbag in Syria

Goal: To invent a device that can be produced in the field to rescue trapped people in destroyed buildings.

Problem framing: The Syrian civil war has claimed many lives and caused untold human suffering. Urban warfare means that people inhabiting multi-storey buildings are at risk of becoming entombed in structures that have been directly hit by artillery, aerial strikes, or 'barrel bombs'. People trapped by rubble and collapsed buildings can survive the attack but frequently do not because they cannot be rescued in time.

The extremes of the war make rescuing trapped civilians a nearly impossible task. Special equipment is needed to lift heavy debris, such as concrete slabs weighing several tons. While lifting airbags are available to well-supplied search and rescue teams worldwide, these can be prohibitively expensive.

Working with a number of excellent partners, Field Ready identified specific parameters – locally produced airbags needed to be small, portable, easy-to-use, robust, and inexpensive – using sketching, photography and prioritization tools. We followed the widely used British Standard for rescue airbags to develop a workable solution that could be implemented within the limitations of cost and the pressures of the combat zone.

Technology: The Field Ready team set out to design a reliable lifting airbag that could be produced from readily available inexpensive materials. Using an iterative design process, a number of prototypes were created and tested. The initial model involved using a reinforced vehicle-tyre inner tube. The second and third prototypes refined this idea, but were still not ideal, so the team prototyped alternative models using thick rubber mats. Along the way, the team created a testing rig capable of applying thousands of pounds of pressure from supplies and compressed air procured locally.

Results: The final prototype was positively received by search and rescue teams in northern Syria. An initial batch of 100 rescue airbags was manufactured and distributed wherever these tools were needed. They were first used successfully in March 2017 to rescue two people following an aerial bombardment. This shows that locally-made rescue technology can be used worldwide to directly save people's lives.

About the author

Tessa Fixsen-Lavdiotis is a programme officer for Field Ready. Tessa holds an MS in Refugee and Forced Migration from DePaul University.

PART V
Summary and challenges for the future

This final part draws together the core themes of the book. In particular, it links the challenges posed in Part II to interesting new approaches in the field described in Parts III and IV. There are some important lessons about actually working in complex non-linear contexts and the tools and approaches which offers promise. This part consists of:

- Expert interviews
- Concluding thoughts on humanitarian innovation.

CHAPTER 26
Q&A with experts in humanitarian innovation

This chapter includes interviews with three leaders – Stanley Chitekwe, Andrew Lamb and Kim Scriven – in the area of humanitarian innovation. They expand on a number of topics covered earlier in this book. These include beginning the process of innovation, the donor's perspective, and dealing with organizational and other barriers to innovation. Their responses provide valuable insight and describe lessons learned through years of experience at a variety of levels and different contexts.

Keywords: humanitarianism, innovation, making, key lessons learned

Editor's interview Kim Scriven, former manager of the Humanitarian Innovation Fund. His leadership and research make Kim a leading figure in advancing the humanitarian innovation agenda.

Q: What does 'humanitarian innovation' mean to you?

A: Innovation has always been hard to pin down and this makes coming to an agreed definition hard, if not impossible. But perhaps that is OK. What is important is that we recognize it as a complex process rather than static moment or thing (a verb not a noun), and approach it as such.

For me, innovation is simply about creatively solving problems to build new value, and for humanitarians this is done with the aim of benefiting people caught up in crises and disasters. This will often involve adapting or developing new technology, but not always. It could equally be about applying new thinking or approaches.

I've always felt the humanitarian system is highly creative and inherently innovative; the humanitarian imperative drives individuals and organizations to extend assistance when local resources are overwhelmed or curtailed. That's as true today as it ever was. But, as the aid sector continues to grow and professionalize, the challenge is to build structures that allow us to harness that innovative spirit in a structured and systematic way.

Q: Why is it important?

A: Innovation is a key driver of growth and prosperity. It is no surprise, then, that innovation has a significant role to play in the aid sector. The key difference is, perhaps, that we're measuring success in terms of lives saved, suffering reduced, and increased resilience, rather than in increased GDP or productivity. Beyond this, I see two related trends that underline how vital innovation is for the humanitarian aid system.

http://dx.doi.org/10.3362/9781780449531.026

On the one hand, changes in the scale and nature of humanitarian crises necessitate new ways of working. As the global population grows and urbanizes rapidly, vulnerability to natural hazards and political instability are shifting and needs are growing. Disasters are becoming increasingly common and impactful because of climate change and, while global conflict may not currently be growing, the nature of conflict and the continued degradation of the humanitarian space are placing new stress on humanitarians. On the other hand, the aid industry itself faces internal challenges. While not keeping pace with need, the global humanitarian system has grown to become a multi-billion dollar industry, and many feel the system has become too bureaucratic and risk averse.

Q: What are the main barriers to successful innovation?

A: I think the main barriers to innovation are institutional and structural. Institutional in the sense that I mentioned above – as organizations have grown and sought to consolidate, they have become less open to new ideas, and more reliant on established ways of working and standard operating procedures. This is also a trend we have seen in the public and private sectors more generally, and was described by Max Weber in his theory of bureaucracy. And a lot of this change has been positive – it is quite right that professional organizations, working in the world's toughest context, do so in ways that are structured and well thought through, and do not expose staff or affected people to unnecessary risk. The trick is to also maintain spaces for experimenting.

More fundamentally, there are structural inhibitors to innovation, meaning that agencies are not incentivized to continually seek to improve their performance. Competition for donor funding means that agencies lack motivation to collaborate, although this appears to be changing. At a deeper level, the system lacks accountability: an agency's income and profile is only loosely (if at all) related to the quality of the service they provide. This takes away a major incentive for improvement which would be a key driver of innovation.

Q: What can donors do to support people and organizations who are trying to innovate?

A: The challenge of accountability is huge, and something that actors need to work on collectively. At its most simple it is about giving up power, which is not something people do easily. But there are more immediate things donors can (and are) doing to support innovation. We are seeing much more funding made available for innovation, which is great. We are also gaining an appreciation that innovation is about more than just money, and this is translating into investment in innovation management – be it specific research or challenge-development work, process facilitation, or funding for communications and diffusion. This should be welcomed, and will need to be taken forward with a willingness to learn from successes and failures.

The final thing I think that donors could usefully do would be to fund the partnerships and collaborations that often fuel innovation. These might include boundary-spanning partnerships with individuals and organizations in academia or business, and efforts to get humanitarian agencies to work collectively on key challenges. This is happening more, but still tends to be on a project-by-project basis.

We have seen huge interest and investment in innovation in recent years, and the challenge for all actors will be to deliver on this as we enter a more mature phase of innovation management in the sector. Without this, there is a risk of disillusionment with the hype around innovation, which would be detrimental to helping the system make the changes needed to remain relevant in the coming decades.

Editor's interview with Stanley Chitekwe, chief of nutrition, UNICEF Nepal. From 2010 to 2015, Stanley led the nutrition unit in the UNICEF mission in Nigeria.

Q: What sparked your interest in innovation?

A: I went to a very average high school and took maths, biology and chemistry A levels. I was worried that the results of this school were historically so poor that I would not be able to go to the University of Harare, as was my ambition. At school I found that a few of my classmates and I were the ones who achieved the best grades and were therefore chosen by the teacher to explain their answers. It then occurred to me that we would be stronger together, if we formed a peer-support group. Competition between the students then became irrelevant and none of us were facing the challenge of going to a very average school alone. The 'study buddies' finished high school not only top of their class in the sciences but with the top four results ever achieved at that school. I was chosen to be head boy of the school in my second year of A levels meaning that I had extra responsibilities – but also some extra leeway to operate the peer-support study group. My leadership practice developed at this time, particularly understanding that the most authentic and effective way is leading by example.

Q: How is innovation supported within UNICEF?

A: UNICEF has provided formal support for innovation over the last decade. The institutional atmosphere is vitally important to fostering an innovative organizational culture. Growth in the perceived value and institutional capital of innovation has come on the back of initial successes that were achieved before that institutional support was formalized.

There is an inherent tension in treating innovation as an integral part of programming, as opposed to having separate innovation staff and structures.

Entrusting innovation to programme staff alone can mean that innovation is abandoned or dropped when programme pressures present themselves. Managing the extra workload, as well as defending and selling to management, is vital when innovation is not a formal part of your remit as an employee. When programme staff are under pressure to deliver, it is easy for innovation to become a lower priority. Creating alliances and finding champions at management level is key in managing this king of off-the-books processes. Once an idea is hatched and has some managerial support, staff can integrate it in work plans to get the innovation into the system.

Q: What barriers have you come up against? What have you learnt in the process of developing and implementing humanitarian innovations?

A: Managing innovation is about persistence, maintaining relationships with other people to explore new ideas, a collaborative approach, and maintaining positive internal relationships. Without the open and collaborative working practices this innovation would have been implemented and then forgotten. The expansion to scale was the result of a measured approach over five and a half years but, even at the end of the project, I was working outside my official remit and was putting a significant amount of my own time into the project. Donor buy-in was a key factor in enabling me to pursue these innovative approaches.

The way innovation can disrupt intricate and complex supply chains – even where new, better, cheaper, locally manufactured products are under consideration – is often enough to discourage logisticians and procurement professionals from endorsing and supporting changes. Resistance comes from those trying to protect large, established, and institutionalized structures, including people's jobs. The form that resistance took was colleagues attacking the quality of data from the surveys. This led us to develop the survey methodology and platform to improve the data quality until it was equal to, and then surpassed, the quality of data generated by established surveys within UNICEF. This required building quality measures into the new survey.

Q: How have you been able to gain traction with innovative initiatives?

A: Having a good personal reputation for maintaining high standards in the day job and as a proven innovator within UNICEF (from my time in Malawi) is important in gaining a license to innovate. However, reputation can be difficult to maintain in a large organization with a rapid turnover of roles. Your own ability to understand an issue, present a solution, convene and motivate a team, and bring reputable partners on board are essential skills in championing an innovation. Innovative solutions should be within the imagining of organizational decision makers.

Innovative ideas and projects in humanitarian responses often come under criticism. The best way to deal with this criticism is to tackle it head-on; criticism can otherwise undermine the programme and staff morale.

In Nigeria, where UNICEF's nutrition programme treated over a million children, I worked to take a therapeutic feeding project to scale. The programme used an innovative peanut-butter-based product, which was an improvement on the milk-based products previously used as it removed the need for mixing with water, had a longer shelf life, and was not confined to hospital settings. The programme was developed to create a replicable pilot. The programme faced internal criticism, questioning why a new method should be implemented in the face of tried and tested methods. The project focus was on feeding, but the broader goal was saving lives. I therefore commissioned a data consultant to devise a model to discover how many lives had been saved and, therefore, justify the programme. Achieving an innovative monitoring and evaluation outcome required programme data to be well managed and accessible. Through the new data advocacy model, we found that the programme had treated 900,000 children and averted 200,000 deaths. Once these facts were known, the discussion around the programme completely changed.

Editor's interview with Andrew Lamb, strategic advisor for Field Ready. A former CEO of Engineers Without Borders UK, and RedR Trustee, Andrew has been instrumental in developing Field Ready's approach and establishing activities in Nepal, Syria, South Sudan, and the Pacific region.

Q: How can an individual and/or an organization be innovative?

A: I think there are a number of important elements. First, recognizing and responding to patterns is essential. An innovator can recognize patterns of behaviour very easily. Normal, linear, grant-donor processes result in the normal, straightforward, linear grant-delivery processes; however complex the situation, you have to report how many people you've helped and how you've helped them. But innovation is basically about trying to find new kinds of patterns of behaviour, of activity, of management, of individuals, and recognizing those patterns and then getting people to work on them. Being able to take a story or idea from one place and play it out in another.

It's possible to tell whether the person you're talking to is the kind of person who is an innovator within a constrained system or is a normal bureaucrat within a constrained system. This insight will help you to know whether you need to meet that person outside of their context in order to unlock innovative opportunities, for example, in a café talking about doing something different or doing something new.

On a project we're working on with a large NGO, the pattern of behaviour I recognized in the people who are leading the consortium was one of risk-aversion. They are project managers: there's a WASH technical specialist and a project manager. They aren't used to having to create spaces for stuff to happen. They don't want to go back to the donor and ask for the amount of money we actually need, because the amount of money we actually need is more than the donor actually wants to give. However, we need to tell the donor the true cost of the project and for them to help us to solve the problem.

The project lead wasn't willing to go back to the donor to have that conversation. The other member of the consortium therefore urged them on and, together, we worked out the language needed to give them the confidence to go to the donor and discuss the situation. We enabled them to explain the situation, how much funding the project actually required and why, in a way that underlines that we (the consortium) know what we're doing.

We had to help equip these people because the pattern of behaviour they were exhibiting was very much: 'we've had a conversation with the donor, now we need to prepare a proposal with a budget that meets the donor's requirements, then we submit it to them'. That process was not going to solve the problem. The new pattern of behaviour was to enter into a more conceptual conversation around how to make something possible, as opposed to the normal management or technical approach to something of working out what the constraints are and then working within those constraints (rather than trying to push those constraints back).

Q: How can you make sure people 'get it' when it comes to innovating new ideas?

A: A big part of managing innovation is creating a sense of possibility. It is related to the idea of abundance thinking (we have all of these resources, just imagine what we could do) rather than scarcity thinking (we have scarce resources so they have to be managed, we can't do anything different or new). Those are the things that a lot of people get really stuck on: because they don't know the answer to the question it can't be done. Or, because we don't have the skills within the team or our organization it can't be done. Whereas you can turn it around and say, 'Well, this is how we are', and turn it into something our organization does or something our organization needs. You can turn something that's innovative into something that looks a bit more straightforward and sensible. Create that sense of possibility, and suddenly you find you're writing concept notes and people get really excited and motivated because they were there creating something new in a conversation. It's not just about a donor asking for a funding bid for year four or a ten-year programme.

I think it is also essential to follow your values. The act of being able to ask the fundamental underlying question creates a sense of possibility because, at some point, you will be able to find a synergy that you can build on. So I would hope that a lot of it is about being able to ask the right questions. Then there's also breadth of experience. A breadth of experience is helpful if you actually want to be able to offer something, because you can talk about ideas for a long time, but you can frustrate people if you can't then turn those ideas into a reality. It's being able to create a sense of possibility and turn it into 'so now what? What do we do now that we've done that exploration? What can we do next?' For Field Ready, this next step is often: 'Let's start a new country programme'; 'Let's start working on a new innovation'; or 'Let's start a new funding bid'. There are things that we can do because we have that internal sense of possibility. It's routine for us to be writing funding bids to try out new ideas – even if it isn't for a large NGO because they're too busy trying to fund their existing operations.

Q: There are so many places to start innovating, where do you begin?

A: There's a few things to unwrap in this in terms of the way we think about these things. Massive numbers of small machines – massive small manufacturing – is a reasonably good litmus test of what we're trying to do. We're not trying to make stuff with big machines, we're trying to make stuff where it's needed – hyperlocal is one of the other words that we use; one of the touchstones in our work.

It is important to first work in abstracts and then in specifics. Generalists deal in abstracts so that you can suddenly turn a monitoring and evaluation issue into a half-million-dollar research project. The specialists are the ones who can make that funding bid sound well informed and accurate, not wishy-washy and idealistic. They're the ones who can provide the references to the papers that back up your argument. You've got to have both: the ability to deal in abstracts is crucial in being able to recognize abstracts and create a sense of possibility, but at some point you have to hand over. The points at which Field Ready has been at its best is when we've had a combination of both of those in the field: someone who can talk the language of humanitarians, someone who can talk the language of technology; someone who can talk the language of the problem, someone who can talk the language of the solution; someone who can talk the language of the abstract and someone who can talk the language of the specific.

Then respond to the world around you. There's that touchstone of local manufacturing – we don't use the phrase massive small manufacturing because it's not something that other people recognize, but I think that, since the industrial revolution, we all recognize the paradigm of having a relatively small number of massive manufacturers. Being able to turn that into a massive number of small manufacturers is a fairly good test.

The trick of managing innovation – besides having the breadth of experience and networks – is just going to conferences, talking, getting out into the world, reading lots of things, signing up to every email list. It's about doing all of those things that standard management practice would tell you not to do ('prioritize your time', 'you should only go to conferences that are directly relevant', 'manage your inbox'). Gathering all the information all the information all the time doesn't work for everyone but I believe in generally sensing what's going on in the world so that you can respond to it.

Finally, you need people on the team who question what we're doing and why. We're much better for it in the longer run. You've got to have diversity in the team.

CHAPTER 27
Concluding thoughts on humanitarian innovation

Eric James and Abigail Taylor

This concluding chapter brings together key aspects of the book. The challenges posed in Part II are being met with interesting new approaches in the field, described in Parts III and IV. The key things to keep in mind include first understanding the problem and context, aligning systems and mindsets, getting the process right, achieving impact through scale, and keeping the humanitarian essence of what we do.

Keywords: humanitarianism, innovation, making, key lessons learned

We started this book with an acknowledgement of the enormous challenges faced by international aid. Those that are commonly acknowledged include issues such as climate change, urbanization, and poor governance. Everyday challenges faced by those trying to manage and improve conditions for affected people are huge. Commonplace examples include sudden spikes in demand, difficult-to-access locations, and disruptions due to conflict or disasters, as well as normal supply-chain problems. Barriers to innovation include static or 'old' mindsets, legacy systems, scaling viable solutions past tests/pilots, funding, failure to learn from previous experience, and the importance of the local.

A key underlying premise has been that opportunities to do something about these challenges are equally large. A number of technologies and approaches will continue to make their way in international aid provision. Examples include advances in additive manufacturing, autonomous and other forms of transportation (e.g. hyperloops), artificial intelligence, medicine and public health, nanotechnology (including sensors, wearable and implanted devices), robotics, software (e.g., blockchains), and ever-improving communications technology and real-time monitoring and evaluation. The opportunities include learning within and across sectors, building momentum and a pipeline of innovations, developing adequate feedback loops and harnessing the potential of localization.

Those who are able to understand this emerging context and manage innovative pathways through it will be the leaders of tomorrow. In this book, the challenges posed in Part II are being met with interesting new approaches in the field, described in Parts III and IV. From these, it is possible to distil core themes. In the fourth chapter, these were introduced as the four Cs: context, complexity, creativity, and culture. Here, the important lessons about actually working in complex non-linear contexts, and the tools and approaches which seem to offer promise, are summarized in six key points.

1. **Understanding first the problem and context**: Everything starts with identifying the problem and understanding the context correctly. There are many good solutions out there looking for problems to solve. Sound awareness of problems and context enables individuals and teams to respond better to weak signals. In this way, developing professional reflexivity will enable a distinction to be made between linear problems (that are decipherable and predictable) and non-linear challenges (within complex systems, where the causes and effects that drive behaviours and outcomes are far more difficult to understand).
2. **Aligning systems and mindsets**: Innovative organizations need to have leadership that understands context, and unleashes (INSPIREs) a culture of diversity and creativity. Even hierarchical organizations can be structured to tame and manage linear problems, in part by developing diverse teams and allowing for boundary-spanning activities. But non-linear problems require a different kind of leadership which is characterized this way: decentralized, empowered, situationally aware, and adaptive. With the right mindsets, and appropriate follow-up actions, innovative leaders can navigate uncertainty and ambiguity like sailors finding the best tack into the wind.
3. **Getting the process right**: The progression of an idea to a useful item for humanitarian purposes can take many routes. Following an effective innovation process means generating new ideas and testing them systematically against clear and meaningful criteria. There is no one right way to manage an innovation across the entire lifecycle. But, when done right, an effective innovation process provides 'ah-ha' moments and opportunities to gain insight from all sorts of sources. Understanding that failure can be an important learning tool is an important part of the process. Focusing on process over product can empower disaster-hit communities and lead to better communication.
4. **Putting technology in its proper place**: The future of technology is hard to predict and even harder to get right. Most technology problems are human problems. In other words, implementation is the key challenge, often requiring greater investment than the technical development. Trends build up hype, take time to gain momentum (often decades), and often simply die or disappear (remembered only, if at all, as a flash in the pan). While getting software solutions to reach scale is a genuine challenge, it is extraordinarily difficult for hardware innovations to take hold and make a difference.

5. **Achieving impact through scale**: Impact is results and scale is replicating these results as widely as possible. Simply put, an innovation needs to scale if it is to have an impact. Therefore, it is important to prioritize and scale the highest-potential ideas. Achieving scale takes significant time and financial investment (having the resources ready to go for scaling the innovation is vital). Seek out feedback and learn as a continual way of working. Partners can be particularly helpful in this process. Through this, replication – ensuring that an increasing number of people and organizations use the innovation – becomes possible.
6. **Maintaining the humanitarian 'essence' while being innovative**: It may be easy to charge off in a direction that appears to be innovative but jeopardizes the spirit and principles of humanitarian aid itself (aid work is about people over things). Perhaps a common way to cross ethical lines is by using new, unproven, and potentially unsafe innovations with affected populations. It can be difficult to balance this with the humanitarian imperative set out in *The Code of Conduct: Principles of Conduct for The International Red Cross and Red Crescent Movement and NGOs in Disaster Response Programmes*. Pressure to meet standards that do not logically apply is common. Other provisions such as 'respect culture and custom', 'relief aid must strive to reduce future vulnerabilities to disaster as well as meeting basic needs', and the need to hold ourselves accountable make this a challenge but also get at the essence of what sets the aid community apart from the commercial and, in too many cases, government sectors. The elements of the Core Humanitarian Standard further spell this out and provide a number of pathways along which humanitarian innovation can be applied. At the very least there is an obligation to identify the risks associated with an innovation and develop mitigation strategies while keeping the age-old dictum, 'first do no harm', to the fore.

About the authors

Eric James, PhD, is the co-founder and executive director of Field Ready. He has over two decades of experience leading humanitarian relief programmes. He has been involved in several business start-ups, holds two patents, and was a fellow/advisor at Singularity University. Eric is an affiliated expert of the Harvard Humanitarian Initiative and an adjunct professor at the DePaul University's Refugee and Forced Migration Studies programme. He is author of *Managing Humanitarian Relief: An Operational Guide for NGOs* (Practical Action Publishing, 2nd Edition, 2017) among other publications.

Abigail Taylor is a strategic advisor for the consulting firm Spark Strategy. She has developed considerable experience in business development and partnership management in Europe and Africa, and, more recently, in Asia. Abigail has worked for NGOs, social enterprises, and UNHCR. She has an MA in Conflict, Security and Development, a degree in Politics, and has worked with the UK government in parliament and through government-focused institutions. She has particular interests in complexity theory, organizational systems, and managing scale-ups.

Useful tools and techniques for humanitarian innovation

Throughout this book, we have presented different means and methods for managing humanitarian innovation. However, bridging the gap between theory and practice can often be a challenge and so having a useful tool to hand for each situation can be helpful. There are literally hundreds of potentially useful tools and techniques. We present two dozen techniques that may be helpful, and Table A.1 shows which challenges each might be appropriate for.

Most of these tools and techniques are designed to be used in groups and require basic office supplies, but use your creativity and available resources (sometimes drawing in earth or sand works just as well as an expensive whiteboard and markers). In all activities, plan ahead and always say 'thank you' to participants.

Table A.1 Useful tools and techniques

We need to ...	Tools and techniques
Understand the situation better	1. Interview 2. Observation 3. Contextual inquiry 4. Immersive empathy
Identify problems	5. Cause diagram 6. Five whys 7. Four-frame approach 8. CATWOE
Generate new ideas	9. Round robin 10. Creative matrix 11. Alternative worlds 12. SCAMPER
Prioritize	13. Visualize the vote 14. Importance/difficulty matrix 15. Bullseye diagramming 16. Theory of change
Develop a clear plan	17. Business plan 18. Blueprint 19. Business-model canvas 20. Promise and potential map
Show others and get feedback	21. Thumbnail sketching 22. Developed images 23. Prototyping 24. Prototype-testing plan

1. Interview

An interview is not much more than an honest conversation. Talking to people is the quickest way to understand their needs and identify opportunities to help to find possible solutions. Interviews can be carried out with nearly any stakeholder, from knowledgeable individuals (known as key informants) to groups of people (in the form of focus-group discussions).

How it works

- Develop a simple list of things you need more information about. While not a precise script, this list can standardize the process across individual interviews. Leave room for notes by each item in the list.
- Plan interviews. Whether conducting one interview or a series, work with someone to identify the candidate(s) and schedule when to talk to them. It is always better to get more than one perspective, especially when talking about complex challenges.
- Conduct the interview. Introduce yourself, the purpose of the interview, and ask if the interviewee has any questions for you before you begin. Then start a conversation in which you ask open-ended questions about each topic in your guide.

Tips

- In some areas, it is not acceptable to record anything – verify whether it is okay to do so beforehand.
- Once you know recording is permitted, get consent (have the interviewee sign a consent form). You can do this when you set up the interview or at the beginning of each interview.
- Pay attention to relevant cultural issues. Have a translator if needed, and make sure your topic or interview guide has been reviewed by an in-country or cultural expert.
- In some cultures, members of different genders may not easily engage with one another.
- Interviews can be conducted over the phone, the internet (using apps like Google Hangouts or Skype), or in person. In-person interviews typically provide the most context and the best information.
- If you can, have an assistant take notes while you conduct the interview. You may need a translator, recorder, or in-country chaperone as well, depending on the situation.

2. Observation

Observation is a technique for gaining insights by viewing people's behaviours, habits, and practices. Naturalistic observation is conducted through unobtrusive field research (not in a lab or simulated environment), whereas participant observation allows for the observer to intervene and change variables in a way that depends on the research aims and methods.

How it works

- Identify a subject area to study and develop a plan to guide the investigation.
- Consider which people, locations, and activities to watch. Try to find situations that are true to everyday situations.
- Obtain the necessary access and permission (it is considered unethical if subjects do not give permission).
- Prepare materials for capturing what you see (e.g., notepad, camera, video or audio recorders).
- Go out, observe, record, and, afterward, analyse the results.

Tips

- This is best done when acting as a fly on the wall and allowing people to act as if you were not there.
- Be aware that this method can be time-consuming and the results can be highly subjective.
- Look at the situation from several vantage points.

3. Contextual inquiry

This technique involves combining interviews and observation. By conducting an interview in your interviewee's environment, it is possible to observe contextual details that are nearly impossible to be aware of otherwise. Contextual inquiry helps to understand people and culture better because it combines the interview with authentic observation. This is important, as those carrying out research typically approach situations with different priorities, perspectives, and experiences to either the affected communities or aid agencies.

How it works

- Create a high-level guide to use during the inquiry. Leave room to take notes and include plenty of white space to document conversations that arise as you see things you did not anticipate or expect.
- Prepare questions. Have a sense of what is being looked for to understand and prepare a list of specific questions that align with the topic guide. It is not necessary to follow these absolutely but it is always better to be prepared.
- Get permission to visit (including photo and video permission) and set a date and location to meet ahead of time. Make sure you ask if there

is a dress code or other safety requirements. Should you wear trousers or are shorts permitted? Do you need steel-toed shoes? A hairnet? Eye protection? Are there cultural aspects of dress you should consider? Talk with your interviewee ahead of time and make a list of the items and spaces that you are interested in learning about.
- Go in pairs (or bring an assistant). It is best to have a second pair of eyes to help take notes, snap photos, and record video or audio if possible. When entering an unknown environment, it is safest to use the buddy system. Be wary of leaders who may create unhelpful dynamics.

Tips

- Be sure to have what might be needed (e.g., paperwork) to enter the area.
- If you are not familiar with the region or culture, find an in-country assistant who can also serve as a translator and/or chaperone (e.g., a local speaker, translator, advocate, or expert).
- Prepare by educating yourself. Who will you interact with? What cultural norms exist? Are there concerns regarding the facilities or environment you will visit? Be safe and follow the rules and customs.
- As you notice potential opportunities, ask detailed questions. Really try to understand how complex and how important each opportunity might be to the affected community.

4. Immersive empathy

This technique can be an effective way of building empathy for people through first-hand experiences. It involves immersion into the roles of others and extrapolating the results to make constructive changes. This tool is useful when the goal is to develop first-hand knowledge of an experience, take a step back and challenge assumptions, or build a shared and aligned understanding within and between teams. This is not the right exercise for picking up small, detail-oriented usability issues but is more valuable when trying to identify higher-level or systemic issues for or with a product or service.

How it works

- Identify whose experience to replicate and choose which tasks or activities to perform.
- Obtain the necessary access and permission.
- If a simulation is used to replicate the experience, assemble what is needed and determine the best location.
- Conduct the targeted tasks. Recruit a handful of product or service users and record their experiences in a carefully prepared probe pack/diary, key activities, time taken, feelings and emotions and taking photos/video where possible.
- Do each activity as realistically as possible and note your findings along the way.

Tips

- The best results will come from committing to the activity fully (e.g., be sure to incorporate any impediments or barriers the actual users live with).
- Be sure to not cut corners or give up early.
- Ask another observer to help capture findings.
- Ensure that those conducting the review are naïve to the product or service and have no prior exposure or allegiance that may bias their experience.

5. Cause diagram

This tool, sometimes called a fishbone diagram, provides a structured way to analyse a problem in a thorough manner. It helps deconstruct all possible causes of the problem beyond the apparent ones. It is a useful method to differentiate cause from effects or symptoms, providing ideas to resolve a problem and helping to build a shared understanding of what it is you are working on. This tool demonstrates that problems can have a number of causes and explores the links between the effects and the possible causes of an issue.

It encourages group problem-solving so is best used as a participatory exercise.

How it works

- Identify the problem, or effect, under consideration and state it in clear and concise terms, agreed by everyone.
- Write the problem in a box on the right and draw a long line pointing to the box.
- Decide the major categories of causes. This may be done through brainstorming or by using standard categories such as the 4Ms (machines, materials, methods, manpower) or STEEP (social, technological, economic, environment, political). When the effect results from a recognisable process or set of activities, the major steps in the process can be used.
- Write the major categories in boxes parallel to, and some distance from, the main line. Connect them to the main line with slanting arrows.
- Consider possible causes and add these to the diagram clustered around the major categories they influence.
- Divide and sub-divide the causes to show how they interact, and draw links between causes that are related. If the diagram becomes too crowded, move one or more categories to a new sheet of paper.
- Evaluate and analyse the possible causes. Decide and act.

Tips

- Large block paper and sticky notes may help but are not required.
- Using this tool will probably involve using other tools. For example, in order to verify some of the possible causes identified you may need to collect data (using checklists) and analyse it.

6. Five whys

The five whys tool works well when problems involve human factors or interactions. By repeatedly asking why (five times is a good rule of thumb), you can peel away the layers of symptoms to reach the root cause of a problem. Very often the ostensible reason for a problem will lead you to another question.

How it works

- Write down the specific problem. Writing the issue helps you formalize the problem and describe it completely. It also helps all members of a team focus on the same problem.
- Ask why the problem happens and write the answer below the problem.
- If the answer you just provided does not identify the root cause of the problem, ask why again and write that answer down.
- Continue doing this until the team is in agreement that the problem's root cause has been identified.

Tips

- Although this technique is called five whys, it may be necessary to ask the question fewer or more times than five before you find the core issue related to a problem.
- This tool can be used in the analysis of new problems and fits with some established methods such as Six Sigma's DMAIC (define, measure, analyse, improve, control).

7. Four-frame approach

This tool is useful when there is a need to identify issues within management functions. The four-frame approach was created by Bolman and Deal in 1991 (see 'Leadership and management effectiveness: A multi-frame, multi-sector analysis', *Human Resource Management*, 30 (4), pp. 509–534, doi: 10.1002/hrm.3930300406). They suggested that leaders display leadership behaviours and operate in one of four frames: structural, human resource, political, or symbolic. This approach suggests that there are times when a particular approach is appropriate – and times when it may not be. Any style can be effective or ineffective, depending upon the situation. Relying on only one of these approaches would be inappropriate, thus we should strive to be conscious of all four.

How it works

- Create a four-by-four matrix of squares on a large sheet of paper, a flipchart, or the ground.
- Label the quadrants of the matrix, identifying the following frames:
  - **Structural leaders** focus on structure, strategy, environment, implementation, experimentation, and adaptation

- **Political leaders** clarify what they want and what they can get, assess the distribution of power and interests, build links to other stakeholders, use persuasion first, but will use negotiation and coercion if necessary
- **Human-resource leaders** believe in people and communicate that belief; they are visible and accessible; they empower, increase participation, support, share information, and move decision-making down into the organization
- **Symbolic leaders** view organizations as a stage on which to play certain roles and give particular impressions, use symbols to capture attention, frame experience by providing plausible interpretations of experiences, and discover and communicate a vision.
* Analyse and discuss the results.

Tips

* It is helpful if stakeholders who have the functional roles identified are open to the examination called for in the tool.

8. CATWOE

This tool is a systematic way of identifying problems. In 1975, David Smyth identified that successful problem-solving has common elements including the people, processes, and environment that contribute to a situation, issue or problem. Having a comprehensive framework enables different perspectives to be revealed.

How it works

* Identify an important problem or issue.
* Use the mnemonic CATWOE as a checklist to identify the various people and elements that are affected:
  - **Customers or stakeholders:** Who are they and how does the issue affect them?
  - **Actors:** Who is involved? Who will be involved in implementing solutions? What will impact their success?
  - **Transformation process:** What processes or systems are affected by the issue?
  - **Worldview:** What is the big picture? What are the wider impacts of the issue?
  - **Owner:** Who owns the process or situation you are investigating? What role will they play in the solution?
  - **Environmental constraints:** What are the constraints and limitations that will impact the solution and its success?

Tips

- This tool works best if used with small groups of key stakeholders.
- Try to be as honest possible in generating responses.
- Capture the results of the analysis in a way that is easily shared.

9. Round robin

This technique allows team members to generate ideas without being unduly influenced by any one person, and takes ideas into the next stages of the problem-solving process. It is a useful tool to get your team to generate ideas and also ensures that everyone within the team has an equal say. It is possible to use this technique in written and verbal variations.

How it works

- Gather a team of creative people. Give each person index cards or small pieces of paper.
- Explain the problem that needs to be solved and how this session will work. Be specific about the objectives. Answer questions, but discourage discussion. The goal in this step is to allow individual people to think creatively without any influence from others.
- Have each team member, in silence, think of one idea and write it down.
- Once everyone has written down an idea, have each person pass their idea to the person next to them. Everyone should now be holding a new card or piece of paper with their neighbour's idea written down on it.
- Have each person use their neighbour's idea as inspiration to create another idea. They should write this on another card or piece of paper. Then ask each person to hand in their neighbour's idea and pass their own new idea to the next person along.
- Continue this for as long as is necessary to gather a good amount of ideas. Collate the responses, eliminate any duplicates, and discuss them further as required.

Tips

- It may help to make the session anonymous by gathering the ideas at each stage, shuffling them, and then passing them out again, rather than having group members pass their ideas to the person next to them.
- Limit the time for each step to two or three minutes.
- Encourage participants to suggest wild ideas.
- Invite a presentation and discussion of new ideas.
- When using this technique with a large number of people, split the group into smaller groups.

10. Creative matrix

This is a tool for sparking new ideas at the intersections of distinct categories. It can help narrow a problem that is too broad and help people depart from conventional thinking. It can also help generate many ideas.

How it works

- Identify a problem or challenge that is in need of fresh ideas.
- Use a poster (or something similar) to make a large grid (no more than five by five) where the columns consist of categories that relate to people, groups, or organizations and the rows consist of categories that are for enabling solutions (e.g., programme, communications, technology).
- Introduce the tool, form teams of participants, and give each team a grid along with pens and sticky notes for each participant.
- Give participants 15–20 minutes to come up with ideas for each cell in the grid, writing each idea on a separate sticky note.
- Discuss the findings.

Tips

- Urge participants to draw pictures of the ideas.
- Encourage the teams to fill every cell of the grid.
- Tally the number of ideas per team. Reward quantity.

11. Alternative worlds

This tool is a way of using different perspectives to help generate fresh ideas. It can work well as a benchmarking exercise.

How it works

- Identify a topic for exploration and bring together a diverse group of people.
- Create a list of similar or comparable topics.
- Select a few alternative worlds to explore such as health clinics, refugee settlements, distribution centres, or WASH stations.
- Describe the key attributes of each world to the group and try to immerse them in the details of that world to the greatest extent possible.
- Ask: How would [the idea] solve our challenge?
- Seek various ideas inspired by the new perspective.

Tips

- To generate new ideas effectively, choose a world that is very different from that being faced.
- Resist the temptation to use obvious competitors.
- Try to interview people from this alternative world.

12. SCAMPER

SCAMPER is a tool to help creative thinking that is particularly useful when used with other tools and techniques. Originally developed by an educational administrator named Bob Eberle, SCAMPER is a simple aid to exploring possible solutions to a problem. It can be used in the context of a brainstorming session or as a standalone technique. (For more details, see Eberle's 1996 book, *Games for Imagination Development*, Prufrock Press Inc.)

How it works

- Gather a small group to work on developing new ideas for a mutual problem.
- Use the mnemonic SCAMPER to move thinking in new directions. To do this, simply go down the list and answer the questions. Not every response will be viable but good ideas to explore further may be identified. For example, when thinking about developing a new product or service idea can we:
  - **Substitute:** Is there another way we can do this, or a different thing we could put in place? Could we take some of the underlying assumptions about the problem and change them?
  - **Combine:** Add elements from somewhere or something else. Can we combine some of the problem elements we have with others to give us a redefined problem? Can we bring together different people or skills to help solve it?
  - **Adapt:** Take an existing idea and shape it to help with our context. Are there related worlds with a problem like this? Is there a different context where our ideas could be usefully applied?
  - **Modify:** Rework the idea. Are there dimensions of our idea we can expand/reduce? How might we change the way our idea is perceived – shape, story, look, feel?
  - **Can we apply other verbs?** For example: magnify, minimize, or manipulate?
  - **Put to another use:** Is it possible to use our original idea in a new context? Who else might be interested in a version of our idea? Could we recycle our product and use it for something else at the end of its life?
  - **Eliminate:** Is it possible to get rid of unnecessary elements, streamline the core idea? What would happen if we took away parts of the idea, what would that look like, how would people react?
  - **Reverse:** What about turning our idea around, to make it do the opposite of our original intention? Can we change the sequence or direction in which things work?

Tips

- Be sure to have someone to facilitate and another to record.
- If the problem has to do with hardware, it often helps to have the object or device there for people to observe and reflect upon.
- Because the aim of this tool is to generate new ways of looking at a problem, some ideas may be impractical or not well suited to the circumstances.

13. Visualize the vote

This tool is useful for building consensus and reaching collective decisions. It involves taking a quick poll of available team members in a way that can reveal preferences and opinions, democratize decision-making and harness, a group's collective intelligence.

How it works

- Identify the subject of your polling activity and explain to participants how the tool works.
- Have presenters describe each concept.
- Give everyone one sticky note to use to cast an overall vote, and two sticky notes of another colour to cast as detail votes.
- Announce the criteria for voting.
- Instruct everyone to vote simultaneously. This helps ensure people do not average early and focus on just a few ideas.
- Tally the votes and invite discussion.

Tips

- Use multiple colours for voting. One common method is to use one colour for the overall concept and another for details. Another is to use one colour for ideas people like and another for those they would be willing to invest in solving.
- Use bold colours that stand out.
- An alternative is to use small stones, dried seeds, or similar objects for the voting. Be creative with the resources available.
- Let people vote more than once on the same thing if they really value it.
- After voting, try to think of clever ways to combine solutions to solve more than one high-priority item.

14. Importance/difficulty matrix

Plotting importance against difficulty helps categorize tasks based on key considerations. This technique is therefore helpful in prioritizing tasks during planning or when an impasse has been reached.

How it works

- Create a matrix on a poster, whiteboard, or other large working surface. Make the x-axis represent importance (increasing from left to right) and the y-axis represent difficulty (increasing from bottom to top).
- List all possible problems using sticky notes, index cards, or small pieces of paper.
- Prioritize them based on importance. Consider: how much impact will solving each problem have?
- Prioritize them along the vertical axis based on difficulty. How complex is each problem? How much time, money, expertise and effort will each require?
- Items that are very important and low difficulty are where to focus first. Items that are both high importance and high difficulty are strategic. Anything that is very difficult or not that important should be postponed until other priorities can be resolved.

Tips

- When plotting problems on the matrix, remember they are relative.
- Avoid placing all of the problems in the same quadrant. This exercise is about making tough choices and figuring out what is truly most important and really most difficult.
- Work as a team and reach consensus. If people disagree, have a conversation to understand why.

15. Bullseye diagramming

This tool can be a useful way of ranking items in order of importance using a target diagram. It works well in small groups when weighing a range of considerations.

How it works

- Identify a project that requires prioritization and gather a team of stakeholders.
- Draw three concentric circles on a large poster or similar visual tool.
- Label the circles, from the centre out, as critical, important, peripheral.
- Gather a set of data (e.g., issues, features, etc.) and divide the data into small units.
- Print each piece of data on a small strip of paper or write it on a sticky note.
- Discuss the relative importance of each item.
- Plot the data on the target and set priorities.

USEFUL TOOLS AND TECHNIQUES FOR HUMANITARIAN INNOVATION   225

Tips

- Size the centre ring to fit a limited number of items.
- Enforce a time limit for each round of deliberation.
- Remind participants that peripheral does not mean irrelevant.

16. Theory of change

A theory-of-change (ToC) tool outlines the steps in reaching a social change. It helps articulate and connect work being done with the overarching goal, and identifies potential risks by clarifying the underlying assumptions in each step (see Figure A.1). This tool can help align team members to the larger goal and help them understand their role in achieving it. In complex programmes, or when there are several projects running simultaneously, ToC can help to map different activities and show how they fit together and relate to each other.

How it works

- Gather a group of stakeholders and provide basic office supplies (this tool can be completed using a whiteboard, or large or small sheets of paper).
- Start by identifying the end state desired. This the impact sought. Note the main problem you are attempting to solve along with the long-term vision for change.
- Then, working from that impact, identify the outcome (the eventual and usually long-term result), output (what will be seen tangibly and can be measured), activities (those tasks that will be carried out), and the inputs needed (such as resources).
- Try to think of some practical steps to take to make changes – like creating partnerships or making tweaks to existing processes. Try to keep these as action-oriented as possible.
- As each box is filled in, it is important to also reflect on the key assumptions that underpin these steps in your work. This may help you to spot potential risks or connections between the different projects.

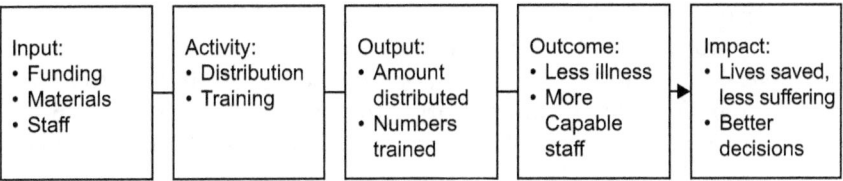

Figure A.1 Theory of change

Tips

- Try to be as specific as possible because it will help make the actions you come up with more effective.
- The final product (i.e., the ToC document) should look well-polished and be easily understood even by people who were not present during its preparation.
- The document produced using the ToC tool can come in many different forms. What is important is the discussion and understanding that it generates.

17. Business Plan

A business plan describes a problem a business group proposes to solve, a vision for how that will be accomplished, and what uniquely qualifies that group. The plan should also include an introduction to the management team, a marketing plan, an operations and financial plan, and any other requirements. It is a common starting point for a business start-up. In most instances, a proposal for funding serves much the same function for non-profit organizations, even though these tend to focus on specific projects. A business plan therefore covers the aspects that a funding partner might be interested in, using the kind of language they will be looking out for.

How it works

- Writing an overview is a good place to start. This includes a few paragraphs about the main idea, and the need and market for it. This will be followed up by a plan for action and the strengths of the team identified for the task.
- When approaching funders or donors, a key component of the business plan is to have a clear statement of why you need the money, how the money will be spent, and, when appropriate, an exit plan.
- An important element of the business plan is the executive summary. This usually sits at the start of the document but is seldom written first.

Tips

- It is often easiest to first write a quick draft of your business plan and then keep re-writing.
- Try not to spend too long getting the draft – or even the next few versions – 'just right' because it is very likely you will have to re-write the plan numerous times. During the process you will come up with much better ways of explaining what makes your idea for social good a feasible one.
- It is easier to write the introduction or summary after you have completed a first draft of your business plan.

- Once the business plan is written, get others to read it. A fresh perspective helps to identify any issues that might have missed.

18. Blueprint

A blueprint gives an overview of an organization's operations, such as key activities, products, services, and points of interaction with the intended audience, stakeholders and beneficiaries. Blueprints clarify how existing resources can be repurposed or recycled, and what new resources will be needed. They also give a sense of the overall impact activities might have. Whereas a business plan is generally descriptive, a blueprint structures the analysis by showing a line of interaction. This line represents the distinction between the activities of the intended audience, beneficiaries, and other stakeholders, and the activities that take place within an organization.

How it works

- Using paper or a whiteboard, write down key aspects of the interactions between your organization and its audience or other beneficiaries. The stages shown at the top of Table A.2 represent the stages the interaction with your audience may go through over time (engagement, hand over, use period, follow-up). The blocks at the left represent the external activities by the people you interact with and the internal activities of your team. The line of interaction demarcates external and internal activities.
- At the bottom of the page, note down which activities your team do internally while they are interacting with your audience. Briefly describe who does what and why, and also what instruments or systems they use for this.

Table A.2 Blueprint

		Engagement	Hand over	Use period	Sign off
External Activities	Things, media and devices being used				
	What people do, know, feel and think				
Internal Activities	What people in the team do, know, feel and think				
	Supporting instruments and systems used				

- At the top of the page, note down which activities are done externally, by the people your organization interacts with, and describe in a similar way who does what and why, and what instruments they may be using for that.
- Working from left to right, consider which of these activities, actors, and instruments are typical for the various stages. By mapping this out you can generate an overview of your key activities, the resources needed, and how these are related.
- Completing the blueprint enables you to see through the different ingredients involved in creating, communicating, and providing your service or product.
- Use the blueprint to analyse a current or future situation. In either case, it will help you highlight key resources and processes that are required and to link these with the people or organizations involved.

Tips

- Try to produce a blueprint from the perspective of different stakeholders you are working with, and anticipate what their activities and responses to your work might be.

19. Business-model canvas

The business-model canvas (BMC) is a one-page overview that lays out both what an organization does (or wants to do), and how they go about doing it. The BMC builds common understanding and tests assumptions that are often unstated. It enables focused discussions about management and strategy by laying out the crucial activities and challenges involved with initiative and how they relate to each other. Created by Alexander Osterwalder and Yves Pigneur in 2008 (see *Business Model Generation: A Handbook for Visionaries, Game Changers, and Challengers*, Wiley, 2010), the BMC is useful for both existing and new organizations and businesses. Existing programmes can develop new initiatives and identify opportunities while becoming more efficient by illustrating potential trade-offs and aligning activities. New programmes can use it to plan and work out how to make their offering real.

How it works

- The BMC follows a standard format (see Figure A.2). Use a blank canvas and add notes with keywords to each building block of the canvas.
- Start in the centre and work outwards answering each question by filling in the boxes. This helps keep the focus on the main goal while a group fills out the other building blocks of the canvas. It is then possible to see how it can be achieved by adding details about the other activities and resources available.
- Discuss, reflect, and act.

USEFUL TOOLS AND TECHNIQUES FOR HUMANITARIAN INNOVATION

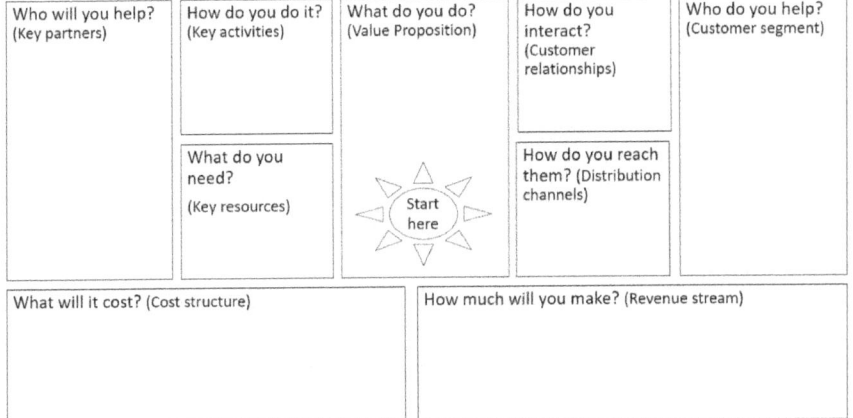

Figure A.2 Business-model canvas

Tips

- Print a large canvas that can be put on a wall for discussion and reflection.
- Practise and learn new ways of doing things by mapping out new canvases. Consider the first draft to be only the first effort. Be ready to challenge the assumptions of that first draft and sketch out alternative business models for the same product, service, or technology.
- Using sticky notes can help move ideas around as elements are filled out in each building block in the canvas. It may be useful to colour-code elements related to a specific segment.
- Tailor so it is applicable to contextual and organizational purposes.

20. Promise and potential map

The tool is a simple way to define added value by mapping the relationship between what you do and who you do it for. The tool provides a diagram on which to plot each idea or solution being considered for R&D. Each idea is classified as being completely new or something that builds upon what you do already. In this way, any potential new solutions developed are mapped alongside the promise of existing solutions, showing how both relate to those who might be affected. Sometimes mapping things out in this way is useful for understanding how much work – and how much benefit – a potential solution might bring. It can be used as an interesting way to brainstorm ideas – and help prioritize them into a product development pipeline for an organization.

How it works

- Decide on which innovation or idea will be evaluated and bring a group together to develop a map.

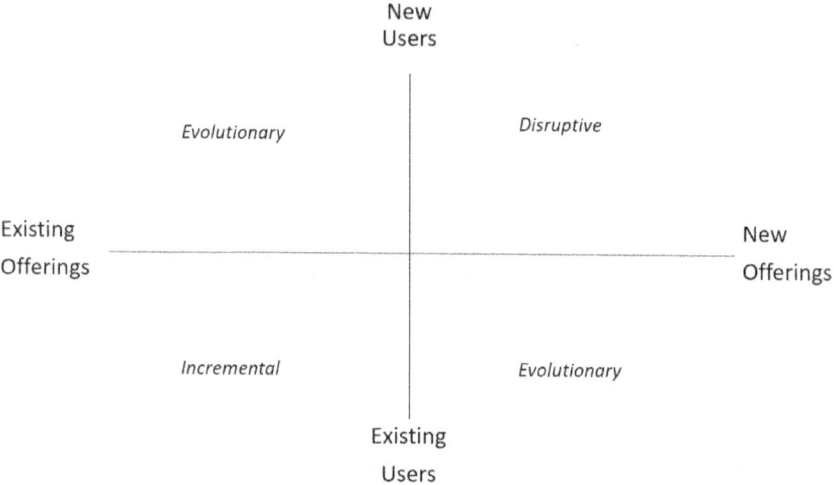

Figure A.3 Promise and potential map

- Create a diagram as shown in Figure A.3. Decide where a specific offering is positioned, considering each axis independently. Is it a new or existing offering? Is it for new or existing users? Then find a spot on the map where these two positions cross.
- Where the idea is plotted will give you a sense of whether it is disruptive or building on something existing, i.e. incremental. This can help you understand whether the innovation or idea is high-risk because it involves doing something radically new, or low-risk because it builds on what is already there.

Tips

- The innovation or idea can have several sub-elements and each of these can be placed in a different position on the map. Using the tool can give a sense of the spread of different ideas.

21. Thumbnail sketching

This technique is the most basic means of prototyping as it involves a series of small drawings used to quickly explore a variety of ideas. It can be fast, allows for a high degree of creativity, and can be fun for participants.

How it works

- Identify a topic of exploration and assemble a team who are provided with basic drawing materials.
- Explain the task and ask each person to work independently.

- Invite them to think about one aspect of the topic and ask them to draw pictures of various possibilities.
- Invite them to consider another aspect of the topic.
- Ask them to draw pictures of various possibilities.
- Invite a group discussion of the sketches.
- Pick a subset to refine with additional sketching.

Tips

- Encourage visual thinking, not perfect drawings. Offerings do not need to rely on a contributor having artistic ability.
- Limit the time for each round of sketching.
- Ask the participants to refrain from editing early.

22. Developed images

When there is more time and information to go beyond basic thumbnail sketches, there are several options for showing others the innovation under development. These include storyboarding (a series of images showing the key elements, sequences, and interactions), a concept poster, or a schematic diagram.

How it works

- As with other tools, identify a topic of exploration and assemble a skilled team with basic drawing materials available.
- Explain the task and ask each person to work independently. Make the first draft quickly.
- Allow time for review and revision.

Tips

- Consider using different media. As well as ink or paint, incorporate more creative media such as clay models, photographs, or videos.
- It may be useful to make a first draft illustrating the idea internally and have the second draft done externally to achieve a more professional appearance. This can reduce the time taken and, ultimately, cost.

23. Prototyping

A prototype is simply an initial model, or sample, to test a concept, and allow you to learn from it. This technique involves rapidly building a model that approximates the appearance and behaviour of a new idea. Prototypes may serve as proof of concept, or show how something looks or functions – either directly or by simulating the user experience. A prototype can take many forms: it may be a rudimentary clay model, a cardboard-and-tape mock-up, or a more sophisticated 3D printed design.

How it works

- Identify an idea or concept to develop and bring together a small team to work on it.
- Depending on the type of prototype, gather basic materials (e.g., pens, paper, tape, etc.).
- Consider what you want to learn from the prototype.
- Select a scenario of how the prototype will normally work and a few key tasks to focus on.
- Build a rough copy of the concept that simulates the appearance, functionality, or both.
- Include some realistic and readable content.
- Indicate the areas that are incomplete.

Tips

- Most successful products go through numerous iterations before they are finalized so expect to make a series of prototypes.
- To make the prototype realistic, spend time on details – but not too much.
- Be resourceful by using objects that are readily available.
- When appropriate, incorporate role-play and demonstration to simulate personal interactions.

24. Prototype-testing plan

This tool gives an overview of the different ways to test a prototype and structure the process through. This provides a means to continually improve the prototype while avoiding getting lost once the feedback collected starts piling up. The tool indicates two periods when it is usually beneficial to test a prototype: in the early stage of development, and just before full implementation.

How it works

- Prototypes should be made as often as possible so keep them easy and cheap to build, focusing more on the core offering than smooth finishing.
- Use what is easily available around you to help you try out your idea rather than just talking or thinking about it.
- Try to clearly specify the main idea you want to test through your prototype.
- Make sure to note down anything you have learnt about how to improve your work by reallocating activities, resources, people or materials.

Tips

- Develop the testing plan with all stakeholders to ensure buy-in and that resources are properly allocated.
- Ensure everyone has access to the plan and that expectations are managed.

ANNEX 1
The principles for ethical humanitarian innovation

These principles were drafted on the basis of discussions at an initial World Humanitarian Summit workshop convened at the University of Oxford on 27 April 2015 by the Humanitarian Innovation Project based at the Refugee Studies Centre.

Principle 1: Humanitarian purpose

Humanitarian innovation has a humanitarian purpose. Humanitarian innovation must be consistent with the humanitarian principles (humanity, impartiality, neutrality, and independence), and the dignity principle. It should be possible for all members of a crisis-affected community to benefit from innovation without discriminatory barriers to use.

Principle 2: Primary relationship

The primary relationship of concern for humanitarian innovation must be the provider/recipient relationship. This primary relationship necessitates both the identification and avoidance of any conflicts of interest as well as the invalidity of any considerations of third party beneficence that would compromise the primary loyalty to recipient populations in any way.

Principle 3: Autonomy

All humanitarian innovation must be conducted with the aim of promoting the rights, dignity and capabilities of the recipient population. Innovation must be based on representative consultation and informed consent. Innovation should be user-driven and based on participatory methods that are sensitive to within-community power dynamics, culture, and language.

Principle 4: Maleficence

Innovation must be based on a 'do no harm' principle. Under no circumstances should humanitarian innovation lead to intentional harm. Risk analysis and mitigation must be used to prevent unintentional harm, including from primary and secondary effects relating to privacy and data security, impacts on local economies, and inter-communal relationships.

Principle 5: Experimentation

Experimentation, piloting and trials must be undertaken in conformity with internationally recognized ethical standards. All innovation activities must be conducted in full conformity with the Declaration of Helsinki of 1964 and the Nuremburg Code of 1947. It must be based on full institutional review board (IRB) assessments.

Principle 6: Justice

Equity and fairness should underpin the distribution of benefits, costs, and risks resulting from innovation. Projects should take into consideration and address the distributive consequences of innovation. Innovation should be sensitive to, and useful for, the most marginalized populations, including sensitivity to age, gender, and disability.

Principle 7: Accountability

Engagement in humanitarian innovation constitutes an obligation to ensure accountability to recipient populations, including establishing process for complaint and recourse relating to unforeseen consequences and maleficence. Humanitarian innovation should take account of the wider effects on the humanitarian system, including on the effectiveness, legitimacy and reputation of the humanitarian system. All aspects of humanitarian innovation should be subject to evaluation and monitoring, including an assessment of primary and secondary impacts of the innovation process. Ethical review and risk analysis should be undertaken prior to embarking on humanitarian innovation projects, and should incorporate external or third party experts where appropriate.

Source: HIP-WHS Oxford Workshop, 2015. *Principles for Ethical Humanitarian Innovation: Draft Principles based on joint HIP-WHS Oxford Workshop*, Occasional Policy Paper, Oxford University – Refugee Studies Centre.

ANNEX 2
UNICEF's principles for innovation and technology in development

According to UNICEF, these principles are not intended as hard and fast rules but meant as best-practice guidelines to inform the design of technology-enabled development programmes.

1. Design with the user
- Develop context-appropriate solutions informed by user needs.
- Include all user groups in planning, development, implementation, and assessment.
- Develop projects in an incremental and iterative manner.
- Design solutions that learn from and enhance existing workflows and plan for organizational adaptation.
- Ensure solutions are sensitive to, and useful for, the most marginalized populations: women, children, those with disabilities, and those affected by conflict and disaster.

2. Understand the existing ecosystem
- Participate in networks and communities of like-minded practitioners.
- Align with existing technological, legal, and regulatory policies.

3. Design for scale
- Design for scale from the start, and assess and mitigate dependencies that might limit ability to scale.
- Employ a systems approach to design, considering implications of design beyond the immediate project.
- Be replicable and customizable in other countries and contexts.
- Demonstrate impact before scaling a solution.
- Analyse all technology choices through the lens of national and regional scale.
- Factor in partnerships from the beginning and start negotiations early.

4. Build for sustainability
- Plan for sustainability from the start, including planning for long-term financial health, i.e., assessing total cost of ownership.
- Utilize and invest in local communities and developers by default and help catalyse their growth.
- Engage with local governments to ensure integration into national strategy and identify high-level government advocates.

5. Be data-driven

- Design projects so that impact can be measured at discrete milestones with a focus on outcomes rather than outputs.
- Evaluate innovative solutions and areas where there are gaps in data and evidence.
- Use real-time information to monitor and inform management decisions at all levels.
- When possible, leverage data for assessments as a by-product of user actions and transactions.

6. Use open standards, open data, open source, and open innovation

- Adopt and expand existing open standards.
- Open data and functionalities and expose them in documented APIs (application programming interfaces) where use by a larger community is possible.
- Invest in software as a public good.
- Develop software to be open source by default with the code made available in public repositories and supported through developer communities.

7. Reuse and improve

- Use, modify, and extend existing tools, platforms, and frameworks when possible.
- Develop in modular ways, favouring approaches that are interoperable over those that are monolithic.

8. Do no harm

- Assess and mitigate risks to the security of users and their data.
- Consider the context and the need for privacy of personally identifiable information when designing solutions and mitigate accordingly.
- Ensure equity and fairness in co-creation, and protect the best interests of the end-users.

9. Be collaborative

- Engage diverse expertise across disciplines and industries at all stages.
- Work across sector silos to create coordinated and more holistic approaches.
- Document work, results, processes, and best practices and share them widely.
- Publish materials under a Creative Commons licence by default, with strong rationale if another licensing approach is taken.

UNICEF innovation principles have been endorsed or adopted by the following partners: UNICEF, USAID, Gates Foundation, EOSG Global Pulse, WFP, WHO, HRP, OCHA, UNDP, SIDA, IKEA Foundation, UN Foundation, and UNHCR.
Source: <https://www.unicef.org/innovation/innovation_73239.html>

ANNEX 3
Technology readiness levels: This is ready ... or is it?

There can be many interpretations of what it means to say an innovation is 'ready'. For example, there can be a chasm between making the first prototype and the intended users using a final product. Therefore, having a common way to measure the status of a technology under development can be helpful. This is especially true when there are potential safety concerns or certain standards need to be met. It is also true when there is a need for dialogue between diverse groups of people with different specialties, and there are different types of technology under consideration.

The US government developed such a tool in the 1970s and the model has since been adopted and adapted by a number of organizations worldwide. The technology readiness level (TRL) scale, and its variants, is based on different levels, most often ranging from one (the initial idea) to nine (the innovation is in use). What appears below is a consolidation of various scales.

Level 1: This is the lowest level of readiness. The basic idea is noted and recognized by moving it to a step past scientific research toward applied research and development (R&D).

Level 2: Validating the potential application is when invention starts. At this stage, studies are limited and without proof or detailed analysis, so the invention is speculative.

Level 3: At this level, there is proof of concept through active R&D. Detailed analytical studies and laboratory studies are done, usually on separate elements of the technology.

Level 4: The rudimentary hardware components are put together to establish that they will work together in a laboratory setting. This is when the first low-fidelity prototype may be available.

Level 5: The basic components are validated in a simulated environment. At this level, the technology will reach a high-fidelity stage with laboratory integration of components.

Level 6: The entire system is validated in a simulated operational environment. This level is a significant step beyond the previous level of readiness.

Level 7: At this level, the prototype is demonstrated in an operational environment, in or near where it will normally be used. This can be considered a field trial or an alpha test of software.

Level 8: This level sees the prototype completed and qualified through test and demonstration which ensures user acceptance (a software beta test). The technology has been proven to work in its final form and under expected conditions.

Level 9: The prototype is proven through successful operations. This means it is available off the shelf and/or is in the hands of intended users. With other factors in place, it may be ready to be taken to scale.

ANNEX 4
Measuring creativity

As noted in Chapter 4, creativity is the ability to come up with novel solutions to problems. There are a variety of methods available to test an individual's level of creativity. These typically look at a number of factors such as originality, number of alternatives developed, and the level of detail in each response. In addition to measuring creativity in others, it can be interesting to use these methods as a self-assessment and in activities to spur innovative thought at workshops and training events. Just three are described below.

Method 1: Alternative uses. Take an ordinary object such as a paperclip, brick, chair, or coffee mug and try to conceive of as many new uses for it as possible in one minute. This can be done by brainstorming and recording the responses on paper. The more alternative uses, the higher level of creativity an individual is thought to have.

Method 2: Word associations. In the Remote Associates Test, three unrelated words are provided and an individual should respond with a fourth word that connects all three words. For example, for the words 'falling', 'actor', and 'dust', the answer is 'star': as in 'falling star,' 'movie star', and 'stardust'. Other examples are shown in Table A.3.

Method 3: Complete a picture. The Torrance test of creative thinking was developed in the 1960s by psychologist Ellis Paul Torrance. He sought to establish an alternative to IQ testing which focused on creativity. Respondents are asked to add to one of the starting shapes shown in Figure A.4 to make a picture, and give their picture a title, within two minutes. The drawing is evaluated based on how original and detailed the drawing is, how many separate ideas it contains, and if the title itself is creative from a verbal perspective.

Table A.3 Word associations

	Words to associate		Answer
Man	Wheel	High	Chair
Back	Go	Light	Stop
Cool	House	Fat	Cat
Spin	Tip	Shape	Top

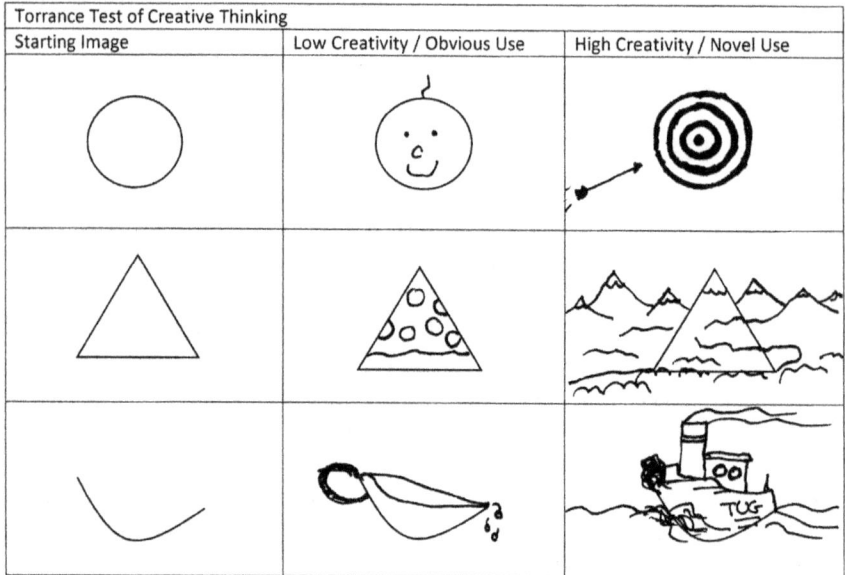

Figure A.4 Torrance test of creative thinking

Reference

Mednick, S.A., and Mednick, M.T. (1967), *Examiner's manual: Remote Associates Test*, Houghton Mifflin, Boston, MA.

ANNEX 5
Innovation-management readiness assessment

The assessment tool shown in Table A.4 is a modified version of that on pages 237–240 of Harvard Business Review's 2009 text, *The Innovator's Toolkit: Practical strategies to help you develop and implement innovation.* As an individual, read each statement and consider your own mindset, habits and performance. The responses might be categorized in one of three areas: 1) strongly agree and simply needs reinforcement; 2) adequate and could use some improvement; or 3) disagree and so the situation is inadequate and needs to change. The lower the number, the more likely you are an innovative leader. It may also be used by turning it into a questionnaire and having staff fill it out independently so the results can be analysed and discussed.

Table A.4 Innovation-management readiness assessment

Key dimensions	Statements indicative of innovative leadership
Leadership style	<ul><li>I can describe my own preferred style of thinking and working</li><li>I have talked with my teammates about their preferred modes of problem-solving</li><li>I encourage intellectual conflict within my team</li><li>When team members disagree, I help them determine the source of their differences</li><li>When communicating with others, I take into consideration their preferred thinking style</li></ul>
Orientation and focus	<ul><li>We routinely do things that help us focus on the 'why' of what we do (helping other people) but have space to work on the 'how'</li><li>I have reminders and ways to make sure problem-solving for people in need is at the centre of what we do</li><li>We have space to change, experiment, and fail while keeping a clear end state in mind</li></ul>
Diversity of styles	<ul><li>I am aware of the creative value of diverse thinking styles and try to incorporate this diversity in teams</li><li>I actively seek out or hire people with diverse backgrounds and thinking styles</li><li>Our team recognizes the conflict that creative abrasion can cause but also recognizes its value</li><li>We have taken formal diagnostic tests to identify thinking or learning styles and discussed the results of these assessments</li></ul>
Teamwork	<ul><li>There is a shared sense of ownership within the team</li><li>In my team, the majority never ignores the opinions of the minority</li><li>I have added someone to the team specifically because s/he brings a fresh perspective</li></ul>

(Continued)

Table A.4 Continued

Key dimensions	Statements indicative of innovative leadership
Teamwork	• I actively look for team members whose thinking styles differ from my own • I help my team establish and agree upon a clear goal at the start of each project • My team has formally agreed upon behaviour guidelines stating how they should work together and treat each other
Psychological environment	• I support people taking intelligent risks and do not penalize them when they fail • There are opportunities for people to take on assignments or tasks that involve risk and stretch their potential • We openly discuss risk-taking, assess the risk potential of projects, and make contingency plans or identify risk-management strategies • Rewards and/or recognition are given for creative ideas • As long as they show learning from the experience, team members are not penalized for experimentation and risk-taking
Physical workspace	• Our workspace includes stimulating objects such as journals, art, and other items that are not directly related to our work • I have made changes to our physical workspace to improve communication and creative interaction • I provide team members with a wide variety of traditional and non-traditional communication tools (email, whiteboards, crayons and paper, etc.) • Team members are encouraged to make their workspaces reflect their individuality • Our workspace includes both areas for boisterous interaction and areas for quiet reflection (if the workspace does not accommodate this, team members feel empowered to find places for reflection or interaction)
Outsiders and alternative perspectives	• Our team makes visits to people outside the organization in order to find different perspectives and ideas • Our team has observed aid workers/affected people actually using our product or service in their own environment • I have arranged for speakers from other organizations and sectors to talk to or work with our team • Our team has observed people using products or services from other organizations whose innovations are similar to our own • Our team has benchmarked the functions and characteristics of our innovations against those of other sectors
Promoting group convergence	• I encourage team members to bring up and discuss non-work-related subjects, especially when they interfere with work • When a project has been completed, I hold a debrief meeting to determine specifically what to do differently (or the same) next time • When I hold a debrief meeting, I always make sure that all members can be present • Project schedules allow enough time for group brainstorming and discussion of ideas • When my team is stuck on a problem, I make sure they get down time or time off to step back, relax, and allow their subconscious minds to work • At the end of a project, I provide a way for my group to celebrate and rejuvenate

ANNEX 6
Useful links and websites

Appropedia: http://www.appropedia.org

Blog about innovation: http://www.game-changer.net/blog/

Business -model canvas: http://www.businessmodelgeneration.com/canvas

Design thinking created by IDEO: http://www.designthinkingforeducators.com/

Development Impact and You, created by Nesta: http://diytoolkit.org/

Failforward: https://failforward.org/

Global innovation community: http://innovationexcellence.com/

Handbook on Participatory Methods for Community-Based Projects: http://www.uwyo.edu/girlmotherspar/_files/pubs-handbook.pdf

IDEO human-centred design kit: http://www.designkit.org/

Innovation articles, tools and inspiration: http://www.innovationmanagement.se/Innovation

Portal created by John Bessant and Joseph Tidd: http://www.innovation-portal.info/

InnovationLabs: http://www.innovationlabs.com/

Methods of the Stanford Design School: http://dschool.stanford.edu/use-our-methods/

Paper on the concept of anti-fragility: http://cpor.org/af/Taleb_Antifragile.pdf

Participatory Methods Toolkit: http://archive.unu.edu/hq/library/Collection/PDF_files/CRIS/PMT.pdf

Theory of change: http://www.theoryofchange.org/what-is-theory-of-change/

Tools for Participatory Development: http://toolkit.ineesite.org/toolkit/INEEcms/uploads/1033/Participatory_Development_Tools_EN.pdf

VARK questionnaire: http://vark-learn.com/the-vark-questionnaire/

Glossary

Abundance thinking: A paradigm that embraces choice, opportunity, creativity, and an understanding of what is possible as opposed to restricted, zero-sum and scarce.

Adaptive pluralism: An approach to programme design and management that recognizes and embraces human-centeredness and the complexity of the wider system.

Additive manufacturing: A process by which machines create new objects in layers (i.e., by adding or printing material one layer at a time). Complex shapes and forms can be made this way. 3D printing is a type of additive manufacturing.

Anti-fragile: Technically, anti-fragile is something that becomes stronger when it is stressed, as distinct from fragile, which breaks when it is stressed. Term coined by Nassim Nicolas Taleb.

Appropriate technology: Technology that fits the socio-economic, cultural, and environmental contexts in which it is used and promotes the self-sufficiency of those who use it. Term coined by Fritz Schumacher.

Champion: A person who moves a promising idea, project or innovation forward to acceptance and wider use. This person is usually not the creator but has the interest and ability to promote the idea so it is ultimately successful. In humanitarian innovation, this person will ideally have sufficient influence to clear obstacles and decision-making authority over resources.

Channel: The supporters, but not necessarily the end-users, of a product or service. In humanitarian innovation, these are likely to be donors who fund activities that others (aid workers and affected people) benefit from.

Complexity: A scientific theory, applied to different fields such as organizations and management, that examines uncertainty and non-linearity, viewing groups as networks, collections of strategies, and structures.

Convergence thinking: Occurs when there is a well-defined, straightforward, correct answer to a problem. Convergent thinking focuses on known facts, not creative responses.

Creativity: A process of conceiving and developing novel and useful ideas.

Design thinking: An approach to complex problems that focuses on solutions (particularly technological solutions), actions, and users of the solutions.

In humanitarian innovation, this involves the creation of a useful item, system, or way in which people are engaged to save lives and reduce human suffering.

Differentiation: Sets a product or service apart from what already exists in a way that the users find of value.

Divergent thinking: Involves solving new or abstract problems with many possible answers, solutions, or outcomes and takes place when creative thinking is required (such as when writing poetry).

Emergence: When new, unplanned, or unexpected behaviours appear. Evolution and technology typically act on the form of a system, enabling new functions to emerge.

Empathic design: An idea-generating technique where those seeking to solve a problem observe how people use existing local products and services.

Exponential technology: Technology which follows the law of accelerating returns in terms that its capacity and cost effectiveness increases in higher and higher amounts. Smartphones and 3D printers are examples.

Generative framework: The organic ecosystem for production supported by a number of systems, institutions, and organizations.

Hyperlocal manufacturing: Fabrication that happens at or very near (e.g., within a few kilometres of) the point of use, as opposed to at central points where supply chains must be relied upon.

Idea funnel: A framework for product development which takes many ideas and gradually reduces them to the few (possibly just one) that comes into use. It is part of the process of innovation.

Innovation: The process of introducing new products, processes, positions, or paradigms. Humanitarian innovation is simply the application of innovation for humanitarian purposes.

Incubator: A programme designed to support new ideas for products or services until they become successful businesses. **Accelerators** take existing firms and try to help them scale.

Intellectual property (IP): Any idea or work that can be considered proprietary in nature and is thus protected from infringement by others.

Lab: A workspace designed to optimize innovation. The word is short for laboratory, a place where scientific and technological research and experimentation occur. It can take many forms, including a **makerspace** used for fabrication, and a **hackspace** used for coding and other learning and forms of collaboration.

Massive small change: The process whereby discrete, seemingly unconnected, developments come together creating larger phenomena. This can take place through networks and affect any number of fields (e.g., hyperlocal manufacturing that is replicated at scale).

Neo-Newtonian: A paradigm that approaches programme design and management in a way that is characterized by linear thinking and a focus on things not people.

Network effect: When the value of an innovation is increased through increasing use. Social media, for example, relies on this phenomenon whereby the more people that are using a particular platform (e.g., Facebook or Twitter), the more they find it useful and interesting.

Pilot: A trial phase done in the field, often over a period of time. In a pilot, the product or services are used by the intended users in a site or situation that mimics or actually is a site of intended use.

Prototype: An initial model that approximates the appearance, behaviour, and functionality of an innovation.

Scale: Is when an innovation goes into wide use, meaning that it has been replicated beyond the prototype and pilot site. The Humanitarian Innovation Fund defines this as: 'building on demonstrated successes to ensure solutions reach their maximum potential, have the greatest possible impact, and lead to widespread change'.

Systems thinking: The way of understanding the linkages and interactions of components that form an intricate whole (i.e., a system).

Trim tab: A metaphor based on the idea that it is possible to help resolve overwhelming challenges by influencing larger forces in a positive way. First suggested by Buckminster Fuller.

TRIZ: Theory of inventive problem-solving; a means to develop innovation not by intuition and creativity but by identifying and eliminating technical contradictions.

Value: The relative worth of an innovation as determined by the impact it will have on different stakeholders.

Weak signal: An early indication of change, used in scenario-planning efforts and early warning.

Index

Page numbers in *italics* refer to figures.

abundance
   and acceleration 7–8
   and scarcity mindsets 31–2, 206
academic institutions 13, 101–2
adaptive iteration approach 72
adaptive pluralism 8, 74
   and Neo-Newtonian paradigms 69–71
adaptive strategy and adaptive organizations 62–3
additive manufacturing (AM) framework 118–19
   3D printing 120–8
agility and bureaucracy balance 90–1
ambiguity, dealing with 82
anonymized data 95–6
Ansoff matrix 14, 15, *16*, 17, 18
assessment 34
   Field Innovation Team (FIT) 163–4, 165
   Field Ready approach 194
   innovation-management readiness 241–2
assumptions
   ICT 94
   partnership 104
   replication problem 57
awareness-raising and marketing phase of innovation process 39–41

barriers to innovation 202, 204
biases 71, 72–3, 86, 87, 186–7
black swan concept and typology 81
blind spots 72–3
blueprint tool 227–8
boundary spanning 49
bright-line rules: data- and ICT-based interventions 96
Brookwood 3D-Design Problem Bank 168
Buffalo Bicycles 16–17
bullseye diagramming tool 224–5
bureaucracy
   and agility balance 90–1
   as barrier 202, 152–3
business plan 226–7
business-model canvas 228

capacity building 105, 135, 178–9
CATWOE tool 219–20
cause diagram tool 217
change 89–91
   replication problem 57
   theory of 90, 225–6

Chitekwe, Stanley (interview) 203–5
co-creation 136, 139
communication
   conversation to opportunity 151–6
   and partnerships 101, 103, 105
Communitere International: collaboration and process 157–61
community development 135–6
community development centres 102
community engagement/involvement 135–6, 137, 158, 159–60
community wellbeing 138
completeness stage of innovation lifecycle 56
complexity/complexity theory 8, 28–9
   adaptive manufacturing (AM) 125
   beautiful complexity 22–3
   case studies 29–31
   embracing 73
   emergencies and adaptive strategies 61–3
   emergency management principles 63–6
   HELIOS (SCM) software 184
   and inclusive rigour 72
   and non-linearity 33
   systems for distilling 58–9
   volatility, uncertainty, and ambiguity 3, 7
compromise stage of innovation lifecycle 56
connection stage of innovation lifecycle 56
contexts 3–5, 27–8
   leadership and management 80–1
   local 103
   replication problem 57
   understanding 210
contextual inquiry technique 215–6
conversation to opportunity 151–6
coordination of actors 65
corporate social responsibility (CSR) 12–13
cost innovations 15
creative combining 49
creative community 48
creative makers, local 23, 24
creative matrix 221
creativity 31, 34, 85
   measuring 239–40
culture
   do-it-yourself (DIY) 4
   local 104
   organizational 31–2

customization 58, 123–4, 126–7, 138
Cynefin Framework 62, *63*, 190–1

data use 95–6
decentralized organizations 64–5
decision-making 66, 108, 153–4
design
   double diamond model 35
   Field Ready approach 194
   human-centred design (HCD) 9, 82
   identification 167–9
   thinking 8–9
   three stage process 163–5
   workshop 160–1
Diagnostics for all (dfa.org) 18
diffusion phase of innovation process 41–2
digital fabrication *see* 3D printing; innovation labs
donors *see* funding/investment
double diamond model of design 35
drivers of innovation 12–13

economic development/transformation 125, 126
economies of scale 118–19
education and training
   additive manufacturing (AM) 126
   design identification 167–9
   innovation labs 135, 138, 140
emergencies: strategies and management principles 61–6
empathy 167–8, 169
   immersive empathy technique 216–7
Enable Community Foundation 168
endgames 84
ends vs. means approach 48
entrepreneurship 12–13, 135, 138, 141
Ethical Filament Foundation 173
ethics
   humanitarian 'essence' 211
   and leadership 79
   'missing middle' challenge 47–8
   principles 213–14
   responsible use of ICT 93–7
   safe and appropriate innovations 81
   unintended consequences 37
execution of innovation 86–7
experience, appropriate 66
experimental learning 49
expertise, types of 103
exponential technology 4
extensive search 48–9
extreme making 189–92
eyeglasses (3D printing) 127, 172

fab labs 125, 126, 134–6
   see also innovation labs
failure/mistakes 38, 51–2, 65, 91
feedback 37, 65, 96
Field Innovation Team (FIT) 163–5

Field Ready
   approach to innovation 193–4
   Caribbean 189, 190, 192
   Haiti 196
   Andrew Lamb interview 205–7
   Nepal 122, 194–6
   Syria 197
field-ready phase of innovation process 38–9
five whys tool 218
flexibility 83
four Cs of innovation 27–32
four Ps of innovation 14
four-frame approach: leadership and management effectiveness 218–9
frugal innovations 15
functionality testing 37
funding/investment
   case study 29–30
   HELIOS (SCM) software 186
   innovation labs 140, 149
   Nia (3D printing) 180, 181
   size and time issues 52, 59–60
   supportive role of donors 202–3
'fuzzy front end' challenge 46

gender equity 106–9, 137–8
global practitioners: innovation labs 141
global/international and local connection 100–4, 134, 147–8, 159–60
goals, setting and stretching 80
good-enough innovations 15
government agencies 102–3
'growth mindset' 8

Haiti
   Communitere International 157, 158
   umbilical-cord clamps 196
healthcare innovations 126–7, 196
   nutrition programmes 17, 52, 205
   see also prosthetics (3D printing)
'heart vs. head' challenge 46
HELIOS (SCM) software 183–7
households and villages, as local partners 103
human-centred design (HCD) 9, 82
humanitarian 'essence' 211
humanitarian innovation
   definition of 6
   key challenges and conclusions 209–12
   key concepts 7–9
Humanitarian Innovation Fund (HIF) 48, 51
   Kim Scriven interview 201–3
humanitarian system challenges 3–4, 11–12

ICT, ethical and responsible use of 93–7
IDEO 9, 34, 35, 82
immersion 190
immersive empathy technique 216–7
implementers, local organizations as 100–1
importance/difficulty matrix 223–4

INDEX

improvisation 66
incremental to radical innovation 14
India
  landfill sites/waste-pickers 126
  Rapid Action Learning Units 73–4
  Wello WaterWheel (wellowater.org) 15–16
individual and organizational innovation 205–6
infrastructure, integration with existing 136–7, 184
innovation
  contexts 3–5
  definitions of 5–6, 14
  drivers of 12–13
  key concepts 7–9
  process management 7
  purpose of 6–7
  types of 14–15
innovation adoption 111
  bell-curve 41
  integration cycle 94
  matrix of influence 112–13
  stakeholders 112, 113–14
innovation labs 133
  case study: 3D printing prosthetics 139–40
  elements of good practice 136–8
  fab lab as foundational model 134–6
  local partners 102
  purpose and characteristics 134
  recommendations 140–1
  see also fab labs; Nepal Innovation Lab (NLab)
innovation lifecycle
  missing middle 47–8, 54–5
  scaling-up and scaling out 51–2, 55–9, 59–60
  stages 53–9
innovation process 32–42
innovation-management readiness assessment 241–2
innovators, local organizations as 100
inside out model of leadership 78–80
INSPIRE framework of leadership 78–87
integration
  3D technology 180
  existing and established aid systems 178
  existing infrastructure 136–7, 184
  leadership and management 85
  Nepal Innovation Lab (NLab) 147–8
  phase of innovation 94
  replication problem 57
interviews
  Q&As with experts 201–7
  technique 214
invention/exploration stage of innovation lifecycle 53
Iraq disaster relief 189–90

job creation 138

knowledge
  of context 80–1
  types of 103

labs *see* fab labs; innovation labs; Nepal Innovation Lab (NLab)
Lamb, Andrew (interview) 205–7
landfill sites/waste-pickers 126, 173
leadership 77–8
  appropriate experience 66
  Field Ready approach 194
  and management 77–8
  INSPIRE framework 78–87
  Nepal Innovation Lab (NLab) 148
  women 108
'lean innovation' 53
lean start-up 9
learning 48–50, 83
  experimental 49
  from mistakes 65
  rapid action 73–4
  style 79
linear and non-linear approaches 14, 28, *29*, 33, *64*, 69–72
local capacity building 105, 178–9
local communities *see entries beginning* community
local creative makers 23, 24
local and global/international connection 100–4, 134, 147–8, 159–60
local innovation 125–6
local partners, roles and types 100–3
local recycling for local materials 172–3
Luci Lights 17

'mad mavericks' challenge 47
makers
  local 194
  'maker movement' 4
makerspaces 102, 134–5, 139
marketing phase of innovation process 39–41
matrix of influence 112–13
measures
  of creativity 239–40
  of progress 59
  of success 52
mental models 66
mindsets
  abundance and scarcity 31–2, 206
  beginners 86
  and leader strategy 82–3
  linear and dynamic *64*
  Neo-Newtonian and adaptive pluralism 71
  and systems alignment 210
MINDSPACE framework 40–1
missing middle 47–8, 54–5
mistakes *see* failure/mistakes
mobile banking 125–6
monitoring and evaluation (case study) 30

monitoring and reviewing partnerships 104–5
multipliers, local partners as 101

Neo-Newtonian and adaptive pluralism paradigms 69–71
Nepal earthquakes 163
　radio antennas 194–6
　resource centre 159, 160–1
Nepal Innovation Lab (NLab) 143–4
　design 144–6
　guiding conditions and principles 148–9
　integration into local, international and humanitarian ecosystems 147–8
network creation 159–60
NGOs
　and BINGOs 91
　local and international 102, 159–60
Nia Technology 177–81
non-linearity see linear and non-linear approaches
nutrition programmes 17, 52, 205

observation 214–5
optimization/improvement stage of innovation lifecycle 53–4
organizations
　adaptive 62–3
　culture 31–2
　decentralized 64–5
　and individual innovation 205–6
　large and small see conversation to opportunity
　and leadership 80–1
　limits to competence 186–7
　local 100–1
　private-sector 12–13, 13, 42, 102
　structures and decision-making processes 153–4
outdated legacies 52
Overseas Development Institute 117–18
Oxfam 184–5, 187

packaged solutions 58
paradigm innovation 14
participatory methodologies and statistics 73
partnership building 99–100
　gender equity 106–9
　local and international 100–4
　long-term 153, 154–5, 156
　success indicators 104–5
partnerships 13
passionate owners 59
people-focus 82
pilots/prototypes 36–7
　make it/break it 190–1
　scaling up 56
　START Network 185
　and student learning 169
platform approach 58–9

policy makers: innovation labs 140
position innovation 14
potential of innovation 21–4
practical wisdom 65–6
preparation for innovation 83–4
private-sector organizations 12–13, 13, 42, 102
problem(s)
　definition and opportunity identification 33–4, 35
　identification 155–6
　and potential 45–50
　replication 57
　statement/challenge statement 33–4, 164, 165
　typology 9
　understanding 210
process innovation 14
process of innovation 32–42
process-over-product philosophy 158–9
product innovation 14
professional reflexivity 74
prosthetics (3D printing) 126–7, 139–40, 168, 172, 177
　business model: opportunity and challenges 180–1
　case study 139–40
　design and implementation 177–9
　obstacles 180
　proving and iterating innovation 179–80
prototypes see pilots/prototypes
psychosocial support 136

Q&A interviews with experts 201–7
quality assurance: 3D printing 128

radio antennas, Nepal 194–6
Ramalingam, B. 61, 65
　et al. 6, 8, 14, 28
randomized control trials (RCTs) 71–2
rapid action learning and sharing 73–4
rapid iteration 169
rapid response 82, 191–2
re-examination of innovation 85–6
reality checks 73
recombinant innovation 49
recruitment 30–1, 108
red-button responses: data- and ICT-based interventions 96
reflexivity and rigour 71–2
　paradigm of things (Neo-Newtonian) and people (adaptive pluralism) 69–71
　ways forward 72–4
Refugee Open Ware (ROW) 139
replication problems 57
RepRap 171–2
rescue airbag, Syria 197
research and development (R&D) 138
resource centres 158, 159, 160–1
respect in partnerships 103–4

INDEX 253

Ries, E. 9, 34, 49, 53, 56
risk exposure 154–5
risk management 65
risk-aversion 52
round robin technique for ideas generation 220

scale/scaling
  achieving impact through 211
  failures 51–2
  economies of 118–19
  Nepal Innovation Lab (NLab) 149
  scaling-up and scaling out 51–2, 55–9, 59–60
SCAMPER tool for creative thinking 230–1
Scriven, Kim
  Buchanan-Smith, M. and (ALNAP report) 62, 65, 66
  interview 201–3
search ideas 34–5
search and rescue teams 165, 197
selection bias 186–7
selection phase of innovation process 35–6
self-mastery and leadership 78–80
sharing innovation 194
Signal Program: data disasters typology 95
skills 52, 167
smartphones 4, 23, 41, 125–6
social entrepreneurship 12–13
social media
  crisis-mapping app (Ushahidi) 47, 93
  data collection 164
social transformation 125
software
  HELIOS (SCM) 183–7
  testing 37–8
solar-powered electricity for off-grid households 173
speed *see entries beginning* rapid
stakeholders 112, 113–14
standardization: 3D printers 122–4
standards 59, 94–5
START Network 185
start-ups 9, 82, 158
strategy of innovation 81–3
success skills 167
supply chains 118, 119, 121, 122
supply-chain management (SCM) *see* HELIOS (SCM) software
sustainability: 3D printing 124–5, 127
Syria: rescue airbag 197
Syrian refugees, Lebanon 163, 164

technology 4–5
  development 13
  implementation challenge 210
  readiness levels 237–8
test phase of innovation process 37–9
  partnerships 105
theory of change 90, 225–6

thinking and doing balance 90
thinking and learning style 79
3D printing 119–20
  additive manufacturing (AM) framework 120–8
  design identification 167–9
  healthcare innovations 126–7, 196
  invention and diffusion 41
  open source 171–3
  topographical mapping 165
  see also prosthetics (3D printing)
three stage design process 163–5
time
  change over 57
  and investment 52, 59–60
tolerance of imperfection 49
tool kits 59
tools and techniques 221–36
trade associations, as local partners 102
trade-offs 57–8
training *see* education and training
transparency in data use 96

umbilical-cord clamps, Haiti 196
UN
  Development Program (UNDP) 12
  finance systems and demand 117
  Global Alliance for Humanitarian Innovation (GAHI) 46
  Global Trends: Forced Displacement in 2015 (UNHCR) 11–12
  Office for the Coordination of Humanitarian Affairs (UNOCHA) 12, 95, 96
UNICEF
  principles for innovation and technology in development 235–6
  Stanley Chitekwe interview 203–5
usability testing 38
user engagement 48
  challenge 46–7
Ushahidi app 47, 93

viable solution use 38–9
villages and households, as local partners 103
visualize the vote tool for consensus and decision-making 223

Washington state landslide, US 164–5
waste-pickers/landfill sites 126, 173
water and sanitation (3D printers) 123–4
Wello WaterWheel (wellowater.org) 15–16
women: equity issues 106–9, 137–8
Wooden, J. and Jamison, S. 79
World Bank World Development Report (2015) 71, 72–3
World Bicycle Relief (WBR) 16–17
World Health Organization 124
World Vision 146, 148

www.ingramcontent.com/pod-product-compliance
Lightning Source LLC
LaVergne TN
LVHW020552040426
835515LV00043B/2387